T0347254

Will Europe Work?

In the post-war years European integration was driven by nation-states attempting to stimulate economic growth and social cohesion through European trade and cooperation. The results were prosperous and unified Western European societies based on full employment and redistributive welfare states. In today's Europe – a Europe subject to increasing international competition fuelled by both economic and cultural globalization – the European social model needs to be re-examined, yet its emphasis on cohesion remains crucial for the future of Europe as a unified polity. *Will Europe Work?* brings together some of the leading names in European sociology to look at the construction of this new European social order through changing patterns of employment and welfare and changing definitions of citizenship and identity.

The book is divided into three parts. The first asks how recent developments have changed the old European model of employment and social protection, and outlines a possible new European social model. The second focuses on the questions of European identity and European citizenship, with special emphasis on borders and cultural divisions such as ethnicity. The third concentrates on institutions such as language and the public sphere, and reflects on sociology's ability to address the European process.

Martin Kohli is Professor of Sociology at the Free University of Berlin. **Mojca Novak** is Director of the Social Protection Institute of the Republic of Slovenia and Associate Professor of Sociology and Social Policy at the University of Ljubljana.

Routledge/European Sociological Association Studies in European Societies
Series editors: Thomas P. Boje, Max Haller, Martin Kohli and Alison Woodward

Will Europe Work?

Integration, employment and the social order

Edited by Martin Kohli and Mojca Novak

London and New York

First published 2001
by Routledge
2 Park Square, Milton Park, Abingdon, Oxon, OX14 4RN

Simultaneously published in the USA and Canada
by Routledge
270 Madison Ave, New York NY 10016

Routledge is an imprint of the Taylor & Francis Group

Transferred to Digital Printing 2006

Typeset in Goudy by
M Rules

British Library Cataloguing in Publication Data
A catalogue record for this book is available from the British Library

Library of Congress Cataloging in Publication Data

Will Europe work? : integration, employment and the social order /
edited by Martin Kohli and Mojca Novak.
    p.   cm.
Includes bibliographical references and index.
1. Europe – Economic integration. 2. Europe – Economic policy.
3. Europe – Social policy. 4. Globalization. I. Kohli, Martin.
II. Novak, Mojca, 1948–
HC240 . W48 2001
337.1'4 – dc21   2001019479

ISBN 0–415–26022–1

Contents

Figures

Tables

Contributors

Gösta Esping-Andersen is Professor at the University Pompeu Fabra (Barcelona), and member of the Scientific Council of the Instituto Juan March (Madrid). He has formerly taught at Harvard University, at the European University Institute (Florence) and at the University of Trento, and has worked also with the United Nations and OECD. His highly influential publications include books on comparative social democracies, *Politics against Markets*; on welfare states, *The Three Worlds of Welfare Capitalism* and *Welfare States in Transition*; and on social stratification, *Changing Classes*. His most recent book, *The Social Foundations of Postindustrial Economies*, is an attempt to give a sociological analysis of the emerging new economic order. At present he is actively engaged in the process of reforming Europe's social architecture (last year for the Portuguese, and this year for the Belgian presidency).

Jürgen Gerhards is Professor of Sociology at the University of Leipzig. His recent books include *Soziologie der Kunst* (ed.), *Zwischen Diskurs und Palaver: Strukturen öffentlicher Meinungsbildung am Beispiel des Abtreibungsdiskurses in der Bundesrepublik* (with Friedhelm Neidhardt und Dieter Rucht, 1998), *Interessen und Ideen im Konflikt um das Wahlrecht* (with Jörg Rössel, 1999), *Die Vermessung kultureller Unterschiede. Deutschland und USA im Vergleich* (ed. 2000), *Democracy and the Public Sphere in Germany and the United States: Shaping the Abortion Discourse* (with Myra Marx Ferree, William Gamson and Dieter Rucht, 2001). His present research interests cover the sociology of the public sphere, and the sociology of culture.

Risto Heiskala is Senior Research Fellow at the Department of Sociology, University of Helsinki. In addition to a large number of articles, his publications comprise an English book, *Society as Semiosis: Neostructuralist Theory of Culture and Society* (1997), as well as several books in Finnish: *The Realms of Freedom and Necessity: Emancipation and the Critique of Political Economy* (1986), *Current Sociological Theory* (1994), and *Towards Artifical Society* (1996). His research interests include gender, globalization, economy and society, social theory, and semiotics and cultural studies.

Martin Kohli is Professor of Sociology at the Free University of Berlin, where he directs the Research Group on Aging and the Life Course, and chairs the Graduate School on Comparative Social Research. He has been a Fellow at the Institute for Advanced Study (Princeton), Collegium Budapest and Hanse Institute for Advanced Study (Delmenhorst Bremen), and a Visiting Professor at Harvard University. His recent books include *Time for Retirement: Comparative Studies of Early Exit from the Labour Force* (with others, 1991), *Liebe, Ehe, Elternschaft* (with G. Burkart, 1992), *Der Zusammenbruch der DDR* (ed. with H. Joas, 1993), and *Die zweite Lebenshälfte* (ed. with H. Künemund, 2000). His research interests center on generations and the life course and on the institutions that shape them: families, labor markets and welfare states. He was President of the European Sociological Association from 1997 to 1999.

Walter Korpi is Professor of Sociology at the Swedish Institute for Social Research at Stockholm University. He has been one of the most influential scholars of the development of welfare states, and has published widely on these issues. Currently he is working on a book that summarizes most of his efforts in this field: *Contested Citizenship: A Century of Social Rights in the Western World*. His present research interests cover political sociology, social policy and distributive conflicts.

Mojca Novak is Director of the Social Protection Institute of the Republic of Slovenia and Associate Professor of Sociology and Social Policy at the University of Ljubljana. She has been also a Visiting Professor at the Central European University in Warsaw. She collaborates closely with the Council of Europe, heading an international project on *Policies and Services for Social Prevention and Action*. Her recent work concerns the welfare state development and social policy, pensioners and pension reform. Recent books include (all in Slovene) *Late-Coming Pattern Mix: Slovenia at the European Periphery* (1991), *Good Morning Poverty* (1994) and *Welfare State Development in Europe* (1997). From 1997 to 1999 she was a Vice President of the European Sociological Association and the Chair of its Program Committee.

Liam O'Dowd is Professor of Sociology at Queen's University, Belfast. He was Chairman of the National Committee for Economics and Social Sciences of the Royal Irish Academy (1992–96). His recent books include *Whither the Irish Border?* (1994), *Irish Society: Sociological Perspectives* (1995), *On Intellectuals and Intellectual Life in Ireland* (ed., 1996), and *Borders, Nations and States: Frontiers of National Sovereignty in the New Europe* (co-editor, 1996). He has edited (with J. Anderson) a special issue of *Regional Studies* on "State Borders and Border Regions" (1999). His current research interests focus on state borders and border regions, the sociology of European integration, and British and Irish nationalism.

Joakim Palme is Senior Researcher at the Swedish Institute for Social Research at Stockholm University. He has published widely on pension rights, the public/private mix of welfare provisions, and on health and social insurance.

Recently he has directed a study on *The Welfare State in Crisis* for the Council of Europe, and currently he is Chairman of a government committee on the development of welfare in Sweden in the 1990s. His research focuses on the development of welfare state institutions and on its causes and consequences.

Maria Petmesidou is Professor of Social Policy at Democritus University of Thrace. Previously she was Head of the Department of Sociology at the University of Crete. She has directed a large number of research projects funded by Greek governmental bodies as well as by the European Commission and other European agencies, and is a member of the Scientific Council of the Foundation on Social Quality in Europe (Amsterdam). Her books include *Social Inequalities and Social Policy in Greece* (in Greek, 1991), *Modern Sociological Theory* (ed. in Greek, 2 vols, 1997/98), and *Employment and Labour Market Policies in Southern Europe* (forthcoming). Her research interests are in the fields of social change and development, social protection, labor markets and employment, social inequality, and social exclusion and poverty.

Chiara Saraceno is Professor of Sociology of Family at the University of Torino and Director of the University's Interdepartmental Center for Gender Studies. She is chair of the Italian Commission on Social Exclusion at the Prime Minister's Office, as well as one of the two Italian Delegates in the Committee on Social Protection at the EU. From 1990 to 1994 she was the Italian expert in the EC Observatory on Policies for Combatting Social Exclusion, and is now a member of several EU networks. Among her recent books are *Politiche contro la povertà in Italia* (with N. Negri, 1996), *Mutamenti della famiglia e politiche sociali in Italia* (1998), and *Separarsi in Italia* (with M. Barbagli, 1998). She has published a number of articles in English, e.g., *Family Change, Family Policies and the Restructuring of Welfare* in the OECD Social policy series (1997). Her current research is on social policies and poverty, the social and economic consequences of separation and divorce, and citizenship, gender and the welfare state.

Dominique Schnapper has been Directeur d'études at the Ecole des Hautes Etudes en Sciences Sociales (Paris) since 1981. She has been a member of several government commissions, and from 1995 to 1998 was President of the Société Française de Sociologie. Among her recent books are *Six manières d'être Européen* (ed. with H. Mendras, 1990), *La France de l'intégration* (1990), *L'Europe des immigrés* (1992), *La communauté des citoyens* (1994) for which she was awarded the Prix de l'Assemblée Nationale, *Contre la fin du travail* (1997), and *La relation à l'autre* (1998). Her main interests are in political sociology, citizenship and nationhood, migration, work, and European integration.

Wolfgang Streeck is Director at the Max-Planck-Institute for the Study of Societies in Cologne and Professor of Sociology at Cologne University. Previously he was Professor of Sociology and Industrial Relations at the University of Wisconsin-Madison. He has held Visiting Professorships at the

European University Institute (Florence), the Institut d'Etudes Politiques (Paris), Bocconi University (Milan), the Instituto Juan March (Madrid), and the University of Warwick. From 1998 to 1999, he was President of the Society for the Advancement of Socio-Economics (SASE). Among his recent books in English are *The Political Economy of Modern Capitalism* (with C. Crouch, 1997); *Governance in the European Union* (with others, 1996); *Works Councils* (with J. Rogers, 1995), and *Governing Capitalist Economies* (with R. Hollingsworth and P.C. Schmitter, 1994). His research interests are comparative political economy, comparative industrial relations and European integration.

Abram de Swaan is Chair of the Amsterdam School for Social Science Research, and was its dean from 1987 to 1997. He has been Professor of Sociology at the University of Amsterdam since 1973 and was appointed University Professor in 2001. He has held Visiting Professorships at the New School for Social Research, Columbia University, Cornell University, Ecole des Hautes Etudes en Sciences Sociales, Eötvös Lorand University (Budapest), and occupied the European Chair at the Collège de France in 1997/98. Among his books in English are *In Care of the State: Health Care, Education and Welfare in Europe and the USA in the Modern Era* (1988), *The Management of Normality* (1990), and *Words of the World: The Global Language System* (2001). His present research interests are in transnational society as it concerns social policy, social identifications, and language problems.

Acknowledgements

All but one of the chapters of this book have originally been presented as plenary or semi-plenary contributions to the 4th European Sociological Association Conference in Amsterdam (August 18–21 1999) organized by the European Sociological Association (ESA), and have since been substantially revised. The ESA organizes these biannual Conferences as part of its effort to create a sociological forum for the study of and debate on Europe and its societies.

Our thanks go to the other members of the ESA Program Committee for the Amsterdam Conference – especially Daniel Bertaux, Thomas Boje, Max Haller, Robert Miller, J. P. Roos, and Alison Woodward – as well as to the members of the Local Organizing Committee – especially Marijke Borghardt, Harry Ganzeboom, Erik de Gier, Jantine van Gogh, Cees Knipscheer, Bernard Kruithof, and Bart van Steenbergen – for their manifold contributions and help, both intellectual and practical. We would also like to express our gratitude to SISWO – The Netherlands Institute for the Social Sciences for its continued support in this crucial phase of laying the ground for European sociology.

We are grateful to Catya de Laczkovich at the Free University of Berlin, without whose wide-ranging editing and translation work the production of this volume would not have been possible, and to Jutta Buyse, Sebastian Schnettler and Antje Starke who assisted her with the formal standardization of the articles.

Martin Kohli is indebted to the Hanse Institute for Advanced Study (Delmenhorst/Bremen) for providing the intellectual ambiente and leisure in which editing could be completed.

Introduction
Will Europe work?

Martin Kohli and Mojca Novak

The title of this book links two major themes: the future of the European unification process and the future of the European "work societies". The two sets of issues are significant in their own right, but might at first glance seem to have little to do with each other. Yet in its early stages, the political integration of Western Europe has indeed been pushed forward by concerns of its nation-states over the employment and welfare of their populations, and it is of utmost importance to examine – and, as the result will show, to maintain – this link today.

The history of European integration has had its ups and downs. Fifteen years ago, "Europe" was still a very distant phenomenon for the inhabitants of the societies now forming the European Union, or of the geographical space called Europe. This applied not only to the populations at large but to most of the cultural and political elites as well. As an example, it could be pointed out how difficult it was for Brussels-based journalists to get space and visibility in their home media for articles on European issues (see Chapter 8 by Jürgen Gerhards), or how little the European experience – such as activity in the European administration or membership in the European Parliament – counted in the business of national politics. In other words, Europe was neither a functioning public space nor widely perceived as an autonomous center of political power.

In the meantime, this has been changing. Today, with a massively established common currency for a large part of the EU, and its expansion to the East and South firmly on the agenda, Europe is very much on the mind of those who do and those who may belong. But the public perceptions of its political fortunes vary with the day-to-day (or month-to-month) political process. At the time of this writing, the slim results of the recent Nizza summit give rise (again) to widespread expressions of pessimism. And the scope of the change that has occurred so far also remains controversial.[1] The majority opinion in the social sciences still seems to be that unification among the European nation-states has not gone very deep yet, that it will necessarily be rather limited, and that it may even come apart again under the pressure of future crises. On the other hand, it is rightly pointed out that European integration is already penetrating social life to a much higher degree than is usually assumed but with new institutional forms that are difficult to grasp by traditional conceptual architecture.

Europe on the sociological agenda

In the task of conceptualizing and analyzing these new forms, sociology has so far taken a back seat behind economics and political science. In addition to the rapidly growing number of studies of European economic processes and institutions, there is now also a large body of literature on Europe's political dimensions, such as the new forms of governance that are emerging in the EU – usually subsumed under the term "multi-level system" (Marks *et al.* 1996; Kohler-Koch and Eising 1999) – its policy-making (Wallace and Wallace 2000) or its "democracy deficit" (Scharpf 1999; Bach 2000; for a cautiously optimistic view see Zürn 2000).

European sociology has had little to say on these and other issues.[2] There are a few examples of studies of the new institutional realities on the European level – such as in the fields of social policy (Leibfried and Pierson 1995), policing (Kapteyn 1995), or industrial relations (Streeck and Schmitter 1991). But by and large, sociology's relation to Europe has been one of benign neglect.[3] This might be seen as an expression of what happens in the world of its preferred subjects of analysis. According to this view, sociology lags behind economics and political science in addressing the European process because the integration of European societies – in terms, e.g., of social mobility, networks, and identities – lags behind that of its economies and polities. Such a view may be adequate in describing societal change, but it does not do justice to what drives it forward (Bornschier 2001). If the main dynamics of Europeanization today were economic, political and juridical ones, sociology would need to articulate itself with the relevant approaches of the other social sciences. The latter, on the other hand, depend on sociology for the broader societal dynamics and implications of change.

A key reason why sociology has so far not realized its potential with regard to conceptualizing Europe is that it is mostly still in the grip of what Anthony Smith (1979) has called "methodological nationalism"; of taking the nation-state as the normal and self-evident unit of analysis. This is true not only for the large number of single-country studies that still comprise the bulk of sociological research and where the extension of the society under question is usually implicitly equated with that of the nation-state in which the sociologist works, but also for comparative studies which usually consist of comparisons between nation-state societies.

The purest tangible forms of such comparative methodological nationalism are the quantitative comparisons, often based on institutionally accumulated data sets, where nation-states are coded in terms of the variables under question – dependent variables such as welfare-state development or industrial conflicts, and independent variables such as demographic or economic indicators of "modernization" or political power structure. But even where the focus is on specific social fields and institutions below the level of the state, such as the family or the firm, these are usually examined in their national contexts, so that one then speaks of the "French" family or the "German" firm. Other salient lines of differentiation – in the case of the family, e.g., religion or class – do not appear any more, or reappear as features of whole nation-states. Regional differences also do not come up, except through grouping the nation-state societies themselves under terms such as "Scandinavian" or "Mediterranean", or "conservative" or "liberal".

Where the state as such is concerned, as e.g. in studies of the welfare state, this strategy of focussing on nation-states may have seemed natural. But even here, the consequences of European integration now render such a strategy increasingly inappropriate (see Chapter 1 by Wolfgang Streeck, Chapter 2 by Joakim Palme, and Chapter 3 by Walter Korpi). Direct political regulation in the sense of positive social policy by European institutions is slim, but the impact of the EU on the national welfare states is nevertheless considerable and growing. As Leibfried and Pierson (2000) point out, the EU impact has two novel features. First, it is no longer a reaction against and protection from market failures but is directly connected to the process of market-making itself – to removing the obstacles against the free circulation of goods, services, capital and workers. Second, it is unusually law and court driven. As a result, "national welfare state regimes are now part of a larger, multi-tiered system of social policy. Member governments profoundly influence this structure, but they no longer fully control it" (2000: 289).

Of course there have so far been compelling practical reasons for following the route of methodological nationalism. Data collection usually occurs at the national level. The emergence of the nation-state has resulted in the creation of nationally centralized data-producing administrations, including Statistical Offices. Social science has followed suit, even with data projects that have been organized bottom-up, without the participation of official state bureaucracies, such as the International Social Survey Program (ISSP). The more substantial reason for proceeding along national lines is that the nation-state has indeed come to create national societies and to permeate them with increasingly far-reaching policies and regulations. Over the last two centuries, within-nation differences in Europe have decreased (while some of the between-nation differences have for some time increased). This is true even for such basic processes as demographic reproduction (Watkins 1991). Thus, for many issues the nation-state has indeed been the most appropriate unit of analysis and comparison.

But there is a downside. Sociology, being concerned with societies, has to ask to what extent its societies coincide with nation-states. There are issues where, e.g., regionally or "ethnically" defined units – or units defined along other social criteria – are better suited. Theoretically informed strategies of comparison need to address this problem explicitly. It is compounded by the fact that the "true" boundaries of a society are not only an analytical problem but also a battleground for political strategies of domination, inclusion and exclusion (as shown in Chapter 5 by Liam O'Dowd) – identity politics in all its forms. Methodological nationalism tends to assume clear-cut and stable boundaries and identities, thereby neglecting the recreation and shifting of boundaries and the emergence of hybrid forms of attachment and identification. Moreover, by claiming the mutual independence of national units it downplays the various interactions between them (what historians have termed "relational history"): the multitude of contacts, exchanges, hegemonic imposition or mutual learning, and assertions of identity by taking the other as a reference case (to be emulated or to be avoided).

The problems are visualized by the question of whether (all or some) European societies have become more similar to each other; in other words, whether they have developed towards a common structure – and if yes, what have been the driving forces. As noted above, the emergence of the nation-states has increased their internal homogeneity, and to some extent the heterogeneity among them. On the other hand, Western European societies through their common history share some basic characteristics, and their rapid modernization since the economic boom years of the 1950s and 1960s has brought them closer to each other, thereby creating the common features of what may be called a "European social model". Whether such a model exists has not been one of the preoccupations of sociology; comparative research has instead given priority to the differences among societies (or among clusters of them). The first to offer a social-structural analysis of whether we are moving towards a European society has not been a sociologist but a social historian, Hartmut Kaelble (1987). It is only recently that the question has been taken up in sociology as well, first with regard to the welfare state and work organization of European societies, and then in the more general sense outlined above. Mayer (2001) points to convergence in life course regimes. Crouch (1999: chapter 14) discusses the evidence for the domains of religious, ethnic, and party blocs, class cleavages, the family, concern for social consensus, the city, and economic structures and institutions, and concludes that if there is a unity among Western European societies, it lies in their forms of diversity: an "ordered, limited, and structured diversity" (1999: 404). As our discussion has shown, however, convergence alone is not a sufficient criterion for the broader issue of social Europeanization. Becoming more alike does not yet mean becoming one society – the relational aspects need also to be taken into account.

The impressive career of the concept of globalization in recent years (e.g., Beck 1997; Cohen and Kennedy 2000) would seem to indicate that the sociological focus on national societies is becoming a thing of the past. Sociology has discovered the world society and its articulation with the nation-state (Meyer *et al.* 1997). The literature on globalization indeed takes up many of the points mentioned above, those of the relations among societies as well as those of contested borders and hybridization. But regarding Europe, it is clearly unsatisfactory; it jumps too easily over what is the most salient supranational level, European integration, and situates itself on a level, world society, which is a much less powerful reality. Transnationalization turns out to be mostly Europeanization, not only in institutional terms but also in those of the flows of goods and people (see Chapter 8 by Jürgen Gerhards; also Beisheim *et al.* 1999). This is not to say that sociology should now focus exclusively on European integration, and thereby reproduce the exclusionary effects of the EU itself. The experience of globalization provides a healthy antidote by locating Europe on the global map and making it visible from the perspective of its outsiders as well.

What is the distinctive contribution that we may expect from sociology in addressing these issues? One way of asserting this distinctiveness is to say that sociology is concerned with the social "embeddedness" of the economy and the polity. This concept, made popular by the seminal work of Karl Polanyi (e.g., Polanyi

1944), is more than an easy metaphor; it can serve to highlight the institutions that condition and moderate economic and political change even while in turn being influenced by it. For economic change, the institutions of the "work society" are a restraining context and a buffer at the same time. This applies to social protection and the organization of work itself (see Chapter 1 by Streeck, Chapter 2 by Palme, and Chapter 4 by Petmesidou) as well as to gender cleavages and the gender contract (as in Chapter 3 by Korpi and Chapter 9 by Esping-Andersen). For political change, the conflicts over borders and their legitimacy (O'Dowd in Chapter 5), the patterns of identity and citizenship (Heiskala in Chapter 6 and Saraceno in Chapter 7), and the institutions of cultural communication (Gerhards in Chapter 8, de Swaan in Chapter 10, and Schnapper in Chapter 11) have a similar role.

European work societies and welfare states

In its early stages after the Second World War, Western European political integration was driven by the attempts of nation-states to create the conditions for economic growth and social cohesion through a stable framework for European trade and cooperation. As Milward (1992) in his penetrating study of the first two decades of the integration process shows, these were the roots of the – at first sight highly unlikely – partial sacrifice of sovereignty that integration implied. The nation-states were not following a death drive by giving themselves up into a new supra-structure; they were on the contrary trying to rescue themselves by agreeing to just the loss of sovereignty necessary for their own survival.

Western European societies at the end of the Second World War were in ruins, physically but even more economically and socially. Political and economic power had shifted to North America and the Soviet Union. To achieve economic growth and social pacification in this threatening situation of losing ground seemed possible only through a renewed social contract, with massive protection of those groups that were particularly at risk and at the same time had particular political weight and thus presented a potential threat to political and social stability. These groups were above all those of mining, heavy industry and agriculture. The new social contract took the form of a social model based on full employment for male bread-winners and strong social protection for those at risk of being excluded; in other words, the form of what came later to be known as the European model of the "work society". But to implement such a model was not possible for the weak nation-states alone; it seemed feasible only in an institutionally secure framework of economic exchange and cooperation (including Germany which economically was still no *quantité négligeable*). This is the story that led six of the countries of continental Western Europe on the path towards economic and political integration which through several – partly successful, partly abortive – institutional steps resulted in the Treaty of Rome.

The welfare state has a crucial role in this story; it offered a form of protection that made it possible to run the risk of exposing the economy to the cold winds of international competition. What Rieger and Leibfried (2001) aptly call "welfare mercantilism" was the attempt to use the welfare state as a functional equivalent for trade protectionism, and thus as a form of social protection that would allow the opening up of the economy to European (and even global) cooperation and competition.

In the literature on international relations, what has come to be known as the "realist" approach to European unity sees the latter as a product of political elites. It has often been formulated in terms of international security, presenting the emerging Western European unification process as an attempt to contain the continuing threat posed by even a defeated Germany and/or as a reaction to the new threat posed by the Soviet Union. In the latter view, the successive take-over of the Central European countries by the Soviet Union in the years after the Second World War was experienced by the countries of Western European as a challenge to their own independence which could be stopped only through giving up some of their sovereignty in favor of a common political framework. Even after the project of a European Defense Community between France and Germany had failed, the impetus remained, leading to a form of integration in which economic coordination for the time being took precedence over a strictly political one. Arguments along this line should not be neglected, but as Milward (1992) rightly points out, they are not a sufficient explanation for the European process because there would have been other ways to achieve the security goals than through political and economic integration.

During the boom decades of the 1950s and 1960s – variously called the "Golden Age" or (in France) the "Trente glorieuses" – Western European societies perfected their model of the work society based on full (male) employment and a redistributive welfare state. It may have seemed at the end of this period that relinquishing national sovereignty in favor of European integration would become expendable – a feeling that nourished a growing Euroscepticism. Thus, the very success of European integration in promoting economic growth and political stability would have allowed it to be relinquished again. But in the early 1980s, the experience of Mitterand's France showed once more that it was not possible to maintain the conditions for economic prosperity and growth on a national level alone, with only loose coupling to the other European exchange partners. This led to a renewed push for European integration, with its (provisional) culmination points in the Maastricht and Amsterdam treaties.

Today, of the trias that was at the origin of European integration – free trade, political protection for key industries, and a welfare state to cushion the deprived – only the first seems to have survived. The European social model has come under increasing pressure. However, while it clearly needs to be reexamined and redesigned, some of its basic principles remain critical for the future of Europe as a relatively unified polity and society. Whether the welfare state contributes to or restricts economic growth is open to debate (see, e.g., Atkinson 1999), but the fact that it is a necessary buffer to protect those at risk of being marginalized and excluded by it has not changed. Without such a buffer, the legitimacy of opening the economy to international competition will wane, and be replaced by growing popular support for protectionism and isolationism. Public welfare is needed as a resource for social pacification and integration just as strongly as before. But the conditions for it have hardened from both sides: from the demand side in terms of the increasing number of those at risk through unemployment or under-employment, and the increasing burden on the welfare state posed by its use as a means of assuring the integration of disadvantaged regions;[4] and from the supply side in terms of the decreasing tax and contribution base available for redistribution. In addition, there are other challenges posed by major societal changes now under way (see the chapter by Joakim Palme). One is the demographic challenge of aging populations common (in somewhat varying degree) to all European societies, which is by now well known but whose possible solutions are highly contentious. A second challenge is that of changing work participation and organization, especially through the incorporation of women into the labor force which is part of the renegotiation of the gender contract (as shown by Gösta Esping-Andersen), and through the changing work career patterns towards what some observers see as the demise of the "normal work biography" (even though its extent is under dispute).[5]

Even more than the old welfare regime, the new model is predicated upon ability for and access to work. This can be argued in two different variants: by stressing the move from redistributive and protective policies to competitive and productive solidarity (as outlined by Wolfgang Streeck), or by insisting on the continued viability of a universal welfare state model (as Joakim Palme does) which then increasingly depends on a well-functioning work nexus, exemplified by the active labor market policies of the Nordic countries. In both variants, the welfare state can no longer operate as "politics against markets" (Esping-Andersen 1985); it has to be reconceptualized – in the words of Streeck – as politics *within* and *with* the markets.

Identity, citizenship and communication in Europe

For the question of identity, the restrictions imposed by focussing on the nation-state are especially pertinent. It is often claimed that national identification is the pre-eminent form of collective solidarity in the modern age (Smith 1991).[6] It may be doubted to what extent this has really been the case in national societies, given the multiple identity referents that have existed: territorial referents such as region and local community as well as confessional, ethnic or class-based referents. It is with the new transnational referents, however, that the restrictions of the traditional perspective become most obvious.

Will Europe work only if it is based on a European identity?[7] On a general level, the question asks whether a widespread sense of collective identity is at all necessary for a political or social community – whether it needs its members to identify with it in order to be viable. Sociology is divided on this question. In some theoretical approaches, the answer is clearly no. If societies are seen to be held together by the results of strategic exchange based on individual preferences (as in utilitarian or rational choice approaches), or by systemic features without resort to individual action (as, e.g., in Luhmann's brand of systems theories), then identity is not needed for social integration. If, on the other hand, societies are seen to be integrated by culture, identity is a major prerequisite for a society to exist as such. In Parsons' view, for example, a "societal community" defined by drawing a boundary anchored in the experience of its members is a necessary component of all societies.

The question is posed in political science as well, and much of the current literature leans to the second answer, stressing the importance of political culture and identity for political integration. The broadly diagnosed "crises of legitimacy" of modern political systems are often reframed as crises of political identity. Conversely, the massive mobilizing potential of political identities has become evident in the recent surges of ethnonationalism. Some authors even claim that everything now turns around identity. A radical example is Huntington's (1997) much-publicized view of the imminent clash of civilizations, where identity becomes the main motivating force. For him, the key question that modern individuals try to solve, and to which only the large religiously based civilizations provide the answer, is "Where do I really belong?".

It is doubtful, however, whether political communities always need the full force of this mobilizing potential. For the European level, this issue is especially pertinent. "As long as the European Union does not require extensive and far-reaching solidaristic behavior from its peoples, full-fledged collective identity is hardly needed. This would change dramatically if the Union begins to levy high taxes and to redistribute major resources" (Armingeon 1999: 236), as, e.g., through a fully developed European welfare system. Even more far-reaching would be for the Union to demand that its citizens (its male citizens, usually) give their lives for the public interest – a demand that until now has been reserved to the nation-state. Yet even for the latter, attachment need not be total. In modern democratic polities, citizens tend to conceive of their loyalties not as natural and boundless but as reflexive and conditional. This may be one of the key reasons why democracies have so far never waged war against each other.

A second line of argument that questions the importance of collective identities is to view them not as an antecedent but as a (more or less automatic) consequence of the development of institutions. Thus, a European identity would not be a precondition for a European society but a by-product of its institutional construction – of its growing cultural networks of communication and exchange, its common economy and money, its political framework of governance and representation, its institutions of redistribution and solidarity, or its European-level organizations, from enterprises and unions to scientific associations and football leagues. Especially salient here would be the establishment of a European public sphere (see Chapter 8 by Jürgen Gerhards) – itself dependent on changes in the political institutions of the Union. All this of course requires some commonality in the linguistic bases for communication (see Chapter 10 by Abram de Swaan).

A third line of argument – taking its clues from both preceding ones – contrasts identity as a sense of belonging with the institutions of personhood themselves, such as citizenship and the rights and duties that go with it. In this view, identity is a rather soft and fluctuating surface aspect of political belonging, while the hard and stable deep structure consists of the legal attachments of citizens to their political community – legal categorizations being much more consequential for social inclusion/exclusion than cultural ones. The problem is thus shifted to the conditions for constructing European-level citizenship (see Chapter 7 by Chiara Saraceno; also Bauböck 2001).

The political actors of European integration – whatever their theoretical inclinations – seem unwilling to take chances: they go by the assumption that European identity does matter, and needs to be constructed and nurtured. There is a broad range of efforts on this behalf, on the aggregate level of politics and culture as well as on the individual level of the citizens. First, there is the constitutional meaning – as expressed in various official documents – of identity as the political identity of the Community itself in terms of what might be called its "statehood". A second understanding of European identity, more relevant to our present concerns, centers on what is often called the "idea" of Europe – what Europe is, or what it could or should be, as manifested in the texts by or discourses among various groups of intellectuals and politicians. On a third level, we move from the cultural meaning systems as accessible in written texts to the cultural practices through which these meanings are created and maintained. This is the broad field, much in evidence in recent scholarship since Nora's (1984) path-breaking compilation, of the *lieux de mémoire*: monuments, celebrations, myths, heroes, holidays, hymns, flags, museums, pilgrimages. While it is often claimed that Europe is still very deficient in these respects, there are also some unquestionable successes, such as the European flag which has become a popular symbol of unity permeating many layers of everyday life (including car license plates). And there is no inherent reason why it should not be possible to repeat this success with other domains, e.g., that of European founding myths and holidays (except perhaps that they would have to be added to an already crowded calendar of religious and national holidays).

The fourth level is that of individual identity proper, or more precisely, of collective identity as experienced and expressed by the individual citizens. Whether understood as a consequence of the political identity or cultural "idea" of Europe, as a result of institutional processes, or as the outcome of conscious constructive efforts, it needs to be assessed as a phenomenon of its own. This has been the focus of much attention by the European integrationists, leading to the public opinion surveys conducted by Eurobarometer since 1972. The results show that Europe is no match yet for the more powerful territorial referents of locality, region and nation. The feeling of attachment towards Europe is not even higher than that towards the world; in contrast to what has been found for economic exchange, Europeanization and globalization in identity terms are on a par.

If a working Europe depended on a strong and uncontested sense of European identity among its peoples, its chances at present would look slim. However, the standard Eurobarometer measurements are somewhat misleading because conceptually too simple. In collective identities, multiple or even conflicting attachments are the rule rather than the exception. Accordingly, European identity should be conceived as multi-level or multi-layered, comprising global and national (and possibly regional and local) attachments as well. Of particular interest is the concept of "hybrid" identity which has been coined for situations of cultural overlap and interpenetration. Hybridity means that contradictory logics of action linked to separate practices are recombined in new patterns in which the contradictory referents remain visible and powerful. With such patterns, changes in situational opportunities lead to switching the referent that is most salient.

Europe as a post-national entity may offer a focus for such contradictory feelings of belonging. Their obvious potential carrier groups are those with conflicting or fuzzy territorial attachments: border populations, international migrants, people in diaspora situations, those with multiple citizenship, or those in multinational or multi-ethnic marriages – situations which are increasingly prevalent today. In border situations between nation-states (see Chapter 5 by Liam O'Dowd) or in those of large-scale migration, where the territorial referent may be the focus of bitter struggles and which are cultural battlegrounds as well, one would expect a hardening of national identities. But even here, there is some evidence that the European level of identity may become more salient. Whether this is the case depends on the link between the two sets of issues that we have discussed here: those of identity and those of social protection. Conflicts are likely to fundamentalize themselves under conditions of exclusion, economic deprivation and moral devaluation. The conditions for avoiding such an outcome are the granting of status, economic security and respect. What this means is that for the new agenda of Europeanization, the old agenda of inclusion and welfare remains critical (see Woodward and Kohli 2001).

The contributions

A single volume such as this one is obviously not able to cover all the issues of the sociological agenda. Through selective examples, the present volume nevertheless aims to touch upon the critical points for establishing whether Europe will work.

The book is organized so that it answers to three dimensions of the question posed by its title. The first part concerns the future of the European work and welfare societies, asking how current developments have changed the conditions on which the old European model of employment and social protection was based, and drawing the outlines of a possible new European social model. The second part focusses on the questions of identity and citizenship in Europe and of European borders. The third part addresses the construction of institutions, especially those of communication such as language or the public sphere, and reflects on the capacity of sociology to conceptualize the European process.

In the first part of the book, three authors – Wolfgang Streeck, Joakim Palme, and Walter Korpi – consider the changes in welfare structures and policies, while Maria Petmesidou concentrates on those of the labor market.

Wolfgang Streeck sets the tone in his contribution on the link between international competition and supranational integration. Economic competition in his view is reinforced, not contained, by European integration. Cost and other pressures faced by the highly productive sectors of the European economies reduce the potential for redistributive politics. This means that there will be no supranational replication of the post-war national welfare state. Centralization of social policy at the European level is highly unlikely; we are instead witnessing a process of post-hierarchical integration characterized by coordination among national polities rather than harmonization, and by competitive adjustment managed at the national level. As a result the traditional European model of social solidarity is changing. National and subnational communities increasingly seek to defend their cohesion, rather than through protection and redistribution, through joint competitive and productive success – through politics, not *against* markets, but *within* and *with* them. The chapter outlines the main contours of what seems to be an emerging new "European social model".

Joakim Palme in his answer to the question "Will social Europe work?" reaches a similar conclusion. The crisis of the welfare state in Europe has caused great uncertainty about the future of social protection. The past decade has been marked by mass unemployment and increasing social inequalities. Large groups are threatened by social exclusion while the benefit entitlements and social services are being reduced. The similarities among the various parts of Europe in this respect are striking. Palme first discusses the present challenges to the systems of social protection: globalization, population aging, exit/entry problems on labor markets, the end of the full employment era, social exclusion, and the Europeanization of politics. He then demonstrates how sociology can empirically evaluate the effects of the various social policy strategies, and how it can design the elements of a reform strategy aimed at joining social policy goals (reduction of poverty and inequality) with efficiency considerations. Such a reform needs to maintain the universal approach to social protection, but also to increase the number of tax-payers and decrease the number of benefit recipients. For this, it is critical to provide the proper incentives, resources and opportunities for people to enter the labor market. In this respect, the Nordic model of improving human resources and of active labor market policy provides a fruitful example for other countries as well.

Walter Korpi takes up the new forms of inequality as a challenge to the welfare state. He aims to broaden the concept of inequality beyond its traditional focus on social class by including gender as another major dimension, and examines how gender and class interact with welfare states in distributive processes. His empirical basis is a unique comparative data set for eighteen OECD countries since the Second World War, assembled to make possible fine-grained analyses of welfare state development. Korpi shows that with respect to gender, inequality cannot be restricted to material standards of living but must include aspects of social agency: access to democratic politics, higher education and labor force participation. A welfare state typology appropriate for gender inequality – distinguishing between market orientation, general family support, and dual earnership – needs to be different from typologies developed for class inequality. Together, these two typologies can serve to describe major constellations of welfare state institutions in Europe, and to explain their development over time. During the last quarter of the twentieth century, the OECD countries have witnessed a more substantial decrease in gender than in class inequality, linked in part to the return of mass unemployment which disproportionally hits lower social classes.

Maria Petmesidou investigates the employment and labor market policies of Southern Europe, which present a challenge to the current debate on "Social Europe" both with respect to work and welfare regimes and with respect to the corresponding policy issues. She first discusses how the study of European welfare state regimes can allow for the peculiarities of the European South (Portugal, Spain, Italy and Greece). The emphasis is on how responses – emanating from the national, supranational and local/regional level – to new challenges modify traditional forms of socio-economic regulation. The second part deals with labor market policy reform and industrial relations in the four South European countries in the 1980s and 1990s (especially under the pressure of EU convergence criteria). Convergence or divergence in labor market regulation among these countries is examined in the light of recent debates on alternative policy paradigms. Italy and to some extent Portugal are examples for macro-level consensus building, while Spain and Greece are characterized by highly politicized industrial relations with rather weak social concertation. But even in Italy, the prospects of a model of "competitive corporatism" are slim.

In the second part of the book, Liam O'Dowd, Risto Heiskala and Chiara Saraceno discuss identity and citizenship as key dimensions in the construction of Europe.

Liam O'Dowd links the construction of European identity to the question of borders and border regions. He shows that the study of state border issues is a *sine qua non* for an adequate understanding of the European Union as an emergent transnational polity and society. In the twentieth century Europe has been a factory of state borders as its great multinational empires and many of its multinational states fragmented often violently. The project of European integration may be seen partly as a response to this fragmentation and as an attempt to develop a more negotiated and consensual approach to border change in its geographical, functional and symbolic forms. O'Dowd first outlines why sociology has generally tended to either 'normalize' or discount state borders, thereby failing to question them for analytical purposes. He then locates the EC-EU in the context of the historically volatile nature of European borders. In the third section he examines the development of transfrontier regionalism as one indicator of the way borders are being reconfigured. Finally, he reflects on the new, more complex and specialised architecture of borders. He concludes that the European Union's lack of stable political borders militates against the emergence of a coherent European identity.

For *Risto Heiskala*, Europe already exists in some sense but its identity remains ambiguous. What makes this ambiguous identity flow even more is the process of globalization. Heiskala discusses the articulation and dearticulation of the identity of Europe in terms of economical, political and cultural power. This is followed by an examination of the issues of globalization and their implications for European identity. Special consideration is given to the network properties of the emerging world society, and to the extent to which individuals, states and world regions are included in or excluded from these global networks. Heiskala thus raises, in a new context, Karl Polanyi's question: What kind of a time is our time? On the chances of a unified European identity to emerge he is highly skeptical. In his view (as in that of Gerhards) Europe is characterized by a cultural lag: it is economically strongly and politically to some extent integrated while culturally it remains highly fragmented.

Chiara Saraceno addresses the ambivalences and contradictions in the twin issues of constructing Europe and constructing European citizenship. She points to the intrinsic tensions between nation-state and supra-state polity, and between national citizenship and European citizenship. She also underlines the contrast between an instrumental view of the European Union and a view which sees the Union as the society constituted by its citizens, not by the member countries' citizens. The argument is developed on the basis of three examples. The first two illustrate the ways in which gender is included in the fabric of citizenship: the constitutionalization of gender equality rights in the EU (increasingly hampered by the weakening resources for implementing them) and "mainstreaming" (the requirement that women be present in substantial numbers in all relevant areas of decision-making and agenda-setting). If the gender aspect is ignored, the social rights may be incomplete. The third example concerns the fragmentation and displacement of decision-making by bringing in actors from outside the institutional policy framework (such as those from civil society). Saraceno concludes that the process of European unification is far from being straightforward and that the "gender lens" brings out its ambivalent features (including the divergent interests among European women themselves) especially well.

The third part of the book assembles chapters by Jürgen Gerhards, Gösta Esping-Andersen, Abram de Swaan and Dominique Schnapper that focus on cultural institutions on the European level, and on the reorientation of the sociological perspective itself.

Jürgen Gerhards asserts and deplores the lack of a European public sphere. In view of the dramatic changes through the EU's planned enlargement and internal consolidation, the non-existence of a broad public debate is astonishing. For the case of West Germany, Gerhards empirically traces the development of transnationalization from 1950 to 1996 in three societal subsystems: the economy, the polity and the public sphere. He shows that during this period there has indeed been a moderate transnationalization of the economy which turns out to have been mainly a process of Europeanization. Contrary to many assumptions, the markets have not run away from political control; economic Europeanization has been paralleled by Europeanization of political decision-making. The development of a European public sphere, however, lags behind these processes; the public sphere is still nationally bound and therefore unable to control the Europeanized political system. This lag can partly be explained by the democracy deficit of the EU; a stronger democratization of the EU would also lead to a stronger European public sphere.

Gösta Esping-Andersen projects a new model of the micro-foundations of post-industrial transformation. His starting-point is the backwardness of the implicit models of European society held by sociology and their inability to assess the ruptures that are currently occurring. Institutions such as the family are massively changing, as do motivations and incentives which drive human behavior, scarce resources and claims on them, productivity and the production of wealth. The dominant sociological responses to these transformations consist either in the navel-gazing of micro-level analyses, in switching to history or in the over-determinism of path dependency. Another approach is represented by Manuel Castell's latest work which begins with a preconceived vision in the sense of an imagined Gestalt in which to fit the empirical pieces of information. Against these approaches, Esping-Andersen opts for his own methodology of directed empiricism and variation-finding based on weak theory and loose hypotheses. He illustrates his methodological proposition by focussing on the family – a fundamental sociological institution which is linked to the transformation of gender relations and the emergence of the service economy, and thus reveals the core dilemmas of the present society and the arrival of a new social logic.

Abram de Swaan delineates the language constellation of the European Union. The human species is fragmented into some five thousand mutually unintelligible language groups. As they are connected by multilingual individuals, these groups nevertheless form a surprisingly coherent system. The many thousands of mostly unwritten, small peripheral languages are connected in clusters to a central (state or national) language. At the transnational level, the central languages are each connected to one of a dozen supercentral languages, with English at the hub of the system. A simple measure, the Q-value, characterizes both the position of a language within this system and its utility as a means of communication. These are the background notions needed for analyzing the European language constellation. The political discussion at the European level is defined by the dilemma between the wish for conservation of a multiplicity of languages and the need for efficient communication. A latent "voting cycle" operates in the European Parliament, leading to an immobilism that paradoxically may reinforce the Europeans' gravitation towards English.

Dominique Schnapper concludes the book with the question 'Is there a European sociology?'. Sociology is a child of the modern democratic society, and thus of Europe and of the Europeans dispersed around the world, particularly in North America. It has a close link to the social problems at the level of the nation-states, and there has always been a tension between these particularistic experiences and sociology's rationalistic and therefore universal ambition – similar to the tension between the rationality of democratic society's principle of citizenship and its exclusionary practices. Schnapper demonstrates this tension by examining the approaches to interethnic relations and inequalities that have emerged in the different national sociologies. It is fitting that with the construction of the European Union there is also a European sociology being constituted. The latter is confronted by the same problems as the social and political construction of Europe: managing the link to North America and maintaining its national traditions (such as in the field of culture and language) while remaining open to its universalism.

We thus end up with a self-reflexive look at the themes and languages of European sociology itself as an example of whether Europe will work. And we are appropriately enough also reminded that our use of language must accommodate divergent and possibly irreconcilable criteria. On the one hand we need to maximize our potential for efficient communication, and this leads Europeans of all mother tongues inexorably towards English. The present book is a document of this fatal attraction, as is the language "policy" of the European Sociological Association itself where the absence of any formal rules coexists with the almost total *de facto* domination of English. On the other hand we know and feel that language is more than a means of communication, and that giving up our languages would be tantamount to losing the cultural plurality which is constitutive for European unity. European sociology in this respect is no better off than European society.

Notes

1 The book by Leibfried and Pierson (1995) presents the parties to this controversy in the domain of "Social Europe".
2 It is to redress this shortcoming that the European Sociological Association (ESA) has been formed, and organizes its biannual conferences. The topic for the 4th ESA Conference in Amsterdam (August 1999), *Will Europe work?*, was chosen with the ideas presented in this introduction in mind. As noted in the Acknowledgements, all but one of the chapters of this book have originally been presented as plenary or semi-plenary contributions to this conference, and have since been substantially revised. The conference theme generated a large amount of intellectual reflection and debate, highlighting the ways in which sociology can and should imprint on issues that it has so far mostly left to other disciplines.
3 There is as yet no systematic sociological treatment of Europe, comparable, e.g., to what Wallace and Wallace (2000) have done for the analysis of the policy process. A case in point is Crouch's (1999) recent broad overview of social change in Western Europe from the early 1960s to the mid-1990s. This ambitious study – highly commendable in its comprehensive approach to the whole territory of Western Europe – discusses the extent of "sociological Europeanization" in the sense of the emergence of a "typically European social form" (1999: 396) of national societies, but almost completely dismisses the European level as such.
4 The political utilization – some would say exploitation – of the welfare state in the process of German unification is a case in point, and foreshadows the demands that will be posed by the EU's extension to the East.
5 See the contributions in Kocka and Offe (2000) and especially Kohli (2000b).
6 Niethammer (2000) in his recent critical semantic history of "collective identity" has also taken national identity to be the primary modern form of this concept, and the one where its (to him) highly problematic political undertones manifest themselves most clearly.
7 The following arguments are taken from (and more fully developed in) Kohli (2000a).

References

Armingeon, K. (1999) "From the Europe of nations to the European nation: Introduction", in Kriesi, H., Armingeon, K., Siegrist, H., and Wimmer, A. (eds) *Nation and National Identity: The European Experience in Perspective*, Chur/Zürich: Rüegger: 235–41.

Atkinson, A.B. (1999) *The Economic Consequences of Rolling Back the Welfare State*, Cambridge, MA: MIT Press.

Bach, M. (2000) "Die europäische Integration und die unerfüllten Versprechen der Demokratie", in Klingemann, H.-D. and Neidhardt, F. (eds) *Zur Zukunft der Demokratie. Herausforderungen im Zeitalter der Globalisierung* (WZB-Jahrbuch 2000), Berlin: edition sigma: 185–213.

Bauböck, R. (2001) "Recombinant citizenship", in Woodward, A. and Kohli, M. (eds) *Inclusions and Exclusions in European Societies*, London: Routledge.

Beck, U. (1997) *Was ist Globalisierung? Irrtümer des Globalismus – Antworten auf Globalisierung*, Frankfurt/M: Suhrkamp.

Beisheim, M., Dreher, S., Walter, G., Zangl, B., and Zürn, M. (1999) *Im Zeitalter der Globalisierung? Thesen und Daten zur gesellschaftlichen und politischen Denationalisierung*, Baden-Baden: Nomos.

Bornschier, V. (2001), "European processes and the state of the European Union" in Woodward, A. and Kohli, M. (eds) *Inclusions and Exclusions in European Societies*, London: Routledge.

Cohen, R. and Kennedy, P. (2000), *Global Sociology*, Basingstoke: Macmillan.

Crouch, C. (1999) *Social Change in Western Europe*, Oxford: Oxford University Press.

Esping-Andersen, G. (1985) *Politics Against Markets: The Social Democratic Road to Power*, Princeton, NJ: Princeton University Press.

Huntington, S.P. (1997) *The Clash of Civilizations and the Remaking of World Order*, New York: Touchstone.

Kaelble, H. (1987) *Auf dem Weg zu einer europäischen Gesellschaft?*, München: Beck.

Kapteyn, P. (1995) *The Stateless Market: The European Dilemma of Integration and Civilization*, London: Routledge.

Kohler-Koch, B. and Eising, R. (eds) (1999) *The Transformation of Governance in the European Union*, London: Routledge.

Kocka, J. and Offe, C. (eds) (2000) *Geschichte und Zukunft der Arbeit*, Frankfurt/M: Campus.

Kohli, M. (2000a) "The Battlegrounds of European Identity", *European Societies* 2: 113–37.

—— (2000b) "Arbeit im Lebenslauf: Alte und neue Paradoxien", in Kocka, J. and Offe, C. (eds) *Geschichte und Zukunft der Arbeit*, Frankfurt/M: Campus: 362–82.

Leibfried, S. and Pierson, P. (eds) (1995) *European Social Policy: Between Fragmentation and Integration*, Washington, DC: Brookings.

—— (2000) "Social policy: Left to courts and markets?", in Wallace, H. and Wallace, W. (eds) *Policy-Making in the European Union*, 4th ed., Oxford: Oxford University Press: 267–92.

Marks, G., Hooghe, L., and Blank, K. (1996) "European integration since the 1980s: State-centric versus multi-level governance", *Journal of Common Market Studies* 34: 343–78.

Mayer, K.U. (2001) "The paradox of global social change and national path dependencies: Lifecourse patterns in advanced societies" in Woodward, A. and Kohli, M. (eds) *Inclusions and Exclusions in European Societies*, London: Routledge.

Meyer, J.W., Boli, J., Thomas, G.M., and Ramirez, F.O. (1997) "World society and the nation-state", *American Journal of Sociology* 103: 144–81.

Milward, A.S. (1992) *The European Rescue of the Nation-State*, Berkeley: University of California Press.

Niethammer, L. (2000) *Kollektive Identität: Heimliche Quellen einer unheimlichen Konjunktur*, Reinbek bei Hamburg: Rowohlt Taschenbuch Verlag.

Nora, P. (ed.) (1984) *Les lieux de mémoire*, 4 vols, Paris: Gallimard.

Polanyi, K. (1967 [1944]) *The Great Transformation*, Boston: Beacon Press.

Rieger, E. and Leibfried, S. (2001) *Grundlagen der Globalisierung. Perspektiven des Wohlfahrtsstaats*, Frankfurt/M: Suhrkamp.

Scharpf, F.W. (1999) *Governing in Europe: Effective and Democratic?*, Oxford: Oxford University Press.

Smith, A.D. (1979) *Nationalism in the Twentieth Century*, Oxford: Martin Robertson.

—— (1991) *National Identity*, London: Penguin.

Streeck, W. and Schmitter, P.C. "From national corporatism to transnational pluralism: Organized interests in the Single European Market", *Politics and Society* 19: 133–64.

Wallace, H. and Wallace, W. (eds) (2000) *Policy-Making in the European Union*, 4th ed., Oxford: Oxford University Press.

Watkins, S.C. (1991) *From Provinces into Nations: Demographic Integration in Western Europe 1870–1960*, Princeton: Princeton University Press.

Woodward, A. and Kohli, M. (eds) *Inclusions and Exclusions in European Societies*, London: Routledge.

Zürn, M. (2000) "Democratic governance beyond the nation-state: The EU and other international institutions", *European Journal of International Relations* 6: 183–221.

Part I

Working in Europe
Towards a new social model

1 International competition, supranational integration, national solidarity

The emerging constitution of "Social Europe"

Wolfgang Streeck

Whatever other consequences European integration may have had, it has vastly increased the competitiveness of the European economy. Competition is a pervasive social force. Not only do its effects extend far beyond the firms and sectors directly exposed to it, but they are beginning to transform the institutional base and indeed the very concept of social solidarity. There is no reason why Europe, in spite of its high labor costs, should not continue to have highly profitable firms and industries even in a global economy. But there is also no doubt that the internationally exposed manufacturing sector of the European economy will in future absorb only a declining share of the European workforce. In fact, where restructuring in response to the new competitive conditions is successful, it entails the ruthless elimination of slack, above all of surplus labor. What was jokingly said of the German railway system before privatization – that it was "a social fund with a railway attached to it" (*eine Sozialkasse mit angeschlossener Eisenbahn*) – to some extent also applied to the large oligopolists of Fordist mass production: given the manifold protections from competition they were able to devise for themselves, they could afford to sustain unused resources and allow unions and works councils to divert them to redistributive solidarity (Kochan *et al.* 1986). The labor shedding of the 1990s, even in an immensely successful manufacturing country like Germany, shows that this period has come to an end.

Today's large firms perceive the social solidarity functions they were enlisted to perform by unions and governments in the Fordist era as a cost burden that they must externalize to society if they are to survive in their new, more competitive environments. Less productive workers, for which unions used to be able to negotiate secure employment in overpaid marginal jobs, have long been retired or placed on unemployment benefit, at public rather than private expense. Inside companies workers now tend to be employed, trained and paid strictly according to their productive contribution, ending redistribution at the point of production and turning over responsibility for economic equality and social cohesion to public policy. At the same time, the ability of the latter to extract resources for social purposes from the competitive sector is declining. Facing more demanding markets and capital givers, exposed firms have only little to spare for "outsiders" if they are to remain leading competitors. That in an international economy they can easily shift their taxable activities to more friendly jurisdictions provides them in addition with the capacity to get their will.

Intensified competition in the exposed sector and the subsequent restructuring of the latter radiate into the domestic sector, which has gradually ceased to be a "sheltered" one (Scharpf 1999a). Firms operating in today's more competitive international markets have no choice but pass on the cost pressures they are experiencing, not only to their domestic suppliers, but also to the public sector. In all European countries, this has resulted in intense rationalization of public admin-istration, as well as the privatization of large segments of national infrastructures. Usually this is, again, accompanied by significant employment losses, although there is often no direct international competition. Underlying the elimination of slack in the formerly sheltered part of the economy is, again, the declining capac-ity of redistributive politics to appropriate surplus resources from the exposed, private, and manufacturing sectors in order to support high wages and high employment in low-productivity domestic, public and service activities, avoiding both wage disparities and unemployment and thereby defending national solidarity.

Competition is reinforced, not contained, by European integration. In the 1990s even "integration theory" has come to realize that at the end of the integration process, whenever this will be, we will not find ourselves in a supranational repli-cation of the post-war national welfare state, with its capacity to insulate social entitlements from economic pressure and take social and labor standards "out of competition". Rather than political centralization suspending competition, com-petition stands in the way of centralization. Nation-states have continued to be the principal sites of political organization, identification and action in Europe, and especially so with respect to issues of social security, equality and justice. In part this is because international competition affects countries differently, and is differently received by different national institutions. The rethinking of solidarity that is under way in Europe thus takes its own course in each country, reinforcing the importance of national political arenas inside the European "social model" and reflecting the fact that European integration remains stuck half way between international relations and the emergence of a supranational state. Moreover, while European countries have been able to agree on opening their markets to each other and to the outside world, they continue to find it impossible to define common interests in the protection of oligopolistic slack and agree on its joint political appropriation and consensual division for shared purposes of social justice.

Whatever the "European social model" will turn out to be, it will be embedded in a more competitive and more market-driven economy, and it will only in part be vested in centralized European institutions (Scharpf 1999b; Streeck 1995). "Social Europe" as an institutional architecture will not be nearly as centralized as some of its centralized member states, like France and Germany. That the border of the European Union, the European market and European solidarity – the dis-tinction between Europe's inside and outside – is itself not fixed but fluid, as illustrated by the impending Eastern enlargement, adds to institutional fragmentation as well as to the intensity of economic competition. Absent of any realistic option of border control *vis-à-vis* the world economy, and lacking a meaningful internal consensus on protective redistribution, the Union remains largely confined to policing the adherence of its member states to the "four freedoms" of the Internal Market, or in any case can do little that would interfere with such freedoms. Centralization and harmonization beyond joint "market-making" are further impeded by the vast variety of national institutions, which are deeply rooted in long and complex, and highly distinct, histories. Any step towards harmonization, if at all significant, is therefore bound to generate different effects in different national systems – which is usually enough to elicit sufficient opposition for it to fail.

Post-hierarchical integration

The politics of social solidarity in Europe will thus for the foreseeable future remain embedded primarily in national institutions, of social policy and of industrial relations, which are in turn embedded in a competitive international market and constrained by supranational institutions devoted to safeguarding that market (Streeck 1998). How European society – or better, European socie*ties* – will respond to the challenges of unprecedented competitiveness, to the elimination of slack and the destruction of the economic base of Fordist solidarity will be decided in a complex, horizontal as well as vertical interplay between increasingly interdependent national systems and a new and unique layer of supranational institutions and commitments. The lasting significance of the national, as distinguished from the supranational, is visible in a number of *historical trends in the evolution of European Union policies and institutions*, four of which I want to mention briefly.

1   *A new approach to social regulation.* In the 1990s the number of significant social policy regulations issued at European level has *decreased*, despite a growing problem load and regardless of the Maastricht co-decision procedure, which was supposed to accelerate the pace of social policy-making. More importantly, the nature of regulatory acts has also changed. In the 1970s the Union tried to impose on its member states binding regulations stipulating common standards. Today's social policy directives, by comparison, typically allow for wide discretion in their implementation, with the Union increasingly restricting itself to issuing legally non-binding recommendations. This approach – which often involves European Directives being formulated in such a way that no changes are necessary at all in extant national legislation – has been described as "neo-voluntaristic" (Streeck 1995). A neo-voluntarist style of governance fits the principle of "subsidiarity" which, since the Maastricht Treaty came into force, has reversed the former centralizing tendencies in a number of areas of Union policy-making, especially in social policy – at a time when other areas, such as monetary policy, were being completely centralized.

2   *Coordination instead of harmonization.* Within the multi-layered European polity, supranational intervention in national systems is increasingly confined to measures of coordination (Eichhorst 1999). The model seems to be the successful European legislation on mobility of labor, which required member states to remove restrictions on cross-border mobility of workers without otherwise intervening in national labor market regimes. A more recent example is the Directive on European Works Councils. The Directive, which is regarded as the most significant achievement of European-level social policy in the 1990s, leaves national systems of workplace representation essentially untouched and merely supplements them with individually negotiable, company-specific arrangements to provide employees in foreign subsidiaries with a minimum level of representation *vis-à-vis* the central management of the company. Rather than granting all European workers a common floor of rights of industrial citizenship, European works councils serve to link different national systems of representation inside large European companies, without intervening in any of them.

3   *Europeanization of national systems, instead of the emergence of a unified European system.* While national systems remain pivotal especially for the defense of social solidarity, European societies are undoubtedly becoming "more European" (Falkner 1999). The Europe of the 1990s is being "Europeanized", not through hierarchical centralization, but through growing awareness of national actors and institutions of their European context, as conditioned by their national interests and circumstances. Here we can speak of a process of *polycentric horizontal* – or *post-hierarchical* – *Europeanization*, in which the horizons of perception and action of national actors are beginning to transcend national borders in the same way as their social contacts ("networks"). For example, current attempts at horizontal coordination of collective bargaining do not occur "via Brussels" but instead involve specific regional constellations with a "variable geometry" of participants. They seem much more in line with the real character of the European integration process than the traditional, and uniquely unsuccessful, efforts of Brussels authorities or peak organizations at hierarchical centralization.

4   *Cooperative adjustment at national level.* As neo-voluntarism, coordination of national diversity and the turn from hierarchical to horizontal Europeanization have redefined the integration process, national systems of social policy and industrial relations are undergoing far-reaching *cooperative adjustment* to the pressures of international competition (Visser and Hemerijck 1997). Although the spectacularly successful reforms in the Netherlands and Denmark carefully observed the new economic framework of the Single Market, they remained strictly national affairs, drawing on national political and economic resources and avoiding as much as possible interference "from above", including in particular from "Brussels". Dominant in national reform efforts was and is a general determination on all parts to make optimal use of cooperative national institutions and traditions, also at company level, in order to improve the common condition in an increasingly internationalized

and competitive economy. Binding European legislation on social policy or European-level collective agreements would only add further complexity to, and reduce the degrees of freedom available to national actors in, already extremely complex negotiations. This to me seems the most important explanation for the, at first, astonishing fact that also trade unions throughout Europe, when it comes to the difficult process of restructuring, usually insist that as much room for maneuver as possible should be preserved at national level and within the familiar and predictable national institutions.

Competitive solidarity

The irreversibly increased competitiveness of their integrated economies forces European societies to scrutinize the rules and management practices they have in the past devised to govern the marketplace. Above all, the search for a new concept of solidarity responds to what one could call *the declining significance of the national average* as an egalitarian measure of economic reward or entitlement, like in traditional solidarity wage policy. Pursuing social justice by giving those with low productivity a right to be paid more than they have earned, while allowing those with high productivity to be paid less, presupposes that the resulting surplus profits in strong sectors can be redistributed to the weaker sectors to cover their rising costs and protect them from losses. But in the new competitive conditions, those with above-average performance need their resources for themselves, or at least have the ability to hold on to them. As slack disappears, or ceases to be taxable, solidarity based on compulsory subsidization becomes ever more difficult to enforce. This applies all the more to Europe as a whole where centralized political capacities hardly exist, and are not likely to emerge in the foreseeable future.

While solidarity remains a national *Hausaufgabe*, its substance, given the by now firmly established trajectory of European integration, is transforming under the pressure of intensified international competition. In trying to adapt to the new economic circumstances, national communities increasingly seek to defend their cohesion, rather than through protection and redistribution, through joint competitive and productive success – through politics, not *against* markets, but *within* and *with* them, replacing protective and re-distributive with what could be called competitive and productive solidarity. The details of this process, which seems to involve nothing less than a deep redefinition of the "European social model" and of the ideas and practices of solidarity inherent in it, are still far from clear, and so are its results. Moreover, both process and outcomes are likely to differ widely from country to country, and indeed reinforcement of national diversity would seem an important element of the sort of competitive adjustment into which European social policy has become enmeshed.

In the following I will try to outline the main contours of what I see as an emerging new "European social model". In doing so I am not making a prediction. Rather than a necessary and inevitable future condition, I regard what I describe as a *really existing tendency* that may or may not, and in some places more than in others, prevail over competing tendencies, such as entrenched distributionism, institutional inertia, or neo-liberal deregulation. Nor is what I will be presenting my view of an ideal or normatively preferable social order; indeed it is not at all clear whether what I see as perhaps the dominant possibility in the evolution of social policy in Europe, will always and in all respects measure up to standards of, especially, social equality to which many continental Europeans have grown accustomed in the post-war era. I hasten to add that I also do not presume that the emergence of the "European social model" that I am describing will be without conflict, or that its operation, if it will ever become a dominant reality, would necessarily be any less conflictual and internally contradictory than that of alternative models.

1   As redistributive social policies are increasingly perceived by Europe's political classes as excessively expensive, the emphasis of the political discourse is shifting towards *investment* in the ability of individuals and communities to survive in intensified international competition (Jessop 1997). Not just prosperity, but also equality and justice are increasingly expected, no longer from redistribution of individual means of consumption, but from investment in individual and collective means of production, in particular in infrastructures of all sorts. Redress of inequality in the absence of redistributable slack is sought through broad and equitable investment in productive capacities, especially in the "human capital" of individuals which is considered a productive asset for the community as a whole and whose optimal development therefore becomes a public and collective concern. Ideally, equalizing through public investment the starting positions of individuals as they face the demands of the market would make *ex post* political redistribution largely redundant – or so it is hoped, given that the capacities for such intervention are in any case melting down. Social policy would then be fortuitously preempted by economic, or structural adjustment, policy, with rough equality of outcomes – or less ambitious, a level of inequality that is still compatible with social cohesion – being achieved through *rough equality of initial endowments*. A possible label for this would be "supply-side egalitarianism", where political capacities are deployed to improve and equalize the marketability of individuals and their ability to compete, instead of protecting them from the market (Cohen and Rogers 1998). Note that the new political key-word, "employability", defines the responsibility of public policy, not in terms of *decommodification* of individuals, but to the contrary of creation of *equal opportunities for commodification*. Social democracy, of the "Third Way", thus seems to become indistinguishable from an activist liberalism which pursues social justice through intervention in the distribution, not of market outcomes, but of the capacities for successful market participation (Giddens 1998).

2   Note also, however, that the new policy of *equal marketability* operates under the same resource constraints that have made redistributive social policies increasingly untenable and that reflect the declining capacities of governments to tax firms, even successful ones, that produce on their territory. Supply-side egalitarianism therefore tends to be associated with both

rationalization of public services and an increase in user fees of all sorts, neither of which sits easily with traditional Social-Democratic constituencies. For example, political commitment to "employability" typically coincides with heavy pressures on educational institutions to improve their efficiency and adjust their output to market demands, as well as with potentially far-reaching decentralization of responsibility for human capital development to its individual "owners". It also often involves attempts to enlist market forces and market incentives for the production of infrastructural goods, with a tendency to rely much more than in the past on private resources, efforts and interests for the achievement of collective objectives. The fundamental puzzle facing the new Social Democracy is whether large-scale public reliance on private investment for infrastructural purposes will not in the long run bring about, *if not required*, a level of inequality that is incompatible with the egalitarian component of supply-side egalitarianism.

3 The emerging new compound of social and economic policy – or better, of *economic as social policy* – involves a strategy of *specialization* as a dominant response to competition (Porter 1990). Governments following that strategy try to discharge their social responsibility by moving their communities into specialized niches in a market that extends far beyond their borders and against which redistributive policies cannot offer meaningful protection. Classical social policy is increasingly replaced by public cultivation of the productive assets of economic communities, to enable them to become privileged providers of products attractive enough for others to be willing to pay a surcharge for them. Developing a community's comparative advantages and investing in the quality and uniqueness of its products – instead of competing on lower prices of identical products, which would ultimately require a competitive lowering of social standards – may enable it to appropriate monopoly rents underwriting a mode of production and distribution that allows its members to participate and benefit equally, according to the community's historical standards of fairness.

4 Countries striving for comparative advantage in sectoral niches of an encompassing international market tend to treat their *social regimes* as part of an economic infrastructure that they may find necessary or expedient to revise in support of their respective productive specialization. Everywhere in Europe the systems of social citizenship and industrial justice inherited from the post-war period are being scrutinized in terms of their implications for the productivity and competitiveness of national economies facing the international marketplace. Elimination of institutional "rigidities" – i.e., of arrangements that impose an efficiency toll on sectors important for a country's economic performance – has moved to the top of the political agenda, not just of those who want to reduce social rights in order to cut costs, but also of governments placing their hopes on productive specialization as a way of defending collective prosperity and solidarity. *Customization of rules*, so as to make social regimes take into account the special needs of individual firms and sectors, in particular those that define a political community's

market chances in the larger world economy, is today becoming a major instrument of economic policy.

5 The politics of supply-side egalitarianism and comparative advantage seem to imply an interesting new configuration between industrial sectors and political-territorial rule. Where sectoral specialization is organized through territorially based political governance, in an effort to defend the economic viability of a spatially defined and functionally diffuse community, economic sectors become *regionally concentrated*, and trading relations between them become intermingled with and regulated by international politics. Territorially based political sovereignty can thus be deployed both to devise optimally efficient sectoral regimes and protect and extend a sector's international market access. Moreover, as specialization proceeds, the sectors on which a particular territorial community has chosen to specialize tend to grow with the size of the market, which *ceteris paribus* will make political communities more homogeneous in terms of their productive activities; this, in turn, vastly simplifies the political task of sectoral customization of national regimes. Collective identity and interest, especially in relation to the outside world, as a result become organized around particular sectors or products, whose fortunes in the world economy become largely identical with those of the territorial communities that produce them (Amin and Thrift 1994). On an extended scale, this invokes the image of the "industrial districts" first described by Alfred Marshall and later rediscovered by students of the "Third Italy" and other successful economic areas of Europe.

6 Both sectoral specialization and efforts at optimization of institutional regimes in relation to sector-specific efficiency requirements increase the diversity between jurisdictions and militate against international convergence; at the same time they tend to make productive communities more internally homogeneous. *Externalization of heterogeneity* enables political communities to found their internal cohesion on, in Durkheim's term, "mechanical solidarity" (Durkheim 1966 [1893]) – which is further increased by supply-side egalitarian intervention aimed at leveling differences in initial endowments. Relations *between* communities, on the other hand, would have to be based on "organic solidarity", that is, on the attractions of complementarity and the mutual benefits of free exchange between participants that are different if not unequal.

7 Obviously small countries find sectoral specialization and elimination of institutional rigidities through regime customization easier than larger ones which cannot normally expect their entire population to earn their living mainly in one or two sectors. Economic homogeneity, which tends to go together with small size, has the great advantage that it makes it possible to have rules and social standards that are both nationally unified and sectorally specialized (Katzenstein 1985). This helps protect governments pursuing customization of regimes in order to make them more flexible and productivity-enhancing, from political conflicts on the necessary and desirable degree of equality of rights and obligations for all citizens. Small and

sectorally homogeneous countries are also less likely than large and hetero-geneous ones to have to impose redistributive obligations on their leading sectors, as inequality tends to increase with sectoral diversity. Governments of countries whose sectoral composition is comparatively homogeneous can also pay more attention to the infra-structural needs of "their" sectors, just as they can draw on an ample supply of solidarity among their populations that is fed by shared perceptions of a need to stand together and defend the com-munity against much larger and more powerful neighbors. In an international economy governed by fragmented sovereignty, more fragmentation seems to be better than less, and it is a striking fact that the small countries of Europe have recently been doing much better economically and politically than the large ones. Moreover, in the process of European integration, small countries, apparently paradoxically, tend to be the most vigorous defenders of national sovereignty while at the same insisting on the strictest adherence of all, spe-cially the large countries, to the principles of a free international market.

8 Large and heterogeneous countries, by comparison, face the problem that uni-fied national regimes that satisfy political requirements of national solidarity and identity are likely to be unable to take into account the specific produc-tive requirements of individual sectors and firms. This makes them "rigid" from the perspective of the latter and imposes an efficiency toll on a national economy that can no longer afford not to use its resources to the fullest. Current pressures for decentralization of economic and social policy through regionalization of political governance inside the nation-state respond to growing diseconomies of political scale that derive from the negative pro-ductivity effects of general rules insensitive to specific market constraints or technological opportunities. Political federalism, widely defined, is becoming attractive as it may enable smaller sub-national jurisdictions to imitate the sectoral specialization strategies characteristic of small sovereign countries, such as seeking out a niche in a larger market; customizing policies and rules to accommodate the requirements of production for that niche; building social and political cohesion around the productive success of selected sectors; developing national solidarity out of structural homogeneity, economic and institutional distinctiveness, and collectively experienced dependence on an international market; and avoiding the efficiency costs of internal redistrib-ution by externalizing heterogeneity and letting less productive sectors, or sectors with different political needs, migrate beyond regional borders. Decentralization within large nation-states may thus be a way of re-territori-alizing economic governance in a borderless international economy, as an alternative to market and management-driven de-politicized governance of internationally integrated sectors cross-cutting territorial boundaries. While nations remain central to the European integration process, then, they clearly come under pressure to reorganize, with national politics turning into a pol-itics of *decentralization in national colors*.

9 Decentralization of governance within large nation-states is typically accom-panied by debates on the *national obligations of federal subunits*, or regions, in

particular of rich in relation to poor ones. Just as profitable and competitive firms, regions with a successful economy increasingly seem to feel that they can no longer afford subsidizing on any major scale others that are doing less well. Here, too, the declining significance of the national average as a guide-post of redistributive solidarity is apparent. As a substitute for equalizing transfer payments, decentralization offers weak regions political autonomy to rebuild their institutions and develop new policies in support of a sectorally specialized regional economy that can be successful within the larger market. To what extent other regions within the same country should or can be obliged to help the weak to get up on their feet is an open question in a debate dominated by the same rhetoric of self-responsibility and self-suffi-ciency, including warnings against "dependency traps" being created by too lavish redistributive support, that has come to dominate the discourse on social policy. National debates on central responsibilities for regional devel-opment in principle resemble the long discussion between the member states of the European Union on the level of European subsidies required for weak regions to participate successfully in the Internal Market, although the amounts involved in inter-regional transfers within nation-states still vastly exceed those at the disposal of European regional policy.

10 Apart, perhaps, from limited injections of regional aid, inter-regional equity and cohesion in a decentralized economic regime like the European Union depend mainly on the benefits of free trade for those invited to participate in it. Solidarity between fragmented jurisdictions is basically reduced to allow each other's free access to one's markets, thereby underwriting local strategies of sectoral specialization conditioned on large market size. It also involves territorial communities optimally developing their productive capacities, not just in their own interest, but also in that of their trading partners. Whether or not the standard of living of sectorally specialized nations or sub-national regions will converge or grow apart, will depend mainly on whether the *law of comparative advantage* can keep its promise and, in the long run, equalize the incomes of unequal traders. In the absence of a political center, fair terms of inter-regional trade can evolve only out of the interplay of supply and demand, perhaps marginally modified by international side-payments, the management of international or inter-regional heterogeneity becoming mostly a matter of developing to the fullest the productive complementarities of specialized territorial communities. This is different *within* the latter where domestic homogeneity may be pursued through political intervention in the distribution of initial endowments, with the objective of broadly equalizing the productive capacities of the citizenry and thereby alleviate pressures for efficiency-diminishing *ex post* redistribution.

Summing up so far, the 1990s have witnessed a rediscovery of the *economic value of social policy*, and indeed a reorientation of the latter to economic purposes, even among those who in the past used to defend political intervention in the market primarily or exclusively on grounds of social justice. In the rising productivistic concept of social policy and solidarity, with its *Wahlverwandtschaft* with the emerging new configuration between both state and markets and national and supranational institutions, egalitarianism comes to be premised on the hope that all or almost all members of a society, national or regional, are by and large equally able and motivated to acquire, if need be with public support, a roughly equal endowment of human capital – in other words, on highly optimistic assumptions on the capacity of human beings to benefit from education and educational policy. For those less inclined to make use of their supposed abilities and take responsibility for themselves, the new social policy of *competitive solidarity* relies less on moral persuasion than on market incentives and punishments, turning away from the redistributive indulgence of the 1970s and using as policy instruments reductions in public subsistence for those who refuse to work or be trained on market terms. Scandinavian methods of an "activating" labor market policy are gradually taking root even in a country like Germany, with its Catholic tradition of labor de-commodification through publicly subsidized retirement of large segments of the society's labor supply. Only those who manage to be recognized as truly unable to care for themselves will continue to receive unconditional support – although in the spreading Communitarian thinking, with its rigorous emphasis on balancing rights with responsibilities, no support should ever be *entirely* unconditional. In any case, in the new Europe the needy, whoever they may be, will have to compete for a shrinking base of publicly appropriable and redistributible resources with a welter of other, more investive and wealth-enhancing uses. As the meaning of solidarity is shifting, it is not least traditional social policy that is being scrutinized for slack to be diverted to productive purposes.

A new "European social model"?

Growing competition in an internationalizing economy and the subsequent erosion of the material base of redistributive solidarity in European welfare states are changing the role of politics in the maintenance of social solidarity. As the relationship between markets and political institutions is being transformed, so is the content of social citizenship, shifting from protection and redistribution to collective support for the development and deployment of productive capacities. Within the emerging "European social model", social justice refers more and more to roughly equal distribution of initial endowments, of access to market opportunities, and of responsibility for a community's productive success. This development is intertwined with a complex new configuration, established in the process of European integration, between the national and the supranational that lays public policies open to unprecedented market pressure and thereby deeply redefines post-war notions of the proper role of the state in relation to society and market.

Certainly solidarity is not absent in the new Europe, including commitments to mitigating the cumulative inequalities that tend to result from a free play of market forces. But supranational policies and national reforms throughout the 1990s reflected a widespread search for new political approaches better adjusted to a world in which states are embedded in markets, rather than markets in states. "Modernizing" social-democratic parties and trade unions, often in complex cross-class alliances, have been and are groping for a new politics of solidarity compatible with what has come to be called a "competition state" or "entrepreneurial state". Fundamentally this search is for a social policy that is no longer dissociated from economic policy – one that protects solidarity by opening up market opportunities and enabling citizens to seize on them, and that "gets its incentives right" while avoiding intolerable levels of uncertainty and inequality. Nevertheless, both appear to be on the rise, and it seems increasingly to be understood that this is inevitable. With the disappearance of the redistributive certainties of the Fordist era, European societies are likely to have to live with less predictable and less equal market outcomes than twenty years ago. At unprecedented levels of both national income and foreign immigration – two conditions that are closely related – this may be easier to accept than it might have been in the past.

Particularly interesting among current responses to the pressures of expanding markets are attempts at *productivist reconstruction of solidarity* within national or sub-national communities. Politically organized sectoral specialization, typically accompanied by extensive infra-structural investment, is to shelter territorial communities from head-to-head, cut-throat competition by providing not just for external competitiveness but for internal equality as well, and indeed for *equally distributed competitiveness*. Especially suited to this strategy, which both reacts to and reinforces the absence of a credible prospect for rebuilding centralized political capacity in Europe and beyond, seem to be small and potentially homogeneous political entities.

Productivist-competitive solidarity, as it offers itself as a defense of social cohesion in a polity of fragmented sovereignty and in an economy without expropriable slack, *accommodates* markets rather than overrules them. Instead of taking social regimes out of competition, it rewrites them to make them more competitive. Equality of citizens is pursued, not through *ex post* political intervention in market outcomes, but through *ex ante* equalization of the resource endowments of market participants, especially their "human capital" and "employability". Competition is accepted, not just as a fact of life, but as a useful tool to elicit additional effort, from the community as a whole in relation to the outside world, as well as from its individual members. Indeed communities are formed and restructured so as to best fit the demands of a market that extends far beyond their borders and that they cannot hope to control. Social cohesion is sought, not through equal outcomes, but through equal opportunity; and traditional concepts of solidarity are infused with a bourgeois spirit of efficiency and self-sufficiency, emphasizing individual effort and collective investment in competitiveness at least as much as social entitlements to minimal levels of reward or consumption.

Underlying the potential transformation of the "European social model", as it has become a real possibility with the progress of European integration, is a Durkheimian answer to competition which emphasizes specialization and differentiation. Agents of this response are political communities – small nation-states or sub-national regions inside large countries – that may hope to increase their internal homogeneity while externalizing heterogeneity to the outside world, basing their internal cohesion on a variant of mechanical solidarity while entrusting their external relations to organic solidarity among traders with complementary capacities. Social egalitarianism, communitarian insistence on individual responsibility, national or regional patriotism, defense of the distinctiveness of domestic institutions combined with resistance to pressures for institutional convergence, and a commitment to international free trade may thus enter into a characteristic, lasting association.

Will this be enough to protect the social integration of European society, within the small *communities of economic fate* that are more or less comfortably nested in a much larger market, and especially between them? Whatever the answer, there is reason to believe that attempts to reconstruct social cohesion around competitive solidarity will become a dominant force in the politics of the transforming European welfare-state.

References

Amin, A. and Thrift, N. (eds) (1994) *Globalization, Institutions, and Regional Development in Europe*, Oxford: Oxford University Press.

Cohen, J. and Rogers, J. (1998) "Can egalitarianism survive internationalization?", in Streeck, W. (ed.) *Internationale Wirtschaft, nationale Demokratie. Herausforderungen für die Demokratietheorie*, Frankfurt a.M.: Campus: 175–94.

Durkheim, E. (1966) [1893]: *The Division of Labor in Society*, New York: Free Press.

Eichhorst, W. (1999) "Europäische marktgestaltende Politik zwischen Supranationalität und nationaler Autonomie: Das Beispiel der Entsenderichtlinie", *Industrielle Beziehungen* 6, 3: 340–59.

Falkner, G. (1999) How Pervasive are Euro-Politics? Effects of EU-Membership on a New Member State, *MPIfG Discussion Paper* 99/4, Köln: Max-Planck-Institut für Gesellschaftsforschung.

Giddens, A. (1998) *The Third Way: The Renewal of Social Democracy*, Cambridge: Polity Press.

Jessop, B. (1997) "Die Zukunft des Nationalstaates – Erosion oder Reorganisation? Grundsätzliche Überlegungen zu Westeuropa", in Becker, S., Sablowski, T., and Schumm, W. (eds) *Jenseits der Nationalökonomie? Weltwirtschaft und Nationalstaat zwischen Globalisierung und Regionalisierung*, Berlin: Argument-Verlag, 50–95.

Katzenstein, P. J. (1985) *Small States in World Markets: Industrial Policy in Europe*, Ithaca: Cornell University Press.

Kochan, T. A., Katz, H. C., and McKersie, R. B. (1986) *The Transformation of American Industrial Relations*, New York: Basic Books.

Porter, M. E. (1990) *The Competitive Advantage of Nations*, New York: Free Press.

Rhodes, M. (ed.) (1995) *The Regions and the New Europe: Patterns in Core and Periphery Development*, Manchester, New York: Manchester University Press.

Scharpf, F. W. (1999a) "The Viability of Advanced Welfare States in the International Economy. Vulnerabilities and Options", *MPIfG Working Paper* 99/9, Köln: Max-Planck-Institut für Gesellschaftsforschung.

—— (1999b) *Governing in Europe: Effective and Democratic?*, Oxford, New York: Oxford University Press.

Streeck, W. (1995) "From market-making to state-building? Reflections on the political economy of European social policy", in Leibfried, S. and Pierson, P. (eds) *European Social Policy: Between Fragmentation and Integration*, Washington, DC: The Brookings Institution: 389–431.

—— (1998) "The internationalization of industrial relations in Europe: Prospects and problems", *Politics and Society* 26, 4: 429–59.

Visser, J. and Hemerijck, A. (1997) *'A Dutch Miracle'. Job Growth, Welfare Reform and Corporatism in the Netherlands*, Amsterdam: Amsterdam University Press.

2 Will Social Europe work?

Joakim Palme

Introduction

It is evident that the crisis of the welfare state in Europe, and elsewhere, has caused great uncertainty about the future for social protection in the twenty-first century. The prospects appear to be heavily influenced by the past decade, marked by mass unemployment and increasing social inequalities. Large groups in society are threatened by social exclusion at the same time as the state is reducing the benefit entitlements and social services, sometimes as a consequence of reduced public social expenditures, often just as a result of increased needs. The similarities of the development in the various parts of Europe are striking. This evokes a critical question about the future of the European welfare states: Will Social Europe work?

The aim here is not to make projections about the future of "Social Europe". Instead, the purpose of this chapter is to discuss the challenges to the European systems of social protection and identify elements of a reform-strategy that can join social policy goals with efficiency considerations. The aim of the chapter is further to explore if sociology can make a contribution to such a strategy by examining the intended and unintended effects of various social policy strategies. In other words, the aim is to identify the challenges and dilemmas that face the European welfare states and suggest a strategy, informed by empirical research, for responding to them without diluting the content of "Social Europe". However, a caveat needs to be added; what can be offered here is nothing more than preliminary reflections.

The chapter is organized as follows. First, I argue for an understanding of "Social Europe" as an inclusive strategy of equality. Second, major challenges to the systems of social protection are outlined. Third, it is discussed how "the modernization of social protection" – as launched by the European Commission – is responding to these challenges. Fourth, some reflections are made concerning the question if sociology can contribute to improve policy design by analyzing the intended and unintended consequences of welfare state programs. This brings the chapter to the last section where some principles for how the framework for reform can be developed further are put forward.

"Social Europe" as a strategy of equality

If we want to discuss and respond to the challenges to the systems of social protection, we should of course have an idea about what, in this context, constitutes "Social Europe". This is notwithstanding the huge variation in how the various European countries have designed their systems of social protection, which makes it difficult to talk about one single European model. There are, however, aspects which make Europe different from, for example, the United States. One such aspect is the degree of inclusion of different groups, also the middle classes, into the programs of social protection. This inclusive strategy could be seen as the essence of the European strategy.

An important challenge for the European countries is thus to accommodate the goals of fighting poverty and providing social insurance; i.e. to both meet the goals of "basic security" and "income security", and to find a balance between, and co-ordinate, non-contributory and contributory benefits. Here the actual *policy design* becomes of crucial importance for how successful different systems are in pursuing the goals. If both kinds of benefits are included in the statutory system of social protection, each of them might actually work better, not least in terms of providing for the social policy goals (see below and Korpi and Palme 1998). The underlying assumption here is that the social protection budget is not fixed but dependent on the content of the entire system; the better the social protection offered by the system the stronger the willingness to pay, and the larger the proportion of the population that gets protection the broader the support for the system.

Even if the systems of social protections have other goals than just fighting poverty, I would still argue that the situation of the worst-off in society is a powerful indicator of how successful the entire system of social protection is. This is really following the philosopher John Rawls' (1971) principle, that we should judge societies on the basis of how they treat those who are worst-off. In the end, the welfare state programs should be most important for those who lack resources derived from the family or the market.

The inclusive nature of the systems of social protection is a possible explanation of the fact that the popular support of them is very widespread in the European populations, despite the fairly widespread critique of how some parts of the systems are managed. This could be interpreted as a message to the reformers to stick to the same kind of underlying social policy approach. The political challenge is thus to design sustainable systems that meet the demands of the citizens without eroding their willingness to pay the economic price for them. If we want to make the welfare state popular in the twenty-first century, it hence appears fruitful to rely on a double strategy of, firstly, tying the self-interest of broad majorities in the population to the programs of health, education and social insurance, and of, secondly, making the systems work in the way they are intended, i.e. making them legitimate.

Following Tawney (1931/1952) and Ferge (1997), it can be argued that the welfare state can, and should, be seen as a project of civilization. This means that the state should re-distribute resources so that the poorest persons can also enjoy the degree of civilization which would otherwise be reserved only for the rich. In this sense the welfare state is also promoting equality. In his classical book *Equality*, R.H. Tawney (1931/1952) consequently portrayed the welfare state as "a strategy of equality". Among the then existing social services, Tawney's attention was directed at health care, education, and policies aimed at providing economic security in the case of work incapacity resulting from old age, sickness, and unemployment. What is argued here is that in this civilization project, the design of the systems of social protection obviously plays a very important role in how successful the policies are.

The challenges

If we want "Social Europe" to work, and consider which strategies to apply in the reform work, it appears important first to consider the many challenges to the systems of social protection. These challenges are not only many but also of different kinds. I will in this chapter restrict the discussion to the following social and economic changes affecting the European countries: the globalization of the economy, the changing working life, the "crisis of the population question", the exit/entry problems on labor markets, the end of the full employment era, social exclusion, and problems of participation along with the Europeanization of politics. These changes create new challenges for the European welfare states when it comes to the design and implementation of reforms. In addressing them it also appears fruitful to take another kind of challenge into consideration, the critique of the welfare state as such.

The globalization of the world economy is most often perceived as a threat to national systems of social protection. It is not all that clear, however, why the welfare state project as such would not be possible for nation-states with open economies. Quite the contrary, the conventional wisdom used to be that the most open economies among the advanced industrial societies had developed the most generous social security systems, in fact as an alternative to the kind of social protection that high tariffs and other import restrictions offered domestic employment (Cameron 1978). The globalization process is still often used as an argument, or excuse, for welfare state retrenchments. It is thus an important challenge to seek reform-strategies that can make welfare state commitments compatible with an exposure to a globalized economy (Esping-Andersen 1997). For many European countries, the current discussion of the future of social protection takes place after a period of economic crisis, and at the same time a crisis for the welfare state. It is worth pointing out that it was in the middle of the global economic crisis of the 1930s that Tawney first published his book on "Equality".

As is argued by Wolfgang Streeck (in this volume), the globalization of the world economy and the increased competition put constraints on the nation-states. To my mind, there are two areas where the limits are clear. The first thing is that the profitability has to be on a competitive level; otherwise, foreign as well as domestic capital will leave the country. The level of income taxation and the size of social security contributions are not of primary importance. Yet the employees and their trade unions must recognize the cost of social security. "There is no such thing as a free lunch." If the cost of social policy, the social wage, is not taken into consideration in the wage-negotiations the result might be inflation and eroded competitiveness. This is a lesson that the labor movements hopefully have learnt from the past decades. The competitiveness is not threatened as long as the cost of the "social wage" is taken into consideration in the wage negotiations. Even if profit levels cannot be reduced in single countries, the division between what is paid as direct wage and what is paid as social wage ought to be flexible.

Under all circumstances, the sharpened competition on global markets makes it urgent to critically examine the effectiveness of the existing programs in order to find ways of achieving both equality and efficiency goals.

The increased participation of women in the labor market is one of the most profound changes of European societies over the past four decades. Even though there is a huge variation in the extent of participation rates among countries, the trend towards increased participation has been universal. The reversal of this trend in Central and Eastern Europe over the most recent decade is relatively modest in a longer time perspective and still leaves these countries with higher levels of female participation than in many Western European countries (Phare Consensus Programme 1999). The increased participation of women in the labor market is often associated with the growth of temporary and part-time work contracts. These contracts are furthermore often improperly covered by the core programs of social protection. This development poses a partly new challenge for any system of social protection that aims at being inclusive. Moreover, temporary contracts increase the social risks and need for protection, and female labor force participation is tied to increased need and demand for social services (cf. Korpi in this volume).

The ageing of populations poses an important challenge. The rising number of people above normal pensionable age is bound to put increased pressure on public finances by increasing the costs of the pension system as well as of health care and other social services – especially when the number of very old people increases. The present very low fertility levels in most European countries adds to the problem of keeping a reasonable balance between workers and retirees but also appear to be a sign of the fundamental problem of giving enough support to families with children. In the inter-war period, declining fertility in many European countries triggered not only a political debate but also, and again, policy initiatives that increased the role of the state for supporting families despite the economic recession (e.g., Myrdal and Myrdal 1934).

The continued very high levels of unemployment are associated with a host of social problems. The risk is very high that older workers are pushed out of the labor market and, because of the severe budget constraints, the social security provisions might not be adequate. The consequences will thus be more serious than when similar processes occurred a couple of decades ago. The problems are even more acute on the "entry" side of the labor market. Newcomers are facing long queues to all vacancies. This is reflected in very high levels of youth unemployment and very high levels of unemployment among immigrants and refugees.

The problems of cost-control are not restricted to the high levels of unemployment. In the longer term the cost control of the public pension systems is, of course, a big challenge.

The problems of high public social expenditures are aggravated by increasing problems of controlling the tax bases in a global economy, although these problems are serious enough on a European level. It is therefore a challenge to use the political mechanism to deal with the problems on the European level. If all European countries are serious about defending the systems of social protection, then they have to leave the rhetoric and take action. On a European level, the most important potential for changing the conditions are presently to be found in the institutions of the European Union. To have a real impact, all the instruments that the Union has, for economic and social policy making, ought to be made employment oriented, including the European Central Bank (ECB), which presently only has other objectives.

The critique as a challenge

The critique of the welfare state *as such* is part of its crisis and, moreover, it is a fundamental challenge for those who believe there are rational grounds for defending the systems of social protection. The critique is not new. In reality, each step in the emergence and development of the various welfare state programs has been followed by critical voices (e.g. Alber 1988). But it is evident that the critique has been particularly strong over the past decades. I think it is useful to distinguish between four kinds of arguments, that, in short, go like this: (1) the welfare state does not deliver the intended social policy outcomes; (2) the unintended efficiency losses, primarily linked to a distorted incentive structure, are too large; (3) severe problems of cost control lead to deficit spending; and (4) the state should not interfere with the family and the market, at least not as much as it does.

The last kind of critique of the welfare state is entirely based on, what I would label, *ethical* grounds. The basic argument is that a big state is bad as such and that state interference as such should be minimized. Such arguments have to be dealt with in terms of what they are based on, i.e. value judgements. The other criticisms, concerning the intended and unintended consequences as well as the issue of cost control, will have to be judged in terms of systematic empirical observations. Even if the theoretical claims about the negative effects are strong, the empirical evidence is sparse (cf. Atkinson 1998).

The efforts to secure social protection of entire populations is undermined by poor cost control of public expenditures. Poor management of welfare state programs has not only wasted resources but also contributed to problems of legitimacy (Palme *et al.* 1998). It is important, though, to distinguish between reasons for eroded legitimacy which have been based on observations of mismanagement, and the critique of the welfare state that has been launched on purely ideological grounds. That "a good state" was equal to "a minimal state" came to dominate much of the debate in the 1980s (World Bank 1997). Such a critique was fuelled by severe problems of under-financing of welfare state programs in some countries, contributing to increasing public debts and financial instability of the entire welfare state. In this situation privatization and marketization have been launched as solutions to an overburdened state. If and how these techniques can be used for securing the welfare of all citizens remains an open question, however.

If the incentive problem is a big issue of the critique, then it should be an important part of the modernization project to deal with these problems. First of all it is necessary to identify where the behavioral effects can be empirically substantiated, and this should of course have an impact on reform priorities. In addition, it is important to take the incentive structure seriously, as a preventive strategy and as a way of accommodating equality and efficiency goals. This is because female labor force participation is such a critical factor and women have been shown to be more sensitive to economic incentives in their supply of labor on the market.

Modernization of social protection in Europe

Europe is larger than the European Union and the notion of "Social Europe" should of course not be confined to the situation within the Union. Reforms aimed at making "Social Europe" work must take the conditions in countries outside the Union into account. Yet there is no other institution on the European level that is likely to have an impact of a magnitude close to that of the Union. Since the effects of decisions within the Union are likely to have effects also on non-member countries in Europe, irrespective of if they are becoming members in the foreseeable future, this motivates a special attention to and concern about EU policies of different kinds.

The "modernization" of social protection (European Commission 1997) has been launched as part of the economic and political integration of the European Union. How is "the modernization of social protection" responding to the challenges and is there really a "common ground" to build on in Europe? The basic feature of it is to adapt the system of social protection to change. Three key areas have been identified by the European Commission: the changing nature of work, the ageing of populations, and the new gender balance. Why then is modernization necessary? One reason is that the systems of social protection, designed decades ago, are no longer effective means to, for example, fight poverty. Another reason given by the Commission is that the system is overburdened financially, and cannot be fully financed, which means taxes cannot be raised without jeopardizing competitiveness on the global market. It is argued by the European Commission concerning the modernization of social protection, that policies have to be seen as a productive factor, they have to be made employment friendly and they have to be financially stable when needs grow stronger as populations are ageing.

Social policy on the European level has historically been modest. From the beginning, the primary objective was to improve the free movement of labor by introducing rules and regulations aimed at protecting migrant workers. Another feature has been the ambition to guarantee that the member countries provide minimum standards on the national level. This can also be seen as part of the "market making" process. More recently, an important ingredient has been the European Court decisions about the equal treatment of men and women. The importance of direct re-distribution via social policies on a European level has declined.

The proposals for reforms which were put forward in the communication from the Commission concern both the benefits and how to finance them. They deal with simplification of the co-ordination of rights for migrant workers, individual-ization of rights and with the transitions both from work to retirement and from unemployment to employment. They do not include large-scale redistributive budgets on a European level; rather the emphasis is on the "re-distribution" of ideas. There are interesting aspects of the proposals for simplification of the reg-ulations for the protection of migrant workers (Palme 1997). However, in the following, the emphasis will be on ideas that concern social policies on the national level.

In comparative welfare state research, diffusion is a largely neglected aspect of the emergence and expansion of the various programs. Despite this, it seems safe to conclude that the diffusion of ideas and program design is an important factor. This goes for the emergence, the expansion as well as the more recent "retrench-ments". It is still an open question if it will work in a constructive way in terms of modernization.

The role of international organizations is one part of the neglected diffusion process. Before World War II the International Labour Office (ILO) undoubtedly played an important role as a forum for discussion and dissemination of ideas. The ILO also actively and systematically collected data on the systems of social pro-tection. After the war, the International Social Security Association took over many of these tasks. OECD is nowadays the only organization beyond the European Union that collects data in any systematic fashion. The question is also if the different international organizations can join forces in the modernization process. From organizations like the International Monetary Fund (IMF) and the World Bank, both the ideological and substantive critique of the various parts of the welfare state has been very strong, but they rarely distinguish between the two kinds of arguments. In this perspective, the European organizations should have the potential to take a more positive and practical part, and there are undoubtedly signs that the World Bank may also have the potential of playing a more constructive role (World Bank 1997).

I believe that the principles laid down in "modernization communication" from the European Commission are compatible with such an approach. They also appear to be responding to several of the challenges that were identified above in an adequate way. Yet I would argue that we need to go further in elabo-rating various elements in a viable strategy. The Commission has the potential for diffusing good ideas, or "best practice" as it is usually labeled by the OECD; but I will not try to advocate that re-distribution of resources is best dealt with at the Union level. The experience with agricultural policy suggests the opposite. However, the European integration creates a momentum for all European countries to take a serious grip on national problems. The internationalization of the economy should also widen our horizons to the social issues. Why should the diffusion of ideas and "learning from others" be restricted to the economic sphere?

Sociological perspectives

The question then is how sociology can make a contribution to the discussion and reform of social protection. I will argue that sociology may be helpful in sorting out the normative and positive arguments for and against various approaches. Moreover, the study of how institutions affect the conditions and behavior of individuals lies at the heart of the sociological inquiry. This makes it highly relevant for the issues that will be discussed in the following, where the focus will be on the study of the intended and unintended consequences of welfare state institutions. Two different approaches to these issues appear to be fruitful to reflect on. The first is the "level of living" approach that has been so influential in Scandinavian welfare research. This tradition is policy relevant since it is resource-oriented and thus focuses on conditions that can be manipulated. It uses micro-level data with a longitudinal design which makes it possible to study behavior in a causal perspective. The second approach is macro-comparative research that by contrasting different policy interventions can help to assess the impact of different kinds of policy regimes on people's welfare. Surprisingly few resources are spent on any kind of evaluation of policy interventions. Here, the chapter may appear biased by the "Nordic" perspective of the author but the main argument for giving attention to the Nordic experience is the good track record in terms of socio-political performance; poverty and inequality are low while labor force participation is high. But the Nordic countries are struggling with unsolved dilemmas, partly in the aftermath of the economic recession of the 1990s, and if there is a scope for political learning it appears reasonable to expect that an exchange of ideas on both policy success and policy failure would be fruitful. A third kind of analysis to be discussed below deals with the potential trade-off between equality and efficiency which has largely been neglected by sociologists.

If we agree that the welfare state is about securing the welfare of all its citizens, it should also be evaluated in these terms, i.e. how it succeeds in promoting welfare in broad terms. In this context the Nordic countries have developed a concept of welfare and methods to study it that has the potential of informing the general debate on the systems of social protection (cf. Johansson 1970; Allardt 1975). Its multidimensional perspective on welfare includes various kinds of resources; health, education, employment, housing, and social relations, in addition to economic ones. This approach to welfare is also action oriented in the sense that all these factors are seen as important for making it possible for individuals to control and steer their own lives. The sociological research perspective is thus close to what Amartya Sen has developed in economics (Sen 1985).

I would argue that this approach also carries the potential to study social exclusion. Following Sen (1998) we may define factors such as low income, ill-health and poor education as risk factors for social exclusion, defining social exclusion in terms of social relations. Social relations may include being tied to family and friends as well as to employment. In this perspective unemployment can be seen as a form of social exclusion. Such perspective is also policy oriented insofar as the risk factors can be affected by broadly defined social policies. If it can be agreed that social policy programs should be judged not from what they intend, but from what they actually achieve, then we have to agree on methods of evaluation. What is argued here is that we should not rely on pure thought experiments; we need empirical data to test our ideas. Moreover, to get accurate assessments we need to assemble data that can actually answer our questions. This data is often costly and time consuming to gather but these costs are small compared to the very large sums that are spent on the system of social protection. However, where the data has been collected, like in Sweden, it appears to be under-explored in terms of analyzing social policies, even if there are exceptions. This undeniably poses a big challenge for social scientists, notably in Sweden.

The other way I propose that sociology can make a contribution is macro-sociological comparisons. Yet in order to be able to evaluate the effects of different kinds of policy designs, it is of central importance to define the goals properly. The goal of the welfare state is often defined in terms of poverty reduction, but some countries appear to have gone further by including the ambition of reducing overall inequalities. The question about what goal should be aimed at is, of course, a matter of values, and in the end a political issue (Erikson 1993). Modern welfare states have additional goals, such as providing social insurance and services of different kinds. However, all social policy boils down to re-distribution. Some of that re-distribution is vertical – that is, from rich to poor through the system of taxation and benefits. A great deal of re-distribution is horizontal, over the life cycle. This is the case with pensions, child allowances and parents' allowance. Another type of re-distribution accompanies the distribution of risks involved by health and work injury insurance and by unemployment insurance. These risks are unevenly distributed throughout the population. Their re-distribution also implies a certain degree of vertical re-distribution, because the risks of illness, work injury and unemployment are greatest among people in the lowest income brackets. Consequently, most parts of the social insurance system also have an important bearing on the fight against poverty.

In the following, I will use the results of a number of analyses of income distribution data from the Luxembourg Income Study (LIS) to illustrate the application of the macro-sociological approach, i.e. how the potential effects of the application of different social policy strategies can be studied. I will start with what has been called "the paradox of re-distribution" and then examine the classical notion of life-cycle poverty. In a third section, the notion of an equality-efficiency trade-off is discussed.

The paradox of re-distribution

Already by the early 1950s, in the preface to the new edition of his book on equality, Tawney appeared to be fairly optimistic about the achievements of public policies in reducing, for example, income inequality. If we share Tawney's passion for equality, which of course is a matter of value judgements, comparative research indicates that there is an important potential for the welfare state as a strategy of equality, a potential which, however, has remained fairly unexplored in most countries. It is important to emphasize how crucial policy design is in this context, and that the size of both the intended and unintended effects of welfare state institutions hinges to a large extent upon the program architecture. This is essential for understanding what has been called "the paradox of redistribution".

The notion of different models of social policy has been very important for comparative research on the welfare state. Richard Titmuss (1974) and Gösta Esping-Andersen (1990) represent perhaps the most influential attempts in this business. In the following, I will rely on another classification scheme which explicitly has been aimed at the institutional characteristics of the social insurance programs among the most advanced industrial nations (see Korpi and Palme 1998, and Korpi Chapter 3 this volume). The aim of this classification as been to see the models as intervening variables and not to confuse them with outcomes, in, for example, distributive terms. The various social policy models, presented below, follow different redistributive strategies. The *targeted* model follows the same principles as Robin Hood applied by following the means-testing principle and only give to the poor, taking from the rich by financing the benefit payments from general taxation. Australia is the clearest exemplar of this model. The *basic security* model follows a simple-egalitarian strategy by paying flat-rate benefits, i.e. providing the same benefit levels to both rich and poor. The British Beveridge system is a typical case of this strategy. The *corporatist* model, in its classical form, re-distributes resources primarily within the different corporations. Germany is of course the pioneer in this category. The *encompassing* model, by relying on universal earnings-related social insurance benefits in fact gives to those who already have economic resources (following the preaching of Matthew rather than that of Robin Hood). Sweden, along with Finland and Norway, can be referred to this category. Even if these models and principles might be central in social insurance they are less applicable in, for example, the provision of social services (see Korpi this volume for an extension of the typology in this regard).

A core issue is whether there are trade-offs between the provision of different kinds of benefits. With Gordon Tullock (1983) we could hypothesize that the more the welfare state programs are directed towards the non-poor the more the worst-off in society will lose out. In reality, and contrary to Tullock's expectations, it seems to be that the more the middle class is involved in the welfare state the better the situation will be for vulnerable groups and the larger the reduction in economic inequalities achieved by the tax/transfer programs. The reason might be found in how interests are organized in different kinds of social policy models. Here a vital distinction has to be made between the distributive profile of benefits (and taxes) and the size of the sums that become subject to re-distribution. Moreover, there appears to be a correlation between the distributive profile and size of sums for re-distribution; the more benefits are targeted the smaller the sums will become. This gives rise to a strongly positive correlation between the size of sums and the size of inequality reduction. Hence, the *paradox of re-distribution* is that the more the benefits are targeted to the poor in a country the smaller is the reduction in inequality achieved by the welfare state. Instead, it appears that protection should be organized within a common framework so that the poor need not stand alone (Korpi 1980).

Life-cycle poverty

In his classical studies of poverty in York at the turn and beginning of this century, Seebohm Rowntree (1901) identified phases in the life cycle that appeared to be more associated with poverty among the inhabitants of York. The problematic phases occurred when there was an unfavorable balance between work-capacity and consumption-needs in the household. Thus, families with small children were facing high poverty risks. When the children grew up and started to contribute to the household income, and when they subsequently moved away from home, the poverty went down. But poverty was also high among the elderly, not primarily as a result of high consumption-needs but rather as a consequence of decreasing work-capacity. How efficient then has the expansion of social protection been in terms of reducing this kind of life-cycle poverty?

The results from a study by Kangas and Palme (2000), based on the Luxembourg Income Study, give some indications. The analysis was based on data from different time points, the first around 1970 and the second around 1990, and different countries representing different social policy traditions. Big differences were found both over time and among countries. A central tendency was that poverty rates showed a more cyclical pattern at the first time point. The cyclical pattern followed the same trajectory Rowntree had observed, i.e. poverty was higher among families with children and among the elderly. In the 1990s, this pattern had vanished in the Nordic countries that were included in the study (Finland and Sweden). In Canada, where old-age poverty had become very low, families with children still faced clearly higher poverty risks. The cyclical component was still strong in the United States. Even if old-age poverty had gone down a little compared to the situation in the 1970s, poverty had gone up among families with children.

What is interesting is that the observed cross-national variation can be linked to the design of social policy programs. In Finland and Sweden the combination of more generous child benefits and wide coverage of subsidized child care – enabling second earners to contribute to the household income – appears to have paid off in low poverty among families with children. Similarly, the generosity of the public pension programs correlates with the poverty rates among the elderly. Here, of course, the universal basic pension in Finland and Sweden and Canada is the most important factor. The results show how the potential of horizontal re-distribution may be explored in a successful way. However, a warning sign here is that poverty rates are high among young people without children – even though there are severe measurement problems (not least concerning Sweden) which should prevent us from drawing very firm conclusions.

Equality and efficiency: sometimes an illusive trade-off

In addition to the classical social policy goals discussed above, there are of course a number of other criteria for evaluating how efficient a system of social protection is. These are important because they are related to the underlying issue of combining efficiency and equality. It is also a way of approaching the issue of intended and unintended consequences of the welfare state institutions. Yet the relationship between the welfare state and efficiency is under-studied both theoretically and empirically, not least within sociology. Several factors contribute to that. One factor is that the intentions are confused with the actual outcomes. Another factor is that the architects behind the systems might have feared a critical examination of the outcomes.

The relationship between equality and efficiency has been given more attention in economics. There is on the other hand an unfortunate bias in neo-classical economics. The neo-classical starting point is that all forms of taxation mean efficiency losses. This starting point leads to a bias towards focusing on the negative aspects of all state intervention. I would argue that it is misleading to compare state intervention in the form of benefits and taxes with no intervention at all. In our kind of society, in fact in all advanced industrial countries, the state intervenes in many but various ways, and all countries have fairly high taxes. This suggests that it is more fruitful to compare different kinds of interventions, i.e. how the size and design of transfers/services and taxation affects equality and efficiency, than to make references to the imagined world of no taxation.

Yet it is in economics, rather than in sociology, that we find the most interesting perspectives on efficiency and the welfare state. Barr (1992) has made an interesting contribution in this direction and has given excellent examples of how the effects on both equality and efficiency can be studied. He points out that the potential advantages of public programs in comparison with private programs are often neglected. With regards to administration they are much cheaper to run, because of scale effects but also because of the uniform conditions. The transaction costs are much lower. The portability is usually much better in the public programs. The possibility of controlling both the incentive structure and the costs should be recognized. This boils down to something which is very similar to the approach advocated by Anthony Atkinson (1998); if we are interested in improving the efficiency of welfare state programs we should worry less about the aggregate social spending and level of taxation and more about the actual design of both programs and methods of financing. This is at least what the empirical research on the behavioral impact of welfare state programs suggests. Public expenditures can of course also promote growth and equality simultaneously by affecting the distribution of at least two aspects of human resources; education and health, in a favorable direction.

What practical lessons can be drawn from efficiency considerations? With regard to the economic criteria mentioned above, the following can be noted concerning universal and earnings-related programs. The administrative cost-efficiency of universal programs is of course one clear advantage. Another strength of the universal systems which are fully earnings-related is that they reduce the so-called transaction costs on the labor market. Individuals, firms and unions do not have to spend time on negotiating about the provision of basic insurance and services like health care. It furthermore promotes mobility and flexibility on the labor market because the universal character of the system means that workers do not lose their earned rights when they move from one job to another – the portability of social insurance is high. One neglected aspect and advantage with public systems is that in principle it is possible to control the incentive structure.

There are hence two critical indicators when it comes to the economics of the welfare state intervention: (1) actual labor force participation; and (2) cost control. When it comes to cost control, I would like to make two remarks from a Scandinavian perspective. First, even during the 1980s the public finances appeared to be in better shape in some of the biggest welfare states. The Nordic countries had better public finances compared to most of the other advanced industrial nations, even those with so-called small welfare states. This development stands in sharp contrast to the problematic development in Finland and Sweden during the first half of the 1990s. However, the situation has improved a lot and the public finances are now roughly in balance in all Nordic countries (Nordic Council of Ministers 1997); they have also been improved in other European countries.

Consolidated public finances is not the ultimate goal of economic policies, and it is not the only instrument for pursuing successful economic policies. However, it is most likely a necessary precondition for making the public commitments – of securing the welfare of all citizens – viable in the longer run. Second, labor force participation appears to be higher in the Nordic countries than in most other countries despite the high levels of taxation. This is not to argue that there is no correlation between taxes and labor supply, only that the empirical evidence suggests that it is possible to combine policies that make high taxes compatible with high participation. In the long run, however, the systems of social protection will experience increased pressure from the ageing of populations and it is urgent to find ways in which we can make them sustainable also when the preconditions are changing. How can the above-mentioned and other findings help us to develop a framework for the reform of social protection?

Framework for reform

If we are serious about fighting poverty and inequality, the empirical research suggests that the underlying ambition with the modernization of the European model of social protection should be to maintain, and when necessary restore, the universal approach to social protection. By this is meant not only that the entire populations should be covered within the same framework, but also that the benefits and services should be adequate enough to provide protection for people in different situations and with different income levels. In order to make the system of protection work in practice, and at the same time ease the burden on taxpayers, it is vital to find techniques that, in essence, contribute to increasing the number of taxpayers and, whenever it is possible, to decreasing the number of benefit recipients. The following concepts will guide the discussion: incentives, resources, opportunities, rights and responsibilities (cf. Palme *et al.* 1998). In short, these are elements in a strategy that attempts to eliminate, or at least reduce, what Arthur Okun labeled as the "big trade-off" between equality and efficiency.

The following questions are central when it comes to the *incentive structure*. How can the poverty traps be avoided? How can the marginal effects be reduced? How can the welfare state programs be designed so that it pays more to work while the entitlements are protected? To put it differently, the question is how can we design the economic rewards so that they induce the desired behaviors? A good rule of thumb is to use universal benefits and services rather than means-tested ones. The reason is that as soon as we start means-testing it will have consequences for how profitable it is for, particularly, low-income people – often women – to engage in paid employment. Another strategy is to make social insurance provisions earnings-related, which makes it profitable for people to work and pay social security contributions. The more they earn and pay, the better the benefit entitlements will be. A technique that has become popular in North America and the United Kingdom is to have earnings disregarded for recipients of means-tested benefits so that benefits will not be fully reduced if the recipient starts to earn an income. This is very different from, for example, the Nordic tradition, where the approach to the problem has been to apply strict activity/work-tests and where no one in principle should be able to say no to a job offer. It appears worthwhile to evaluate the "earnings disregard"/"tax credit"-approach seriously, even if the overall higher tax rates in most of the other European countries are likely to create stronger marginal effects for low to middle income earners than is the case with low-tax countries like the United States.

Once the incentive structure is reformed, the big issue is about the *resources*. It is not enough to make people willing to work, they must also possess the resources to be able to work. This is partly a matter of *skills*, partly of adequate social services making it possible also for adults in families with small children, or frail elderly relatives, to participate in the labor market. In both these respects the achievements of the Nordic countries appear fruitful to reflect on. The classical strategy for improving human resources is education and training, as well as other forms of active labor market policy, such as public relief work and forms of subsidized employment. The aim with these measures is to improve, or at least maintain, the employability of unemployed. This approach has probably contributed to the overall high employment rate. However, when some of the Nordic countries were hit by mass-unemployment in the early 1990s, the problem was that the resources were so restricted that governments often found it necessary to give priority to cheap and "passive" measures.

The universal tendency towards increased female employment and an outspoken political ambition to equalize the participation of men and women appears to be heavily dependent on the provision of another kind of resource, namely subsidized *social services*. If governments fail to respond to the needs of social services, this is likely to reinforce old, and create new, divisions of welfare. Low-income parents are especially dependent on subsidized social services for being able to seek and uphold employment, not to mention lone-parents. I would argue that in this context social services probably provide the most efficient way for lone parents to simultaneously break potential "benefit dependency" and improve the economic standards of their families. In this respect, the modernization of "Social Europe" implies that family support should be designed to make family and work life possible to combine for both parties in two-earner families. Policies aimed at equal opportunities of men and women on the labor market and equal participation and responsibility in family life should be encouraged. The lack of adequate resources in terms of social services, such as child care and care for frail elderly relatives, are effective barriers primarily for the participation of women in the labor market but also in society in general. Social services may also be seen as investments that in a dynamic way provide people with the opportunity to become taxpayers and thus to contribute to balancing state finances.

Even if the labor force is highly skilled and has access to the necessary services and the incentive structure is reasonably sound (i.e. poverty traps, as well as high marginal taxes have been avoided as much as possible), this is of little comfort as long as people do not get the *opportunity* to exercise their skills. If there are no, or too few, jobs to apply for, good skills might not be enough to obtain employment. Social policies cannot make up for economic policy failures. This means that a successful strategy has to be based on successful macro-economic policy making; but the fundamental problem of mass-unemployment is that there are too few jobs. On the other hand, successful macro-economic policies are not likely to be enough either if the skills of the unemployed do not match what the new vacant jobs demand. It is necessary to improve social policy and labor market institutions along several dimensions: incentives, resources (skills and services), responsibilities, opportunities for vulnerable groups. In sum, reforms of the social security systems have to be coupled with macro-economic policy making promoting employment and growth. In this respect, the track-record of the European countries is far from being impressive.

The European discourse on the future of "Social Europe" entails an important theme which concerns the relationship between *rights and responsibilities* in the welfare state, and further what is a proper balance between the two. How successful we are in finding the right balance between rights and responsibilities will ultimately depend on the success in providing the proper incentives, resources and opportunities for people to enter the labor market. Hence, every attempt to find a balance will have to deal with the kinds of obstacles – in terms of incentives, resources and opportunities – that face those who seek employment. Although it is beyond the scope of this chapter to go into details, I will put forward the hypothesis that the balance of rights and responsibilities will be determined at the "street level" in the interface between individuals and bureaucracies. In order to evaluate different social policy strategies, we would therefore have to study the consequences on this level. Citizenship is basically about rights and responsibilities and it is therefore perfectly appropriate that social citizenship should include both rights and responsibilities. Moreover, T. H. Marshall pointed to the fact that social citizenship was a precondition for full political citizenship. This makes the whole issue of "Social Europe" a democratic problem. Adequate social services are, for example, necessary for ensuring the full participation of all citizens in society in general and not only in the labor market.

Conclusion

The conclusion of this chapter is that the answer to the opening question – "Will Social Europe work?" – is still open. What has been argued is that the outcome is heavily dependent on whether we are capable of designing the programs and policies properly. Moreover, if we are serious about making the systems of social protection work, I would claim that it is necessary to consider two different things in addition to finding an adequate program architecture on the basis of the knowledge we have. The first is to critically *evaluate* the design of the existing programs against the goal of promoting the welfare of all citizens. Good intentions are not enough to defend a program. Not only do we have to study if the goals are actually achieved, we also have to consider unintended consequences of the programs. Sociology has an obvious mission here. The second is that it is probably not enough to deal with the programs on a national level. We need to use European arenas for the discussion of common problems of social protection, as well as different solutions. The European Sociological Association is providing one such an arena, deserving to be fully explored in the future.

References

Alber, J. (1988) "Is there a crisis of the welfare state? Cross-national evidence from Europe, North America, and Japan", *European Sociological Review* 4, 3: 181–206.

Allardt, E. (1975) *Att ha, att älska, att vara: Om välfärd i Norden (Having, Loving, Being: Welfare in the Nordic Countries)*, Lund: Argos.

Atkinson, A. (1998) "Does social protection jeopardise European competitiveness?", *Bulletin Luxembourgeois des Questions Sociales* 4.

Barr, N. (1992) "Economic theory and the welfare state: a survey and interpretation", *Journal of Economic Literature* 30: 741–803.

Cameron, D. (1978) "The expansion of the public economy", *American Political Science Review* 72: 1243–61.

Esping-Andersen, G. (1990) *The Three Worlds of Welfare Capitalism*, Cambridge: Polity Press.

Esping-Andersen, G. (ed.) (1997) *Welfare States in Transition*, London: Sage.

Erikson, R. (1993) "Descriptions of inequality: The Swedish approach to welfare research", in Nussbam, M. and Sen, A. (eds) *The Quality of Life*, Oxford: Clarendon Press: 67–83.

European Commission (1997) *Modernising and Improving Social Protection in the European Union*, (COM (97) 102).

European Commission (1998) *Social Protection in Europe 1997*, Luxembourg: Office for Official Publications of the European Communities.
Ferge, Z. (1997) "And what if the state fades away? The civilising process and the state", paper prepared for the European Sociological Association Third Conference Aug. 27–30, Essex University, UK.
Johansson, S. (1970) *Om levnadsnivåundersökningen (About the Level of Living Survey)*, Stockholm: Swedish Institute for Social Research.
Kangas, O. and Palme, J. (2000) "Does social policy matter? Poverty cycles in the OECD countries", *International Journal of Health Services* 30: 335–52.
Korpi, W. (1980) "Social policy and distributional conflict in the capitalist democracies: A preliminary comparative framework", *European Politics* 3, 3: 296–316.
Korpi, W. and Palme, J. (1998) "The paradox of redistribution and strategies of equality: Welfare state institutions, inequality and poverty in the western countries", *American Sociological Review* 63: 661–87.
Myrdal, A. and Myrdal, G. (1934) *Kris i befolkningsfrågan*, (Crisis in the Population Question), Stockholm: Bonniers.
Marshall, T. H. (1950) *Citizenship and Social Class*, Cambridge: Cambridge University Press.
Nordic Council of Ministers (1997) "Fiscal consolidation in the Nordic countries: Fiscal policy for sustainable growth and welfare", *Tema Nord*: 595.
Palme, J. (1997) "Social policy regimes, financing and co-ordination", in *25 Years of Regulation (EEC) No. 1408/71 on Social Security of Migrant Workers*, Stockholm: Swedish National Social Insurance Board and European Commission: 111–30.
Palme, J. (1998) "To find the right balance between contributive and non-contributive schemes", *Bulletin Luxembourgeois des Questions Sociales* 4: 73–81.
Palme, J., Koni, A., Pettinger, R., Predosanu, G., and Todorova, V. (1998) *Welfare State in Crisis: How to Protect the Rights Whilst Controlling the Costs*, Strasbourg: Council of Europe.
Phare Consensus Programme (1999) *Change and Choice in Social Protection. The experience of Central and Eastern Europe. Volumes 1 & 2*, Brussels: European Commission.
Rawls, J. (1971) *A Theory of Justice*, Cambridge: Harvard University Press.
Rowntree, S. (1901) *Poverty. The Study of Town Life*, London: Macmillan.
Sen, A. (1985) *Commodities and Capabilities*, Amsterdam: North Holland.
Sen, A. (1998) "Social exclusion", paper presented at the Ministry for Foreign Affairs in Stockholm, Sweden, December 8.
Tawney, R. H. (1952) [1931] *Equality*, London: Allen & Unwin.
Titmuss, R. M. (1974) *Social Policy – An Introduction*, London: Allen & Unwin.
Tullock, G. (1983) *Economics of Income Redistribution*, Boston: Kluwer-Nijhoff.
World Bank (1997) *World Development Report: The State in a Changing World*, New York: Oxford University Press.

3   Class, gender and inequality
The role of welfare states

Walter Korpi

Inequality is an issue which has always fascinated and energized human beings, in their roles of citizens as well as of social scientists. As Norberto Bobbio (1996) has pointed out, in Western societies views on inequality can serve as a prism separating the political left and the political right. Social scientists have traditionally studied inequality in terms of the distribution of material and other advantages among socio-economic classes or strata. In these distributive conflicts, issues related to the relative roles to be played by markets and democratic politics have been in the forefront. Here social scientists have seen political measures, especially those associated with the welfare state, as being of major relevance for the patterning and degree of inequality. While the mainstream focus in politics as well as in research thus has been on inequality in terms of class, there have long been undercurrents focusing on inequality in terms of gender. A couple of decades ago, these undercurrents came to the surface in the social sciences, where they generated considerable turbulence. Also in the context of gender inequality, however, the role of welfare states has been a central issue.

The turbulence once generated by issues related to gender inequality would now appear to be calming down. There is an emerging consensus that gender as well as class are major bases for inequalities and that both must be included in the analysis without excluding the other (see, for example, Acker 1989; Lister 1997; Williams 1995). Against this background this chapter attempts to integrate gender and class into an analysis of different dimensions of inequality and examines the ways in which these two factors interact with different types of welfare states in distributive processes.[1] In such an effort we face at least three major challenges.

First, we have to tackle the old question: Inequality of what? Is it here enough to look at the distribution of income and material standards of living, or should we also attempt to include aspects of agency? In that case, what areas of agency are important for gender inequalities? Second, we have to develop typologies of welfare states, which can help us to handle and to make sense of the puzzling mosaic of differences between countries that we observe. An important question here is if we can find typologies relevant for gender inequality as well as for class inequality. Third, we have to analyze the relations between gender inequality and class inequality. To what extent do they have similar driving forces? Do they show similar developments over time? I will here discuss these questions and bring in empirical data from comparative analyses of inequalities in 18 OECD countries. These countries are Australia, Austria, Belgium, Canada, Denmark, France, Finland, Germany, Ireland, Italy, Japan, Netherlands, New Zealand, Norway, Sweden, Switzerland, the United Kingdom, and the United States.[2]

Inequality of what?

Inequality in terms of material standards of living has been central for class analysis but has also been important in analysis of gender inequality. In this context a large number of studies have focused on the intra-family distribution of standards of living.[3] These studies indicate that in the affluent Western countries some significant inequalities are likely to remain within nuclear families and that these inequalities are exacerbated in the case of marriage dissolutions, thereby disadvantaging women in terms of material conditions of life. Outside the nuclear family, we also find some significant differences between men and women in these respects.

Yet it would appear that analyses of gender inequality in modern Western societies cannot be limited to standards of living and material achievements but must also consider inequalities with respect to agency. As Amartya Sen (1992) argues, when assessing individual well-being or the goodness of a social order, we must consider not only manifest but also latent or potential aspects of a person's well-being. Sen assumes that freedom to choose is an important component of well-being, and he defines freedom in terms of "alternative sets of accomplishments that we have the power to achieve" (1992: 40). In the context of gender inequality, it is therefore important to consider freedom to choose, that is the range of alternative achievements among which women and men actually have the capability to choose and which thus define their real opportunities to achieve well-being.[4]

Feminist scholars have long highlighted different expressions of gendered agency inequalities with respect to civil and political rights, inequalities which historically have been important in what now are affluent Western countries.[5] Major parts of these inequalities were associated with the institution of coverture, whereby women lost basic parts of their civil rights when entering marriage. Furthermore, women's access to higher education was limited, and marriage bars prevented them from entering the civil service and some of the professions. In many countries women received the right to vote later than men. In several European countries considerable parts of these legally enforced gender inequalities in civil and political rights remained until well after the end of the Second World War.

But at the beginning of the new century, what dimensions of agency can now be assumed to remain most important for gender inequality in the rich Western countries? Without claiming full coverage, I will here concentrate on three arenas in which gendered agency inequalities can be expected to be of central importance, namely democratic politics, higher education, and labor force participation. Most of us would probably agree that these three arenas are worthy of study in their own right, even if they do not exhaust areas in which gendered agency inequality can be of importance.

Gendered agency inequality in politics and education

Gendered agency inequality in the arena of politics can occur at different levels; at the basic level, for example, in terms of differences in the right to vote, and at elite levels in terms of differences between men and women in representation in parliaments and governments. We will here concentrate on elite level gender inequality. As an indicator we will use a simple index of the *equality gap*, showing the percentage point difference between the share of women and the share of men in parliaments (weighted average of both chambers where relevant).[6] In terms of representation in legislatures, the average equality gap among our 18 countries was –90 percentage points in 1950, indicating that women made up only 5 percent of the membership in legislatures (Figure 3.1). Two decades later, in 1970, the average equality gap remained largely unchanged. Thereafter, however, this gap tends to decrease and ends up –50 in 1998, when on average 25 percent of parliamentary members were women.

Behind the average level of the equality gap in 1998 we find major differences among our 18 countries (Figure 3.2). At this time, the equality gap was greatest in France and Japan (–82) with only 9 percent women in the legislature, followed by Italy, the United States and Ireland. The equality gap was lowest in Sweden (–14), with 43 percent women in the parliament, followed by Denmark, Norway,

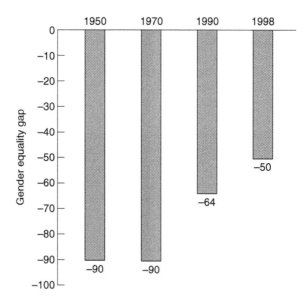

Figure 3.1 Gender equality gap with respect to representation in legislatures, 1950–1998 (average percentage point difference women–men in 18 countries).

Finland and the Netherlands. The gender composition of governments partly follows the patterning of legislatures but with somewhat higher equality gaps. The social democratic cabinets in Norway in 1994 and in Sweden in 1998 were the first ones with a full gender balance.

The above differences in gendered political representation between countries reflect a range of factors, significant among which are electoral systems and the relative strength of different political tendencies. Here party lists and proportional elections appear to favor women relative to single member majority elections. Given the level of voter preference for men, single member districts tend to activate this preference both among voters and among parties in the nominating process. Even with only a relatively small preference for men among voters, voting for individual candidates may thus generate social processes similar to those described by Schelling (1978) in the context of racial segregation, processes which can result in large imbalances in the sex-ratio among elected representatives. Voting for party lists may allow gender preferences to be expressed in a more balanced way. Left parties appear to have been more inclined to elect female candidates than have other political tendencies (Norris 1987). This is somewhat surprising given the traditional tendency for women to vote for confessional parties to a larger extent than men (Tingsten 1937).

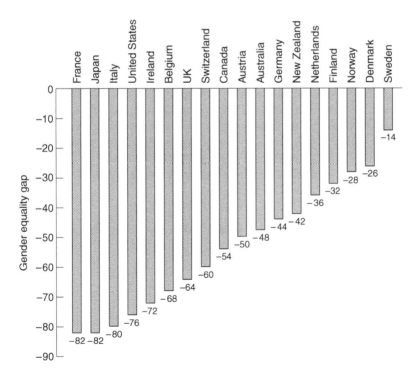

Figure 3.2 Gender equality gap with respect to representation in legislatures in 18 countries, 1998.

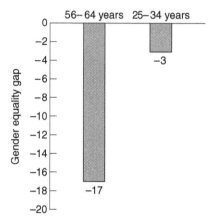

Figure 3.3 Gender equality gap with respect to percentage of university graduates by age in 1994 (average of 17 countries).

As noted above, in several countries women's access to higher education was for a long time limited. During the period after the Second World War, however, in all of our countries in successive cohorts the proportion with university degrees has increased faster among women than among men. Taking the equality gap as the percentage point difference between the proportion of women and the proportion of men with a university degree we find that in 1994, among women 55–64 years (born in the 1930s) this distance was –17 percentage points while it was only –3 percentage points among those 25–34 years (born in the 1960s) (Figure 3.3). Noticeable gender differences are found primarily in Switzerland, Belgium, the United Kingdom, Austria and Germany. In the cohorts from the 1960s, women had on the average a slightly higher cumulative number of years of schooling than did men. Among those with a recent Ph.D. degree, however, women are still a minority and we also find gender differences in terms of more or less prestigious educational specialization.

Labor force participation and agency related gendered policy institutions

In analyses of gendered agency inequality, the role of labor force participation has long been central. Labor force participation is thus a key issue in the vigorous debates on gender inequality in terms of the distinction between paid vs. unpaid work as well as in the debate on strategies to decrease gender inequality captured by the horns of the Wollstonecraft's Dilemma (Pateman 1988: 252). Here we must recognize that behind the distinction between paid and unpaid work looms the fact that the labor force is an arena for the major socio-economic processes of stratification and distribution in modern societies, processes where agency is crucial and which are located outside the family. Individuals who are excluded from participation in the labor force, among them traditionally many women, are disfavored not only in terms of material standards of living but also in terms of social rights. Participation in the labor force is also likely to affect a person's self-perception and identity in ways which influence her capabilities and freedom in many different areas of life. Furthermore such participation is very relevant for interaction patterns and bargaining positions within the nuclear family. It can therefore be argued that in contemporary Western societies, gender differences in terms of labor force participation constitute a crucial area of gendered agency inequality. Being outside the labor force can be seen as a major indicator of agency poverty.

In this context an important question is to what extent different types of welfare states shape patterns of gendered agency inequalities in terms of labor force participation. To discuss these questions we need a gender-relevant typology of welfare states. We all know Gösta Esping-Andersen's (1990) seminal three-fold distinction between "liberal," "conservative," and "social democratic" welfare state regimes. The conceptualization of these broad regime types has proved very fruitful. By opening up new and imaginative perspectives in the comparative study of welfare states, it has stimulated much research. However, this as well as other mainstream typologies have proved problematic in the context of gender relevant analyses, especially when it comes to labor force participation (Lewis 1992; Orloff 1993; Hobson 1991; Sainsbury 1996; Shaver 1989).

Esping-Andersen's typology spans a wide range of factors, from causal forces over aspects of policy programs to policy outcomes, and has therefore been useful primarily for descriptive purposes. To improve the analytic power of a typology it would appear fruitful to focus on welfare state institutions as intervening variables between, on the one hand, driving forces, and, on the other hand, policy outcomes. I will here outline a typology of gender policy aspects of welfare state institutions likely to be of relevance for gendered agency inequality in terms of labor force participation. In this context it must however be remembered that while the typologies we construct can be of heuristic value in helping us to bring out the main contours of the vast empirical mosaic we can observe, such typologies are always great simplifications of the outcomes of complicated historical processes and can only be expected to show a partial fit with reality.

The typology of gender policies proposed here has two dimensions; the degree to which policy institutions give general support to the nuclear family and the degree to which they support a dual earner family model.[7] These two dimensions need not be uncorrelated with each other, but can be used to indicate the relative weight of different types of public policies likely to be of relevance for gendered agency inequality in terms of labor force participation.

The dimension of *general family support* reflects to what degree public policies help to sustain the nuclear family while presuming that, or being neutral to whether or not, wives have the primary responsibility for caring and reproductive work within the family and only have a marginal labor force attachment. As empirical indicators for this dimension we can look at three indicators: (1) the level of cash child allowances to minor children; (2) the level of family tax benefits to minor children and to an economically non-active spouse; and (3) the level of public daycare services for the somewhat older children (from three years up to school age).

While the first two indicators above are self-explanatory in this context, the third one is more problematic. This is because in many countries presently available statistical information does not allow us to distinguish between full-time and part-time day care. In most continental European countries, daycare centers have thus traditionally been organized primarily for the somewhat older pre-school children and on a part-time basis, intended only to complement caring work within the family. Thus they often offer only half-day care, are closed on Wednesdays and do not provide lunches for the children, presuming the presence of a mother at home. In other countries, for example the Nordic ones, daycare is typically provided on a full-day, full-week basis and is intended to enable mothers' continuous work careers. At present it is however not possible to find comparative data reflecting this difference.

The dimension of *dual earner support* reflects the extent to which public policy institutions encourage women's continuous labor force participation; enable parents, men as well as women, to combine parenthood with paid work, and attempt to redistribute caring work within the family. For this dimension we use four indicators, measuring the extent to which public policies provide (1) daycare services for the youngest children (0–2 years); (2) paid maternity leave; (3) public home help to the elderly; and (4) paid paternity leave. The first three indicators reflect policy efforts to enable wives and mothers to carry on a continuous work career while the last one indicates efforts to redistribute caring work within the family.[8]

Because of statistical problems with now available basic data, the above empirical indicators are partly unreliable. We will here therefore treat them as ordinal variables and rank our countries from 1 to 18 in terms of both these dimensions; giving *rank 1* to the country with the *highest* level of support provisions. These rankings in the two-dimensional space are shown in Figure 3.4. It appears that we can here distinguish between three different gender policy models. The figure shows that seven of our countries have chosen to provide very little of general family support as well as of dual earner support, having ranks 12–18 on both these dimensions. The dominant gender policy chosen in these countries can thus be described as a *Market oriented model*; that is, their policy is to allow market forces to dominate the shaping of gender relations by leaving individuals to find private solutions within the context of their market resources and family relations. These seven countries are New Zealand, the United States, Switzerland, Australia, Japan, Canada and the United Kingdom. The remaining eleven countries provide some degree of general family support as well as of dual earner support. Among them, however, only Sweden, Denmark, Finland and Norway, can be described as having a *dual earner support model*. The remaining seven countries; France, Belgium, Germany, Italy, Austria, the Netherlands and Ireland, can then be said to have a *General family support model*. It can here be noted that in terms of these rankings, Norway is relatively similar to France. Among the countries with a general family support model, France thus has the most developed dual earner support policies, while among countries with the dual earner model, Norway has the strongest emphasis on general family support policies.

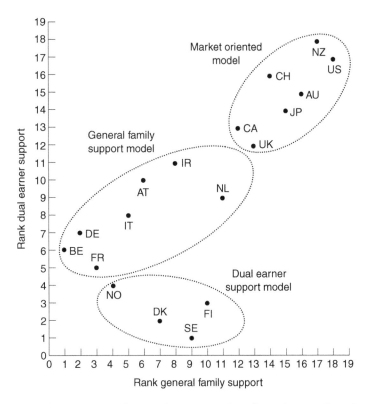

Figure 3.4 Ranks of countries by two dimensions of gender policies and gender policy models, 1985–1990.

Political tendencies, institutions and inequality

In the development of gender policy models many different actors have been involved, among them churches and women's movements acting outside political parties or in close association among them. In many countries women's movements have been important in changing public attitudes and values and in bringing up gender issues to the top of the political agenda. Yet in the countries considered here women have not formed feminist political parties; in recent decades they have instead chosen to attempt to affect the policies of already established parties from the outside or from the inside.

The development of gender policy models is quite clearly related to the strength and longevity of the presence in governments of the main political tendencies in our countries. In this context the most important differences among parties can be roughly described in terms of two dimensions; on the one hand, the left-right dimension centering around the relative role of politics and markets in distributive processes, and, on the other hand, what perhaps could be called a confessional or moral dimension, focusing especially on the role of the family.

During the period after the Second World War, we can thus here distinguish between secular conservative-centrist parties, confessional parties, and left parties.[9]

Secular conservative-centrist parties have generally tended to be wary about introducing policies impinging on market distributive processes, whereas left parties have been inclined to introduce policies to modify market distribution to decrease inequality and poverty. In this context, European confessional parties have often attempted to occupy some kind of a middle ground, especially in terms of counteracting poverty. The confessional or moral dimension is a much less clear one. Of relevance here is that this dimension reflects positions taken with respect to the role of the traditional family form. Confessional parties have seen the preservation of the traditional family as one of their most important goals. While a concern with pro-natalism has also made some secular parties, especially conservative-centrist ones, to occasionally support similar policies, on the whole the preservation of the traditional family form has played a lesser role among the secular parties.

During the period after the Second World War, in the countries of continental Europe confessional parties have been of major importance and they have tended to favor the traditional family and the general family support; a model now found in Austria, Belgium, France, Germany, the Netherlands and Italy but also in Ireland with a very strong position for the Catholic Church. Although having a relatively strong confessional party presence, in this context Switzerland constitutes an exception with a market oriented gender policy model, something probably reflecting that its constitution tends to inhibit political action on the national level.[10] Apart from Ireland, in the English-speaking countries secular conservative-centrist parties have dominated. With their general propensity to avoid meddling with market forces, they have come to favor the market oriented gender policy model. The traditional left parties have been strongest in the four Nordic countries, and in recent decades they have come to support the dual earner model. In this context women's movements have been significant.

Thus, for example, within the Swedish Social Democratic Party women's movements have long worked within the party to affect gender-relevant policies (Hobson and Lindholm 1997). An example of efficient working outside parties was given in the run-up to the 1998 parliamentary elections, when a network of feminists threatened to field a feminist party if the established parties did not increase their nominations of women. This threat was ultimately withdrawn but resulted in the highest proportion so far of women in the parliament and in a government with an equal representation of women and men. In this context it can be noted that Norway, where a confessional party has had a more influential government position than those in other protestant countries, has a combination of gender policies which is relatively similar to the one in France, which is the continental European country where the confessional party impact has been weakest and where secular conservative-centrist parties have dominated postwar governments.

Policy models and gendered agency poverty

As argued above, in modern Western societies being outside the labor force can be seen as an indicator of agency poverty. To what extent are different gender policy models associated with differences in terms of this indicator of agency poverty? We must here limit the discussion to one empirical measure; the female–male differences in percentages outside the labor force in the 25–54 years age category, taken as an average for 1983 and 1990.[11]

According to this measure the range of variation in the overall gendered differences in agency poverty rates among our 18 countries is very large, with almost a 50 percentage point difference between Ireland and Sweden (Figure 3.5). We are here primarily interested in the size of the overall differences among countries with different gender policy institutions rather than in variations within these models. As expected, we tend to find the highest levels of gendered agency poverty in countries with the general family support model, the lowest ones in countries with the dual earner model, while countries with the market oriented model tend to fall in between.

Because of the multitude of factors affecting gender differences in labor force

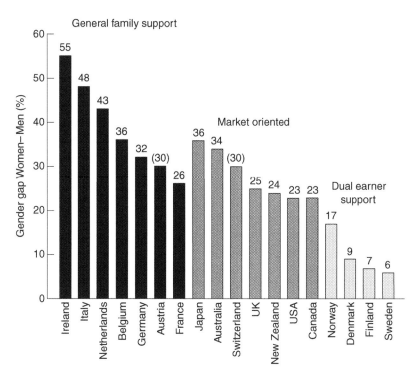

Figure 3.5 Gender equality gaps in agency poverty by gender policy model (indicated by the percentage point differences in proportions outside the labor force, 25–54 years, averages 1983 and 1990).

participation we cannot expect more than a partial fit between our policy models and observed gender differences. Thus Japan and Australia with market oriented gender policy models have higher gender differences than expected. In Japan, gender differences probably to some extent reflect cultural traditions and the still relatively high frequency of three-generation families. During the period after the Second World War, Australia has to a large extent satisfied its labor demand through immigration, something which may have lessened pressures on women to enter the labor force. In this context we can also note that the gender difference is relatively low in France in spite of its general family support model, while this difference is comparatively high in Norway with a dual earner model. A hypothesis in this context is that this pattern reflects the relatively weak government position of the confessional parties in France but again, the comparatively strong position of the confessional party in Norway.

A class-related welfare state typology and income inequality

For the analysis of the role of welfare states in the context of class inequality, we need a different typology. Assuming again that welfare state institutions provide a fruitful basis for analytically oriented typologies, we will here focus on the major social insurance programs, primarily old age pensions and sickness insurance, the development of which has often been associated with major societal conflicts and which are of great importance for the economic security of most citizens. Again it must be remembered that typologies can never be expected to show a perfect fit with existing realities.

In this context we can use a typology keyed to three different aspects of social insurance institutions: (1) criteria for benefit eligibility; (2) principles used for determining benefit levels; and (3) structures for governing social insurance institutions (Korpi and Palme 1998). Eligibility can be determined in terms of proven need, contributions, labor force participation, belongingness to a specific occupational category, and citizenship (residence). Principles for benefit levels result in a continuum running from minimum or flat-rate benefits to benefits which are markedly related to previous income. In terms of structures of governance it is fruitful to make a distinction between programs run by elected representatives for employers and employees and programs governed in other forms. On the bases of these criteria, among the social insurance institutions found in old age pensions and sickness insurance in our 18 countries during the past century, five different ideal-typical institutional forms can be distinguished. These five ideal-typical institutions are the targeted, voluntary state-subsidized, state corporatist, basic security, and encompassing models, and they have emerged roughly in the order stated here. The principle characteristics of these models are outlined in Figure 3.6.

The *targeted model* originates in the old poor laws and relies on a means test before granting benefits at a minimum level (indicated in the figure by horizontal lines). Targeted programs have been important in many countries but are now dominant only in Australia, where however the means test has been gradually

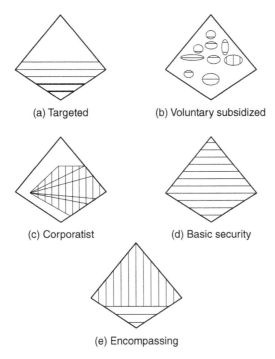

Figure 3.6 Ideal-typical models of social insurance institutions.

relaxed so as to exclude the rich rather than to include only the poor. The *voluntary state-subsidized model* with a multitude of separate mutual-benefit associations has historically been important in sickness as well as unemployment insurance but has not proved practicable in the context of old age pensions. It is therefore no longer dominant in any of our countries. The *state corporatist model*, introduced by Bismarck in Germany in the late nineteenth century, broke with the poor laws as well as with voluntarism by being based on compulsory insurance. In principal, this model is limited to the economically active part of the population; it provides separate programs for selected occupational categories, such as industrial workers, agricultural workers, salaried employees, self-employed, and farmers, each program with different conditions and entitlements. In this model benefits are clearly earnings-related (indicated in the figure by vertical lines). Unlike the other four models, state corporatist social insurance institutions are governed by elected representatives for employers and employees. Catholic confessional parties have traditionally favored the state corporatist model. Pension programs of this type are now found in Austria, Belgium, France, Germany, and Italy with a somewhat differing variant in Japan.

The *basic security model* includes, in principle, all citizens (residents), and insures them within one and the same program. It is thus based on universalism but provides typically only flat-rate benefits, thus a relatively low safety net for all (indicated by horizontal lines). In accordance with principles expressed by William Beveridge, this is to leave room for high-income earners to protect their usual standard of living via various forms of private insurance. The basic security model is now found in Britain, Canada, Denmark, Ireland, Netherlands, New Zealand, Switzerland, and the United States.[12] The *encompassing model* combines the Beveridgian principle of universalism with the Bismarckian principle of clearly earnings-related benefits. This model was first introduced in Sweden in the 1950s, when the universal flat-rate "People's Pension" program was complemented with the clearly earnings-related occupational pension program for all economically active individuals. This model of social insurance is now found also in Finland and Norway.

These different models of social insurance institutions receive their socio-political significance partly because they organize citizens into differing configurations in terms of the distribution of risks and resources. Therefore they are likely to influence the formation of citizens' interests, identities and patterns of collective action. Of socio-political relevance also is that they involve different degrees of political interventions into market distributive processes, something reflected in the relative size of budgets available for redistribution. Furthermore these models can be seen as associated with different types of redistributive strategies. These redistributive strategies can be characterized in terms of the degree to which benefits are targeted to population categories with relatively low incomes, that is what proportion of monies spent goes to the poor.

By having a high degree of low-income targeting, the targeted model relies on a Robin Hood type redistributive strategy of financing benefits to the poor via general taxation. Thereby it tends to drive a wedge between the short-term economic interests of the poor and the rest of the population, which has to finance redistribution but gets very little in material returns. As a result this model tends to produce relatively small redistributive budgets. By limiting itself to a low safety net, the basic security model follows a redistributive strategy of simple egalitarianism in giving the same benefits to all without regard to previous income. Thereby it becomes inefficient for safeguarding accustomed standards of living for middle and high-income earners. In the long run the better off therefore tend to develop various forms of private insurance and come to rely on these additional programs for the major part of their economic security, while mainly manual workers remain dependent on the public programs. In this way the material interests of the economically better off tend to diverge from those of manual workers, also here tending to result in relatively limited redistributive budgets.

Because of its separate programs for different occupational categories, the state corporatist model tends to segment the population according to socio-economic status and can thus be said to follow a strategy of redistribution among relative equals. Since programs are clearly earnings-related, however, this model tends to result in relatively large redistributive budgets.[13] By including all citizens within the same insurance programs and by providing the economically active with clearly earnings-related benefits, the redistributive strategy of the encompassing model can be said to follow the Matthew principle of giving more to those who already have much. However, since it provides all citizens with relatively good protection for accustomed standards of living, the encompassing model tends to limit or to crowed out the various forms of private insurance. Therefore it tends to produce relatively large redistributive budgets.

The total redistributive effect of social insurance institutions can be expected to depend not only on the degree to which monies spent go to low-income citizens but also on the total amount of money to be spent, that is, on the size of redistributive budgets. The relationship between these two factors is likely to be of a multiplicative nature. Furthermore, we can expect a trade-off so that the more highly targeted a program is, the smaller is the redistributive budget likely to be. On the basis of these considerations, we can expect that the lowest degree of redistribution and therefore the highest levels of inequality are likely to be associated with the basic security and the targeted models. The highest degree of redistribution and the lowest levels of inequality are expected to be associated with the encompassing model. The corporatist model is expected to generate middling levels of inequality. It must of course here be remembered that in this context, social insurance institutions provide only one set of intervening variables in the distributive processes generating income inequality; here also many other significant factors are likely to operate.[14]

To provide something of a test for the hypotheses sketched above, we can use data from the Luxembourg Income Study (LIS) to analyze the distribution of household income in 15 of our 18 countries in the 1980s. We have here computed three measures on income inequality and five measures on levels of poverty in different demographic categories.[15] In Table 3.1, countries are grouped by type of

Table 3.1 Average rank of countries in terms of eight indicators of inequality and poverty, by type of social insurance institutions

Country (Year of data set)	Type of social insurance institutions	Average rank*
United States (1986)	Basic security	1
United Kingdom (1989)	Basic security	2
Canada (1987)	Basic security	3
Ireland (1987	Basic security	4
Australia (1989)	Targeted	5
Switzerland (1982)	Basic security	8
Denmark (1987)	Basic security	10
Netherlands (1987)	Basic security	11
Italy (1986)	State corporatist	6
France (1989)	State corporatist	7
Germany (1984)	State corporatist	9
Belgium (1988)	State corporatist	12
Norway (1986)	Encompassing	13
Sweden (1987)	Encompassing	14
Finland (1987)	Encompassing	15

* Gini total population; Gini persons 25–59 years; P90/P10 total population, and poverty measures for total population; persons 25–59 years; persons 65+ years; children, and lone mothers.

social insurance institutions, and the table also gives their rank in terms of the average rank on the above eight indicators of income inequality and poverty. On the whole the expectations sketched above are borne out.

Of the eight countries with the basic security or targeted model, six end up among the highest ranks in terms of inequality (United States, Britain, Canada, Ireland, Australia and Switzerland). The three countries with the encompassing model (Norway, Sweden and Finland) are all found among the three lowest ranks. In the middle of the distribution we do however find some exceptions. Thus Denmark and the Netherlands with basic security models have levels of inequality comparable to the lowest among the state corporatist ones. Among the four countries with the state corporatist model, Germany and Belgium have middling ranks as expected while Italy and France have higher levels of inequality than expected.

On the whole, however, these results point to what can be called "the paradox of redistribution" (Korpi and Palme 1998). The targeted model, giving only to the poor, and the basic security model, giving equally much to all, thus tend to produce higher levels of inequality than the encompassing model giving more to those who already have much. This paradox is to a large extent accounted for by the fact that in the targeted and basic security models, middle and high income earners must attempt to safeguard their accustomed standards of living by private or occupational insurance or by savings, something which tends to produce even higher levels of inequality than those found in the income-related benefits of the encompassing and state corporatist models. By tending to "crowd out" such solutions, the markedly earning-related public programs tend to result in comparatively low levels of inequality.

It is here tempting to advance hypotheses for future research that may help to account for what appear as unexpected results above. Thus in Italy, the well-known regional differences between the North and the South may contribute to increase income inequalities. Unlike Germany and Belgium where Christian democratic parties have dominated during the postwar period, in spite of its state corporatist model French distributive policies have been largely directed by secular conservative-centrist parties with less concern for avoiding poverty than have traditional confessional parties. In the Netherlands with a basic security model, however, confessional parties as well as the social democratic party have been relatively strong, and in Denmark the social democratic party has been stronger than its counterparts in the other countries with a basic security model. Such differences in political constellations may help to account for relatively low levels of inequality in those countries with unexpected levels of inequality.

Types of welfare states and patterns of class and gender inequalities

The above discussion indicates that to account for the role of welfare states in gender inequality and class inequality, we would appear to need two separate typologies reflecting the nature of different aspects of welfare state institutions. In combination these two typologies can serve to describe major constellations of welfare state institutions. As noted above each of the three types of political tendencies, which have dominated governments in our 18 countries during the decades after the Second World War, can be expected to have favored specific constellations of welfare state institutions. With their stress on the primacy of market processes, secular conservative-centrist parties can be expected to have opted for the targeted or basic security models of social insurance institutions as well as the market oriented gender policy model. Confessional parties are likely to have thrown their support behind corporatist social insurance institutions and the general family support model.

Left parties, which were latecomers into the social policy making arena, found themselves in the context of welfare state institutions largely erected by the other political tendencies and these institutions turned out to be difficult to change, especially in countries where left parties were relatively weak. The strategies which the left parties chose have therefore come to differ greatly among our countries, much more so than the strategies adopted by confessional parties and secular conservative-centrist parties. It is thus hardly possible to talk here about a "social democratic model" of welfare state institutions in the sense that it has been adhered to by most social democratic parties. In countries where left parties have had a long-term hold on governments, we would however expect them to have gradually come to support encompassing social insurance institutions and dual earner gender policies. Again it must however be remembered that the types of welfare state institutions we now can observe are the products of the interplay between many different actors, often working at cross-purposes, over long historical periods, and with overlaid effects.

When we combine our typologies of social insurance institutions with gender policy institutions, we find a *targeted/market oriented* constellation of institutions in Australia and *basic security/market oriented* constellations in Canada, Switzerland, Britain, the United States and New Zealand (Table 3.2). With one exception, in these countries the dominance of conservative-centrist secular parties has been marked. The exception here is Switzerland with a relatively strong presence of confessional parties. However, as noted above, the characteristics of the Swiss constitution have contributed to drastically limiting the role of policy making on the national level. The constellation of *state corporatist/general family support* institutions is found in Austria, Belgium, Germany, Italy, which all are countries with a strong presence of Christian democratic parties. Also in France we find a similar constellation, although its Christian democratic parties have been considerably weaker and faded out in the 1960s. Here, the state corporatist social insurance institutions were introduced before the First World War and in the period between the two world wars and have been largely retained, but as noted above, in the general family support institutions have been complemented with a significant dose of dual earner support policies. In Finland, Norway, and Sweden, three countries where social democratic parties have been strong, we find the *encompassing/dual earner* constellation.

An unexpected combination of *basic security/general family support* institutions

Table 3.2 Combinations of institutional models of social insurance and gender policies and of inequality with respect to class and gender in 18 countries, 1985–1990

Country	Institutional models of Social insurance/Gender policy	Class inequality	Gender inequality
Canada	Basic security/Market oriented	High	Medium
Switzerland	Basic security/Market oriented	High	(Medium)
United Kingdom	Basic security/Market oriented	High	Medium
United States	Basic security/Market oriented	High	Medium
New Zealand	Basic security/Market oriented	(High)	Medium
Australia	Targeted/Market oriented	High	High*
Ireland	Basic security/General family support	High	High
Netherlands	Basic security/General family support	Medium*	High
Denmark	Basic security/Dual earner	Medium*	Low
Belgium	State corporatist/General family support	Medium	High
Germany	State corporatist/General family support	Medium	High
Italy	State corporatist/General family support	High*	High
France	State corporatist/General family support	High*	Medium*
Austria	State corporatist/General family support	(Medium)	(Medium*)
Japan	State corporatist/Market oriented	–	High*
Finland	Encompassing/Dual earner	Low	Low
Norway	Encompassing/Dual earner	Low	Low
Sweden	Encompassing/Dual earner	Low	Low

* Unexpected level of inequality, given type of institutions.

is found in Ireland and the Netherlands. Catholic Ireland received its basic security social insurance institutions while it was part of Britain and in the 1930s efforts failed to change them in a state corporatist direction. In the Netherlands, however, the social democratic party with its allied trade unions managed to change its pensions insurance institutions from the state corporatist to basic security one.[16] Denmark has a *basic security/dual earner* combination of institutions. As in the other Nordic countries, during the postwar decades the Danish social democrats attempted to move from basic security to encompassing institutions but these efforts failed. In Japan we find an unusual combination of *state corporatist/market oriented* institutions. Its social insurance institutions became constructed according to a variant of the Bismarckian model during the Meiji Restoration. With cultural and religious traditions differing from those in Europe, however, it gender policies have developed in a different direction.

As discussed above, in terms of class inequality we would expect to find the relatively highest levels in countries with the targeted or basic security model and the lowest ones in the encompassing countries with the corporatist countries somewhere in between. In terms of gendered agency inequality, the relatively highest inequalities are expected in countries with the general family support model, the lowest ones in those with the dual earner model and middling levels in those with market oriented models. In Table 3.2 we have information on 35 of these outcomes, and 27 of them are in accordance with the above predictions.

It can be noted here that it is only the encompassing/dual earner constellation of institutions which tends to generate relatively low class inequality as well as low gender inequality. In the other institutional constellations, we can expect to find asymmetrical patterns of gender and class inequalities. Thus the combinations of targeted or basic security social insurance institutions with market oriented gender policy institutions tend to generate high class inequality but medium level gender inequality, while the state corporatist/general family support constellation tends to yield the opposite pattern. As a result we find relatively low correlations between class inequality and gendered agency inequalities in our countries, something attesting to the fruitfulness of developing separate institutional typologies in these two policy areas. In this context it can be remembered that also in terms of gen-dered agency inequalities in areas of political representation, tertiary education, and labor force participation, we tend to find low levels of "crystallization." Thus, for example, Ireland has the highest gender gap in labor force participation and a relatively high one in terms of political representation but has extinguished the gender gap in access to university education.

A long-term perspective

It is instructive to look at the relationships between class inequality and gender inequality in a long-term perspective. While it is here not possible to compare *levels* of inequalities in these two respects, it is possible to crudely sketch *trends* in the development of inequalities in each of the separate dimensions. Fifty years ago T. H. Marshall (1950) talked about the "modern drive towards social equality," stating that "the modern drive towards social equality is the latest phase of an evo-lution of citizenship which has been in continuous progress for some 250 years." As is well-known, Marshall saw this evolution as containing the gradual devel-opment of the civil, political and social components of citizenship. Although Marshall did not consider gender inequality, it appears that with the gradual emergence of citizenship rights, for long periods inequality with respect to gender as well as class decreased in roughly parallel although not identical ways. What does the situation look like half a century later?

During the period after the Second World War, governments in several Western countries have made strong efforts to decrease class inequality as well as gender inequality. In many respects, however, class inequalities appear to have been considerably more resistant to reform and reduction than have gender inequalities. These differences in reform resistance can be illustrated in different areas. With respect to life expectancy, we know that in Western Europe and North America, women now have considerably longer life expectancy than have men. But in the 1990s in these rich countries, among men, the risk of premature death is clearly greater for manual workers than for men in higher socio-eco-nomic classes. As shown above, the female disadvantage in access to university education has markedly decreased. In all of these countries, however, marked class inequalities in access to higher education remain.

As indicated above, the decreases in class inequality and in gender inequality long followed largely parallel paths. During the last quarter of the twentieth century, however, these paths have come to diverge. As shown above, the decrease in gender inequality appears to have accelerated since the early 1970s, while since the early 1980s inequalities in disposable household income have markedly increased in these countries. In this context it is also important to consider long-term changes in levels of unemployment, an often overlooked indicator of class inequality. As is well-known, unemployment disproportionally hits lower socio-economic categories. Therefore the disappearance of recurring periods of mass unemployment characterizing the industrialized countries up to the Second World War and the arrival in most of our countries of full employment in the decades after 1945 can be seen as a major decrease in class inequality. In the same perspective, however, the return of mass unemployment after the 1970s, especially in the West European countries, is a major reversal of the trend of declining class inequalities.

Those who appreciate equality can rejoice at the tendencies towards decreasing gender inequalities which we can now observe. However, very much remains to be done and since political and economic factors are relevant here, reversals are always possible. Yet, those who appreciate equality should be concerned about the marked tendencies towards increasing class inequalities starting during the last quarter of the twentieth century. For social scientists, it is important to attempt to understand the diverging trends in these two areas. These changes indicate that the development of citizenship is unlikely to be one of evolution. Processes of distributive conflict are at work here.

Notes

1 Race, ethnicity, and immigration are examples of other important factors of relevance for inequality in many countries (see Woodward and Kohli 2001) but cannot be discussed here.
2 These countries have had uninterrupted political democracy after the Second World War and have a population of at least one million. The data presented here come primarily from the *Social Citizenship Indicator Program (SCIP)* which now is in the process of being built up at the Swedish Institute for Social Research, Stockholm University.
3 For example, Cantillon and Nolan 1998; McLanahan, Sorensen and Watson 1989; Millar and Glendinning 1989; Pahl 1989.
4 Needless to say, freedom to choose is of relevance also in the area of class inequality, but where differences in standards of living still remain central.
5 For example, Lewis 1986; O'Connor 1996; Orloff 1993; Pateman 1988; Vogel 1991.
6 Thus *Equality Gap* = % Women–% Men.
7 For a detailed description of the empirical indicators used in constructing this typology, see Korpi 2000.
8 In the measure of dual earner support, the indicators of daycare for the 0–2 year olds and for the character of maternity leave are given a weight twice that of the other two indicators. The three indicators for general family support are all given the same weight.
9 In addition to these three tendencies there have of course also been other types of parties, such as the "green" ones, but in terms of government positions they have been of less importance during the period considered here.
10 See Immergut 1992; Huber *et al.* 1993.

11 For an analysis based on a larger number of indicators, see Korpi 2000.

12 In Britain, Ireland and the United States, benefit eligibility is in principle based on contributions but in the other countries on citizenship or residence. In Britain, Canada, Ireland, Switzerland, and the United States, pension programs are to some extent earnings-related but because of low ceilings for benefits, the degree of earnings-relatedness is much lower than in the encompassing countries.

13 In some countries state corporatist programs have excluded the top income earners, enticing them to look for private insurance.

14 These other factors include, *inter alia*, industrial relations systems, wage setting procedures, and demographic factors.

15 The inequality measures include Gini coefficients for the total population and for the 25–59 year category as well as the P90/P10 ratio for the total population. Defining poverty as the proportion below 50 percent of median income, poverty levels are computed for the total population, the prime working age population (25–59 years), the elderly (65+ years), minor children and lone mothers. In comparing households of different sizes, household income is weighted by the size of family and to account for economies of scale, by giving different weights to the "first" and other family members. The equivalence scale is one used by the OECD and gives a weight of 1.0 to the first adult, 0.7 to the second adult and 0.5 to each additional person, regardless of age. To avoid statistical problems associated with differing practices for including teenagers in the data, we have excluded households with a head below 20 years of age. Countries have then been ranked on each of the seven indicators and the average ranks are given in Table 3.1. Here disposable income refers to net cash income after direct taxes and social security contributions as well as after public transfers.

16 In health insurance, however, state corporatist institutions were retained.

References

Acker, J. (1989) "The problem with patriarchy", *Sociology* 23: 235–40.

Bobbio, N. (1996) *Left and Right. The Significance of a Political Distinction*, Cambridge: Polity Press.

Cantillon, S. and Nolan, B. (1998) "Are married women more deprived than their husbands?", *Journal of Social Policy* 27: 151–71.

Esping-Andersen, G. (1990) *The Three Worlds of Welfare Capitalism*, Cambridge: Polity Press.

Hobson, B. (1991) "Economic dependency and women's social citizenship: Some thoughts on Esping-Andersen's welfare state regimes", paper presented at the Conference on Gender, Citizenship and Social Policy, Social Science History Association Meeting in New Orleans.

Hobson, B. and Lindholm, M. (1997) "Collective identities, women's power resources, the making of welfare states", *Theory and Society* 26: 475–508.

Huber, E., Ragin, C., and Stephens, J. D. (1993) "Social democracy, Christian democracy, constitutional structure, and the welfare state", *American Journal of Sociology* 99: 711–49.

Immergut, E. (1992) *Health Politics. Interests and Institutions in Western Europe*, Cambridge: Cambridge University Press.

Korpi, W. (2000) "Faces of inequality: Gender, class and patterns of inequalities in different types of welfare states", *Social Politics: International Studies in Gender, State and Society*, 7.

Korpi, W. and Palme, J. (1998) "The paradox of redistribution and the strategy of equality: Welfare state institutions, inequality and poverty in the Western countries", *American Sociological Review* 63: 661–87.

Lewis, J. (1992) "Gender and the development of welfare regimes", *Journal of European Social Policy* 2: 159–73.

—— (1986) *Labour and Love. Women's Experience of Home and Family, 1850–1940*, Oxford: Blackwell.

Lister, R. (1997) *Citizenship. Feminist Perspectives*, London: Macmillan.

Marshall, T. H. (1950) "Citizenship and social class", in Marshall, T. H. (ed.) *Citizenship and Social Class and Other Essays*, Cambridge: Cambridge University Press: 1–85.

McLanahan, S., Sorensen, A., and Watson, D. (1989) "Sex differences in poverty, 1950–1980", *Signs: Journal of Women in Culture and Society* 15: 102–22.

Millar, J. and Glendinning, C. (1989) "Gender and poverty", *Journal of Social Policy* 18: 363–81.

Norris, P. (1987) *Politics and Sexual Equality: The Comparative Position of Women in Western Democracies*, Boulder: Rienner & Wheatsheaf.

O'Connor, J. S. (1996) "From women in the welfare state to gendering welfare state regimes", *Current Sociology* 44: 1–124.

Orloff, A. S. (1993) "Gender and the social rights in citizenship: The comparative analysis of gender relations and welfare states", *American Sociological Review* 58: 303–28.

Pahl, J. (1989) *Money and Marriage*, New York: St Martin's Press.

Pateman, C. (1988) "The patriarchal welfare state", in Gutman, A. (ed.) *Democracy and the Welfare State*, Princeton: Princeton University Press: 231–60.

Sainsbury, D. (1996) *Gender Equality and Welfare States*, Cambridge: Cambridge University Press.

Schelling, T. C. (1978) *Micromotives and Macrobehavior*, New York: Norton.

Sen, A. (1992) *Inequality Re-examined*, Oxford: Oxford University Press.

Shaver, S. (1989) "Gender, class and the welfare state: The case of income security in Australia", *Feminist Review* 32: 90–110.

Tingsten, H. (1937) *Political Behaviour. Studies in Election Statistics*, London: P. S. King & Son.

Vogel, U. (1991) "Is citizenship gender-specific?", in Vogel, U. and Moran, M. (eds) *The Frontiers of Citizenship*, London: Macmillan.

Williams, F. (1995) "Race/ethnicity, gender, and class in welfare states: A framework for comparative analysis", *Social Politics: International Studies in Gender, State and Society* 2: 127–59.

Woodward, A. and Kohli, M. (eds) (2001) *Inclusions/Exclusions in European Societies*, London: Routledge.

4 Employment and labor market policies in South Europe

Maria Petmesidou

This chapter examines employment trends, industrial relations and labor market policy reform in South Europe in the last two decades. In the first part the challenges that the European welfare states have been facing since the early 1980s are briefly discussed. The emphasis is on how responses – emanating from the national, supranational and local/regional level – to new challenges modify traditional forms of socio-economic regulation. A classificatory framework is developed that can help us to summarize a wide range of policy strategies. Further, the peculiarities of South European social, employment and welfare structures are highlighted. In the third part convergence or divergence in labor market regulation in South European countries is examined in the light of recent debates on alternative policy paradigms.

Policy options in the European context and the peculiarities of the European South

The change factors confronting European welfare states and their traditional forms of socio-economic regulation have been widely studied in the last few years (Esping-Andersen 1996, 1999; Rhodes 1996). First, a convergence of internal pressures on European welfare states (demographic change, technological transformation, cost explosion of welfare programs coupled with structurally high levels of unemployment, the emergence of non-standard work-careers and changing household and family patterns) makes necessary a common basis of reform and action. Second, pressures created by the globalization of markets call for rapid adjustments of products, technologies and labor markets, while new production regimes transform the world of work and industrial relations. Third, participation in the common currency further restricts the scope of policy choices (i.e. the use of traditional measures of economic leverage like various forms of protection and currency devaluation).

In parallel, significant changes in the policy context are observed, as diagnosis of mounting challenges and tensions of traditional forms of socio-economic regulation, as well as the search for solutions, take place within an emerging multi-tiered system of governance (Pierson and Leibfried 1995, also Streeck in this volume). On the one hand, EU competencies are widening. For instance, regarding employment policy, there is a progressive Europeanization of policy objectives, indicating that the outlines of a supranational labor market policy are in close reach; and some authors even forecast "a supra-nationalization at EU level of unemployment burdens" as a result of the process of achieving monetary union (Leibfried 1994: 243–4). On the other hand, a progressive redrawing of the boundaries of state intervention in most European countries creates more scope for action in matters of socio-economic regulation for the sub-national levels (regional, local, and firm level).

Under these conditions the landscape of European industrial relations and labor management is continuously shifting, while the supranational dimension is strengthened. An example pointing towards this direction is the resolution adopted by the European Metalworkers Federation, which aims to co-ordinate bargaining policy throughout Europe in order to counteract the potential negative effects of monetary union on pay and employment conditions (that is, the potential bidding down of pay and working conditions by employers feared to be "the outcome of the increased transparency and competitiveness of a common currency zone") (EIRR 1999a).

The various policy responses to the above challenges can be conceptualized on the basis of three bipolar distinctions that as ideal-types can synthesize in a useful way actual policy options by European countries. The first bipolar distinction counterposes centralization to de-centralization (e.g. of industrial relations and labor management). The second contrasts concertation to deregulation (unilaterally introduced by governments); while further within the *concertation pole* we distinguish between micro-concertation taking place at the firm-level and macro-concertation consisting in peak level pacts between the government and the industrial partners. The third distinction refers to two different formulae of government: the *active society* or *workfare society* notion puts forward a perspective which redefines the links between social policy and labor markets in a way which sharply contrasts with the de-commodification of labor that the welfare state formula of government embodied in the mid-twentieth century. The *active-society* perspective reflects:

> a fundamentally neo-liberal axiom that associates job growth, economic development and social well-being with wider participation in society and expansion of the entrepreneurial culture . . . it seeks to make all individuals into workers . . . while at the same time it signals the end of the age of the fully-employed, "tenured" worker and the dramatic rise of part-time, irregular and non-standard forms of employment.
>
> (Walters 1997: 225)

Actual policy responses include a range of combinations of elements pertaining to one or the other pole of these ideal-type distinctions. Often responses may include contradictory strategies:

> [as] the new challenges require the European economies to strike some sort of balance between opposing needs of deregulation of labor markets, industrial relations and welfare systems, on the one hand, and of concertation able to provide a social pact for national competitiveness, on the other.
>
> (Regini 1998: 19)

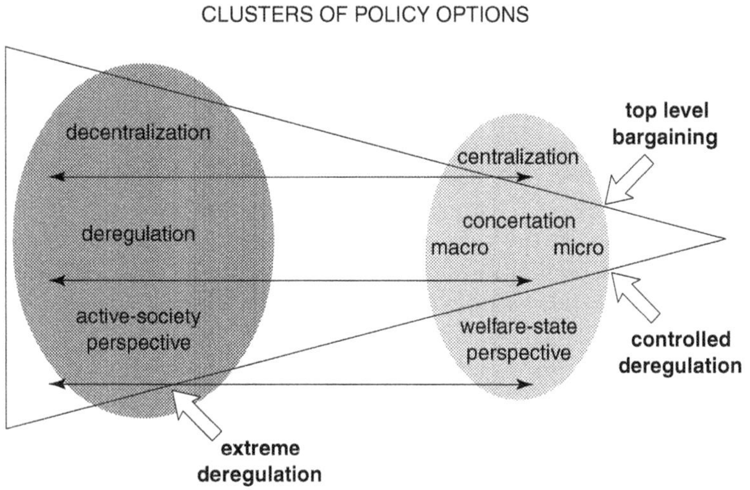

CLUSTERS OF POLICY OPTIONS

Figure 4.1 Clusters of policy options.

It is outside the scope of this chapter to delve deeply into the particular strategies adopted by various European countries (as well as to crucial underlying factors influencing different strategies, such as power relations, institutional traditions and organizational learning, the position of a country in the European/global economy, its capacity to respond to the requirements of monetary union, etc.). Three groupings of policy strategies are schematically defined in Figure 4.1, on the basis of the three bipolar distinctions, as indicative of alternative policy clusters with differing orientations.

The policy strategies subsumed under the heading of "recurrent top-level bargaining" combine wage solidarity within various sectors with a *quid pro quo* political exchange between the partners, encompassing also welfare provisions which decommodified labor. These characteristics were epitomized in the corporatist, Fordist pattern of socio-economic regulation in Europe that has been in decline since the 1980s (such a tradition remained weakest in many parts of South Europe though).

In the last two decades policy responses – conceptualized along the three bipolar distinctions – may take the form of either *extreme deregulation*, or of more or less *controlled deregulation/decentralization*. Among EU countries, the UK offers a striking example of the former policy paradigm: that is, policies of deregulation of labor markets and industrial relations unilaterally introduced by the government, coupled with: (1) the decentralization of bargaining procedures; (2) numerical and functional flexibility; and (3) the dismantling of welfare guarantees.

An alternative policy orientation in European countries tends to re-strengthen social concertation around public policies as a crucial strategy in boosting national competitiveness. This new type of social concertation is considered to depart from the *quid pro quo* logic of an immediate political exchange of benefits between the partners and rather promotes a regulatory framework of policy: it facilitates a controlled debasement of regulations, selective and concerted flexibility as well as regulated welfare state restructuring (Rhodes 1998; Regini and Regalia 1997; Regini 1998). Some authors go so far as to clearly define this policy orientation as a promising alternative to the Anglo-Saxon deregulation strategies, that, on the one hand, attempts "a readjustment of the 'continental' model" so as to respond to market pressures, yet on the other hand it also preserves social consensus and social protection (hence the term "competitive corporatism") (Rhodes 1998: 179).[1]

From this perspective the main questions raised with regard to South European countries are: How do they fit into this classificatory framework? Are there any trends of convergence in labor market policies among the four South European countries, especially as regards the latter paradigm? Is there a significant redrawing of boundaries between central and sub-national policy actors in industrial relations? However, in tackling these issues we must bear in mind that the above range of change factors need also to be linked to the peculiarities of socioeconomic and political structures in South Europe.

Aspects of social, employment and welfare structures

(A) Late industrialization, followed by a rapid shift to post-Fordism since the early 1980s, well before industrialization had deepened and Fordist production structures with their accompanying patterns of collective solidarity and universalist social citizenship had been fully developed, constitutes one important characteristic of South European countries. This is linked to a rather weak tradition in building social consensus (though of course there are significant differences between the four countries) (Petmesidou and Tsoulouvis 1994).

In the 1980s and 1990s de-industrialization coincided with de-ruralization. Coupled with demographic pressures, and a rapidly increasing female participation in the labor market, this condition produced high levels of unemployment in South Europe (striking examples being Spain with a record high unemployment rate, as well as South Italy). Further, significant structural adjustments introduced in the decade 1975–1985 under the pressure of a number of mutually reinforcing factors, such as the two oil shocks, the transition from an agricultural economy to post-Fordism, the opening up of South European economies, combined with the release of pent-up wage pressures and the democratization of union organizations in countries such as Spain, Portugal and Greece, after the fall of dictatorships, were decisive for employment trends. Preparations for EU accession by these three countries constituted an additional pressure.

In the period of the transition to democracy Spain experienced a very serious fall in employment that marked a significant departure from the rest of Europe. In the mid-1980s net employment losses amounted to about 17 percent of total employment in 1974; over two million jobs were lost and these were mostly in the manufacturing, construction and agricultural sectors, while service sector employment slightly increased (OECD 1996b: 57).[2] Unemployment jumped from 5 percent in the late 1970s to 21 percent in the mid-1980s. Job growth during the economic expansion period (of the late 1980s) did not succeed in closing the gap with the labor force, which had kept growing over the previous decade of declining employment opportunities. As the recovery lost momentum in the first half of the 1990s, unemployment reached 22.2 percent in 1996 (of which 53 percent was long-term unemployment).[3] At the end of the decade employment started to show a strong recovery and overall unemployment declined significantly for the first time since the mid-1970s (to 15.3 percent in 1999).

Compared to the other South European countries, Greece experienced low rates of economic growth until the late 1990s. Male participation stagnated, but the female labor force increased rapidly. Unemployment rose sharply between 1975 and 1985, from 1.7 to 7.0 percent of the labor force. It fell slightly in the second half of the 1980s but increased rapidly again in the 1990s reaching 11.6 percent of the labor force (7.8 percent for men and 17.4 percent for women) by the end of the decade. If we also take into account hidden unemployment (about 3 percent according to a report of the European Employment Observatory), total unemployment amounted to about 14 percent of the labor force (over 50 percent of it being long-term unemployment).[4]

In contrast to these trends, the structural adjustments set in motion by the opening up of the Portuguese economy in the late 1970s and early 1980s, as well as special factors linked to accession to the EU, contributed much to absorbing the labor supply in this country. Male and female unemployment fell sharply between 1985 and 1992: from 6.6 to 3.6 percent and from 11.7 to 5.0 percent, respectively. These trends contrasted with developments in most EU countries, where structural labor market conditions worsened throughout the 1980s (OECD 1996a: 77). What is more, the fall of female unemployment at about 7 percentage points in the period 1985–92 was twice as large as that of men, reducing the excess of female over male unemployment to around 1.4 points (even under conditions of comparatively high participation rates for women);[5] the gap slightly increased in the late 1990s, yet it is still one of the lowest among OECD countries.

Italy exhibited a comparatively high annual average rate of growth of GDP from 1975 to 1990 (3.0 percent). Throughout this period employment grew by a yearly average of only 0.5 percent; this rate was above the EU average (0.1 percent) in the decade 1975–85, but well below it in the following period of economic recovery (1985–90). This manifests a comparatively low employment-intensity of growth, and output expansion was achieved largely by raising productivity. During the 1980s far-reaching restructuring and reorganization in the industrial sector decreased labor demand in it, while at the beginning of the 1990s similar trends affected the service sector as well (European Commission 1996a: 1). A substantial fall in employment (by 3.7 percent) between 1990 and 1994 was followed by a period of employment stagnation.[6] In January 1995 unemployment reached the historical height of 12.2 percent (22.0 percent in the South and 7.2 percent in the North). Long-term unemployment also significantly increased to reach 65 percent of the unemployed in 1998. Further, in Italy – as well as in Greece – unemployed young people are more likely to be long-term unemployed than their unemployed elders.[7]

(B) South European countries exhibit strong official rigidities in employment regulations and industrial relations; however, this condition is counterposed to informal flexibilities pertaining to a wide black economy. Greece constitutes a characteristic example of a highly legalistic mode of labor market regulation offset by the functioning of a wide informal sector, as according to a study (Schneider 1999) a little less than a third of GDP is produced in the black economy, ranking Greece at the top of the OECD countries.[8] This phenomenon is also closely linked with labor market fragmentation (across the formal/informal labor market divide and the protected/unprotected sectors). Moreover, Greece, together with Portugal, exhibit a high degree of centralization of collective bargaining coupled with extensive state intervention in industrial relations at least until the early 1990s.[9]

(C) Social protection systems are doubly fragmented in South Europe. Welfare guarantees depend upon a full and uninterrupted occupational career that establishes contributive entitlements, while those who cannot secure such a career in the formal labor market are left unprotected. A policy of a universal income safety net was only introduced in Portugal, it is absent in Greece, while in Spain and Italy some initiatives in this direction at the regional/local level remain uncoordinated. Further, wide inequalities in the level of benefits offered by social security funds increase polarization between groups of hyper-protected and weakly protected beneficiaries (particularly in the case of Greece). What is more, income maintenance programs and welfare service delivery are based upon a particularistic-clientelistic system in which corruption and discretion are endemic characteristics (Ferrera 1996; Petmesidou 1996a). Some authors talk about an "anomic division of political labor" in South European countries, meaning by this term the penetration and exploitation of state institutions and decision-making structures by a wide range of socio-economic interests that greatly limit the state's authority and administrative capacity.[10]

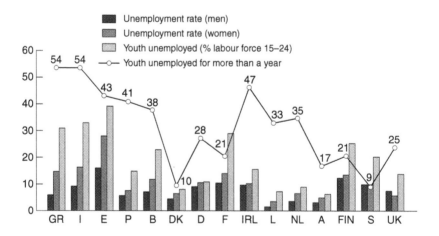

Figure 4.2 Unemployment trends, 1998.

Source: Eurostat 1999 (data for youth unemployment for more than a year refer to 1996).

(D) Another peculiarity of South European countries concerns the central role of the family/household as a strategic unit of decision-making, regarding employment opportunities of its members, and a redistribution unit providing its members with the means to overcome distress, unemployment and bankruptcy. In parallel a familist labor market management gives priority to the protection of the earnings and career continuity of the male breadwinner (in the formal labor market).[11] This is also connected to a major difference in unemployment trends that sets South European countries apart from a good many EU countries. In the latter countries the most significant problems emerged with persons who became unemployed under conditions of recession and were later caught up in the wheels of passive income support policies. In South Europe this situation affects a limited proportion of older workers, whilst the most significant problem is high and persistent unemployment among youths and generally among women (Figure 4.2). Another facet of these conditions is the comparatively low degree of employment polarization among households in South European countries (Gregg and Wadsworth 1998). Although unemployment increased rapidly in Spain, Greece and Italy in the 1990s, this trend was not accompanied by the simultaneous rapid increase over time in both workless and fully employed households and an abrupt decrease of mixed-work households (that is, households in which at least one member is employed); as is for instance the case in some North European societies (e.g. the UK) even under conditions of declining unemployment. Instead, in South European countries we discern a large proportion of mixed-work households.

Major labor market policy reforms in the 1980s and 1990s – social pacts

South European countries embarked upon wide-ranging plans for labor market and welfare policy reform linked to privatization strategies relatively later than other industrialized countries. It is in the decade of the 1990s, under the pressure of EU convergence criteria which weakened social resistance, that governments put through major reforms introducing market forces in the public sector and deregulation measures for labor markets. The time and pacing of these reforms, as well as the extent to which they draw upon a social concertation process, or instead are introduced by governments in a unilateral way, vary among South European countries. On the one hand Italy (and to some extent Portugal) provide examples of a "consensus building process at the macro-level" supporting significant reforms for adjusting public policies to external and internal constraints. On the other hand, in Spain and Greece social concertation is rather weak. Among other factors, the highly politicized and conflictual character of industrial relations in these countries until recently (mostly due to a strong labor market dualization, in the case of Spain, affected by a policy of temporary-contracts) considerably limited the possibility of wide social agreements on policy reform.

Italy

In Italy, from the mid-1970s to the early 1990s, collective bargaining processes repeatedly shifted emphasis between the "center" and the "periphery," that is between peak level political exchange among the social partners on the one hand, and informal, voluntaristic agreements at the firm-level on the other, according to circumstances and power relations (Regalia and Regini 1992). Yet until the early 1990s this dualism in collective bargaining was not linked to well-established rules about the competencies of and the issues addressed at each level. A phase of explosive trade-union mobilization in the late 1960s was followed by a period of political exchange at the central level. By the early 1980s peak level bargaining collapsed, mainly because of the crisis of union representation. The tripartite accord for an anti-inflation policy (that would revise the *scala mobile*, that is the inflation-linked wage escalator), signed in January 1983, hardly produced a stable concertation. Throughout the 1980s industrial adjustment took place through the widespread use of bargaining in the lower tiers of the industrial relations system. Under these circumstances a strategy of micro-concertation emerged which may not have favored large-scale agreements of socio-economic reform, yet it firmly hindered extreme deregulation.[12]

Peak level negotiations over the cost of labor and the collective bargaining structure were resumed in 1989. In the next couple of years new tripartite agreements acknowledged the deadlock of the *scala mobile*; these, however, were once more restricted to declarations of principle, postponing again any significant reform. The situation changed drastically in 1992, when the "Clean Hands" operation was launched as a response to the political crisis that erupted in close connection with widespread economic scandals. Under the conditions of crisis and the pressures exerted by the Maastricht stipulations for joining the EMU, a process of building social consensus across political boundaries emerged in Italian society that consolidated the claim of "removing politics from the budgetary process" as the principal policy option for Italy to enhance national competitiveness and secure its place in the European economic and monetary union.

In 1992 a tripartite agreement was reached which abolished the *scala mobile*; the core of the agreement checked wages growth without however introducing compensatory measures that traditionally accompanied political trade-offs in the 1980s. Despite some resistance by workers in the most unionized factories, the concluded agreement was met in a positive way as bringing about a significant change in the relationships between the social partners and the state.

A year after, the technocratic government led by Ciampi signed a crucial agreement that redefined the overall system of collective bargaining. It introduced an incomes policy based on a joint commitment of the parties to link wage increases to the expected inflation rate; the bipolar character of the Italian collective bargaining system (at the national and company or local level) was consolidated and the roles and competencies of each level were clearly specified. The social actors explicitly confronted the task of regulating collective bargaining, introducing rules as to the relationships between the various levels, and enhancing formalization.

Further, negotiations over pensions reform gave rise to a most severe conflict and then to an agreement between government and unions on a law which introduced significant changes in the social insurance system: such as the shift from the old earnings-related to a new contributions-related formula, the standardization of rules for public and private employees, stricter rules on the cumulative receipt of disability benefits and incomes from work, and tighter controls on beneficiaries. A subsequent reform, agreed in November 1997, brought about substantial savings in the public budget, and thus contributed to Italy's joining the first wave of European economic and monetary union.

The "Employment Pact" concluded in September 1996 constitutes another major development in labor market regulation. It attempted to lift most of labor market rigidities so as to enhance flexibility, in a controlled way though. In mid-1997 the provisions of this accord were incorporated in new legislation (the so-called "Treu package"), which legalized temporary work agencies, yet under controlled guidelines; introduced cuts to the level of employer social security contributions on part-time work; established new types of contracts like area contracts (especially for the South); improved apprenticeship and provided community work for young unemployed people in the South; it also introduced new measures with real innovations in the education and training system. A new social pact on "Development and Employment," signed in December 1998 by a broad range of social partners (and ratified by the Parliament in early 1999), extended the social concertation strategy to the territorial level by involving in it the local administrations in the context of a process of devolution of state tasks to regions, provinces and municipalities.

Evidently, for social concertation to be effective and stable in the long-run, most of these agreements on "rules" need to be "fleshed out" with common views and definitions of socio-economic development and national competitiveness by the social partners (Regini and Regalia 1997: 229). Otherwise the prospects for the co-operative game to yield a stable basis of wide consensus are rather bleak. This is indeed an open issue in Italy, given that the social dialogue has hardly yielded such a common frame of reference up to now. A too narrow focus on market and cost efficiency criteria limit considerably the basis of consensus on a common approach. These conditions create an unstable and precarious equilibrium, in which controversial issues, such as the introduction of the 35-hour working week, or the demand by *Confidustria* (General Confederation of Italian Industry) that the national level of bargaining is abolished can easily threaten social concertation.

Spain

In Spain, in the last two decades, major reforms for tackling the employment crisis supported a growing liberalization of entry in the labor market. Although some of the reforms may have been introduced under the pressure of unions' demands, a practice of social concertation has developed hardly at all. Corporatist arrangements remained contingent and non-institutionalized (Roca 1991). This has given the government considerable flexibility to support negotiations at some conjunctures and keep its distance from them at others. Strategic fluidity has thus been a central feature of economic policy in Spain (Martinez Lucio 1992).

At the time of the transition to democracy, governments sought to establish some kind of "corporatist global agreement" with the unions and the employers' associations (e.g. the Moncloa Pact signed in the late 1970s) in an attempt to prevent future social conflicts and enhance the credibility and legitimacy of governmental policy. Between 1977 and 1984 five such peak level accords were signed mainly as part of a strategy to combat inflation through wage growth moderation.

In the mid-1980s the Spanish authorities opted for a safety valve to the employment crisis, and this consisted in low-cost fixed-term and temporary contracts. Instead of reforming the core of the labor market, this strategy rather allowed the development of a *fringe* where labor market regulations, in particular dismissal procedures, would be much less restrictive. The introduction of low-cost fixed-term contracts resulted in growing labor market dualism, by isolating a core of *insiders* (usually adults with indefinite contracts), from a periphery of *outsiders* (young workers and women, with temporary contracts). Needless to say, wage moderation fell mainly upon the latter.

The social dialogue failed during the economic growth period (1985–90) and any subsequent attempts to restore it, particularly when the Spanish economy entered the recession, had no positive results. Consequently, throughout the 1980s and 1990s governments unilaterally introduced labor market reform.

Reforms in the 1990s further supported a radical deregulation in the labor market: in 1992 new legislation aimed at reducing the budgetary cost of unemployment insurance, while the 1994 reforms sought to improve the firms' ability to allocate labor efficiently by increasing both internal and external flexibility. They also significantly changed the balance between law and collective bargaining by giving the latter a more fundamental role, so as to make wages more responsive to local conditions. In addition, the range of criteria for legitimate collective dismissals was expanded so as to include organizational and production-related reasons; while, at the same time, some attempt was made to tighten the rules for fixed-term contracts. Procedures for small-scale layoffs were revised and the approval process for larger layoffs was streamlined. What is more, internal flexibility increased with the relaxation of the so-called *Ordenanzas Laborales* (since 1994 most of these labor regulations have gradually been abolished) and restrictions on part-time work were lifted.

In the last decade any attempts (though hardly successful) to build peak level social concertation emerged as a response to the challenge of EU integration as well as to changes in the balance of political power following the December 1988 general strike. In an attempt to develop links with the labor movement, especially on specific issues of immediate sensitivity (such as the stabilization of pensions or the creation of more permanent jobs) the conservative party government (in office since 1996) favored peak level bargaining, albeit through a process that separates negotiation fora and issues, rather than through comprehensive pacts covering a range of policy matters (as is the case in Italy). Soon after the conservative party came to power, an important agreement reached between the social partners, after difficult negotiations, can be interpreted along these lines. It further decreased redundancy and dismissal compensations in exchange for a reduction in job precariousness. Public subsidies and reductions of social security contributions were provided to employers as incentives for promoting indefinite contracts and transforming temporary into fixed-term jobs.[13] The conjunctural (and fragile) character of recent accords lends support to the view that these do not manifest a "resurgence of corporatism." Rather they constitute a defensive move on the part of the unions which feared "the potential privatization thrust" of the right-wing government; the weakening of left-wing parties because of heightened internal divisions and corruption scandals constitutes one more important factor influencing the industrial relations scene (Gutiérrez and Guillén 2000: 212).

In a nutshell, successive responses to the employment crisis consisted in a radical deregulation giving rise to casualization of employment and dualization of the labor market. Arguably, these conditions led to the consolidation of "a culture of temporary contracts in Spanish firms" with long-term detrimental effects on employment and national competitiveness (European Commission 1997: 175). In the short term, an increased elasticity of employment over the business cycle was observed. But the sharp distinction between temporary and permanent contracts affected the labor market in a negative way: it created wage pressures and increased the insider power of permanent workers, because they are less likely to suffer the potential dismissals due to wage increases; further, it did little to reduce rigidities in the protected sector (Segura *et al.* 1991). Additional serious negative effects on productivity, training and migration have also been recorded as a consequence of enhanced labor market dualism. In a sense, the Spanish experience clearly reflects most of the potential pitfalls of radical deregulation.

Portugal

In Portugal large-scale revolutionary mass mobilizations in the period of the transition to democracy influenced significantly the industrial relations pattern. The highly politicized stance of the trade unions and the predominance of a relationship of mistrust between the social partners halted the modernization of the Portuguese industrial relations system (Barreto and Naumann 1992).

From the revolutionary period up to the late 1970s the polarized approach of the CGTP[14] trade union (the class-oriented main trade union confederation affiliated to the Communist Party) and extensive state intervention, through legislation and the imposition of limits to pay increases, limited the scope of collective bargaining. In the 1980s union mobilization declined, as union density also did, and the state's direct intervention in collective bargaining decreased; however, the state's intervention in the settlement of conflicts and in support of negotiation is still far from negligible. Significant factors that contributed to these changes were: the shift of power relations in favor of neo-liberal political forces (the forging of a strategic alliance between the Social Democratic and the Socialist Party), the emergence of the UGT union[15] with a moderate stance, and increasing employer power (particularly in the form of employer discretion at the company level).

By the mid-1980s collective bargaining stagnated at the sectoral level. Similarly, at the company level workers' involvement in the regulation of work relations was limited. In 1984 the establishment of the Permanent Council of Social Concertation (CPCS) as an institutionalized basis for peak level tripartite negotiations, aimed at introducing a new dynamism to collective bargaining. Since then the CPCS has become the main vehicle for a process of political exchange between the state and the social partners. However, developments did not measure up to expectations. Tripartite national negotiations failed to lead to a real reform of industrial relations; instead they functioned as a legitimizing process for liberalization and restructuring.

Nevertheless the Portuguese labor market has performed remarkably well since the mid-1980s. In the late 1970s–early 1980s the Portuguese economy suffered from severe structural problems, such as a large and inefficient agricultural sector, the very small size of businesses and inefficient management, large-scale nationalization and state intervention in price regulation and market processes, an archaic tax system, inadequate infrastructure and widespread illiteracy (OECD 1996a: 75). The effect was low overall efficiency and increasing unemployment, which reached its peak in 1985 hitting 8.7 percent of the labor force. The shift to market oriented policies in the 1980s, combined with specific conditions concerning Portugal's accession to the EU and widespread flexibility, achieved mostly in an informal way, contributed much to absorbing the labor supply shock of the 1970s and early 1980s. Particularly between the mid-1980s and early 1990s employment increased sharply and unemployment remained low by EU standards. What is more, such performance was achieved under conditions of high participation rates, particularly so in the case of women, long-term demographic trends of decreasing fertility and increasing life expectancy, as well as large-scale employment shedding in agriculture.[16]

Since the mid-1980s tripartite agreements on incomes, employment and welfare policy laid down guidelines for collective bargaining and legal reforms. The 1987 accord adopted the concept of expected inflation rate as the reference point for wage negotiations. It was followed by the 1990 "Economic and Social Agreement." Due to the wide range of regulations and their significant importance, this accord is by far the most crucial. It focused on the objective of promoting effective growth of real wages towards the EU average, under noninflationary conditions, and improvement of international competitiveness of Portuguese firms. In addition, guiding principles were decided in respect, among others, to budget policy and other macro-economic and industrial policies, earnings policy, legislative reform in social security, working time, safety in the workplace, educational and training, atypical work and dismissals. An official decision was also reached by this accord to reduce working time to 40 hours per week by 1995 in exchange for enhancing flexibility in work schedules.

Further, significant reforms of the Portuguese pensions system were agreed upon in the first half of the 1990s. These raised contributions and contribution periods, but at the same time improved social insurance coverage, while the privileges of public sector workers were removed

The "Short-Term Social Pact" signed in January 1996 under the initiative of the socialist government constitutes another important step in social concertation. The agreement elaborated guidelines for nominal wage growth, taxation and social security, introduced regulations for restricting child labor, adopted a policy of local initiative programs for job creation and facilitated the implementation of measures already agreed upon (i.e. the reduction of standard working time to 40 hours per week and a more flexible organization of working time largely based on reduced job demarcations). It also introduced, on an experimental basis, a minimum income scheme, the features of which have yet to be further elaborated. In addition, the pact formulated training measures, emphasizing on-the-job training and better counseling of the unemployed and owners of small firms. Equally important was the objective of empowering social partners in the design of regional policies and the allocation of EU-funds.[17]

The extent to which these peak level agreements signal a phase of consensus on a regulatory framework of industrial relations and labor market policy is an open question. Given the polarization between the CGTP trade union and the employers association (CIP – Confedaration of Portuguese Industry), and the contradictions within the trade union camp, tripartite peak concertation failed to provide an impetus for a more ambitious reform enlarging the autonomy of collective bargaining at the company and national level. The failure of the 1990 peak tripartite agreement on a reduction to 40 hours working week (with compensating flexibility measures) to stimulate negotiations between the partners for its implementation, and its subsequent enforcement through legislation enacted in 1996, testify to the above point. Similarly, CGTP and CIP refused to support an agreement on the regulation of arbitration. Further, CGTP did not sign the 1996 tripartite agreement and PIS showed limited commitment. This indicates an inability by the social partners to regulate their relations autonomously, a condition that strengthens the role of the state.

Greece

In Greece, until recently, excessive politicization of unionism, deep conflicts within the union camp, as well as extensive state intervention in industrial relations considerable limited the role of organized labor in socio-economic development.

Up to 1990, there was strong government intervention in the wage formation process, through an inflation indexation system and direct mingling in collective negotiation procedures.[18]

Important policy reforms were introduced in a unilateral way. In 1991 the automatic inflation indexation system for wages was abandoned and new legislation on industrial relations was introduced that eliminated direct government intervention in collective negotiations. Legislation supporting part-time and fixed-term employment and the introduction of the possibility for firms to use a fourth shift were the two major labor market reforms in the early 1990s that increased flexibility of working time. However, there was little use of these forms of contracts up to now (European Commission 1996c).

Further, legislation in the social security field passed in the early 1990s (i.e. laws 1902 of 1990, 1976 of 1991 and 2084 of 1992) was targeted mainly at reducing the public debt and social security deficits; yet these laws hardly succeeded in rationalizing the system and overcoming fragmentation in social security (Petmesidou 1996b).

Since 1997 an attempt to initiate peak tripartite agreements was made by the government under the pressure of promoting macro-economic measures and labor market reforms held to be necessary for meeting the Maastricht requirements. The first round of the social dialogue started in spring 1997 and extended over 1998. The policy measures put on the agenda by public authorities concerned primarily employment and labor market flexibility. The "Agreement of Trust" signed by the social partners and the government in November 1997, as the outcome of the first stage of the dialogue, is a rather vague statement with no binding obligations. Disagreement on many of the above issues was strong between the social partners.

A social dialogue on pension reform took place in parallel and also extended into 1998–99. Yet it hardly touched upon incisive changes of the pension system. The so-called mini-reform of pensions through legislation enacted in December 1998 only marginally tackled the issues of fragmentation in social security and fiscal crisis of a number of social funds. A new round of dialogue announced by the government in 1999 was postponed, as the political cost of a major reform appeared to be high at that conjuncture. Similarly, in early 1999, an attempt by the government to develop a social dialogue on significant reform of the tax system did not bear fruit, as GSEE (the General Confederation of Greek Workers) refused to participate.

Given the weakness of the industrial relations system and the rather decorative role of the social dialogue so far, labor market reform was unilaterally introduced by the government through legislation (law 2434 of 1996 on "Policy Measures for Employment, Vocational Education and Training," and its follow-up, law 2639 of 1998 on "Regulating Industrial Relations"). Among the main aims of these laws were: enhancing labor market flexibility and regulating atypical forms of work; linking passive to active labor market policies (so as to promote employability); upgrading OAED (the Manpower Employment Organization) services, as a precondition for a more efficient labor market policy, in parallel with the establishment of private employment offices. The new legislation aimed also to facilitate the design and implementation of a long-term employment strategy that would redistribute resources between passive and active labor market measures through the implementation of continuing training and employment subsidization programs. Although drawing upon the agenda of the social dialogue, these legal developments hardly reflected a consensual process of reform and some issues of the new legislation were vociferously opposed by trade unions (e.g. work time flexibility). This hindered significantly their effective implementation (Petmesidou, 2000: 312–17). The contentious issue of a 35-hour working week (without wage cuts) has persistently been put forward by GSEE as a pre-condition for a serious social concertation process; but this is approached with scepticism by both the employers' association and governmental officials.

Concluding remarks

In an overoptimistic vein some authors (e.g. Rhodes 1998) tend to extrapolate from examples of a revival of peak level concertation around public policies an emerging paradigm of economic governance and labor market regulation that is held to be a potential alternative to policies of extreme deregulation. "Competitive corporatism" is held to be a model of economic governance drawing upon consensus on the necessity of national adjustment to internal and external pressures for increasing competitiveness, through more or less controlled deregulation measures, expected to avoid the detrimental effects on socio-economic inequalities, exclusion and marginalization that extreme deregulation has. Often, examples from South Europe (mainly Italy and Portugal) are elicited in support of this view.[19] On the basis of the above analysis, however, there are serious doubts as to the prospects of peak level concertation even in Italy where the co-operative game took a more systematic form.

Despite attempts to stimulate a social dialogue, mostly influenced by policy trends in the EU, Greece remains greatly distanced from labor market and employment policies drawing upon social concertation. This is mainly due to the immaturity of the industrial relations system and the restricted scope for autonomous bargaining among social partners at both the central and local level; under these conditions the state remains the key locus of action.

Similar conditions characterize Portugal. The peak tripartite concertation policy introduced in the mid-1980s failed to give an impetus for a more dynamic model of industrial relations, as the inability of social partners to conclude agreements on the guidelines set by peak tripartite pacts shows. In the last decade, some examples of initiatives for bi-lateral agreements between the social partners at the local level exhibited a strong potential for exerting pressure for the renewal of the overall framework of labor market and employment regulation, though such a trend is expected to be "an extremely contradictory and protracted process with uncertain outcome" (Barreto and Naumann 1992: 422).

Widespread job insecurity is one of the determining features of the Spanish labor market. A policy of liberalization of entry to the labor market has persistently been pursued by the Spanish governments in a unilateral way since the mid-1980s. Unemployment and high incidence of temporary working are the two prominent issues that have brought unions to the negotiation table. The potential of certain practices of negotiation to lead to durable regulatory agreements is an open question. Besides, the government's strategy to separate negotiation fora and compartmentalize issues manifests that the time of peak level pacts tying a range of policy areas and interventions is over; and indeed in the last two decades in Spain such pacts were a rare phenomenon with not much durability. The increasing importance of collective bargaining and tripartite agreement at the sub-national level, as was for instance manifested by the concluded Basque country employment deal (that provides for early retirement, the recruitment of young unemployed, the elimination of overtime hours and improved rights for temporary workers) (EIRR 1999b) makes the picture more complicated.

Industrial relations reform in Italy comes closer to the direction of regulated flexibility and organized decentralization: macro-concertation on economic and incomes policy, labor market and social policy reform provided the guidelines for more autonomous lower level bargaining (at the regional, district and firm level). However, as stressed above, up to now most of the peak tripartite agreements hardly offered any indication of a common view on social and economic development by the social partners. Given that competitive corporatism distances from a *quid pro quo* logic characterizing traditional corporatist arrangements, the existence of a common view of national goals for social and economic development is a crucial precondition for the durability and effectiveness of social pacts. A too narrow emphasis on market and cost efficiency makes the consensus building process very fragile.

For the potential of this new type of social concertation in Europe to yield durable consensus on joint efforts by the social partners to enhance competitiveness (at the regional, national and supranational level), a European-wide reinvigoration of the social debate around the reconstitution of the role and status of social and employment policy *vis-à-vis* economic policy is required. Overcoming the huge asymmetry between the implementation of efficiency and equity criteria would be the focal point of such a debate. Mounting academic and political pleas for a concerted action to improve the Social Quality of Europe through "a creative reciprocity between European economic and social policies" (Beck *et al.* 1997: 264) offer significant stimulation in this direction. Further, important developments in the European Union, such as steps taken towards a more co-ordinated employment policy framework among EU countries so as to fight unemployment and unacceptable forms of social marginalization, as well as the encouragement of autonomous negotiations of social partners at the European level, may spark off possibilities for a new basis of consensus around joint efforts (consolidated through social agreements) for a more efficient development of human resources. However, one cannot be very optimistic about the prospects of such a trajectory of European integration.

Notes

1 Other authors talk about "organized decentralization" or more loosely about "controlled deregulation" (Traxler 1995; Regini 1998). Streeck (in this volume) in an attempt to grasp the contours of "the new European social model" under conditions of intensified international competition emphasizes the shift from "protective and redistributive" to "competitive and productive solidarity." However, he focuses on the overall change trend of socio-economic regulation in Europe rather than on the patterning of alternative reform strategies.

2 For the causes see Argandona 1997; Rhodes 1997; and European Commission 1997.

3 Regional differences were also high, as unemployment was roughly 50 percent higher than average in Andalusia, and about 50 percent lower in Navarra.

4 Hidden unemployment refers to all those *discouraged* unemployed who become inactive; it also has to do with the large number of self-employed in Greece (about one-third of total employment) among whom unemployment cannot be easily defined and detected (Petmesidou 1998).

5 This was 61.9 percent in 1998 (EU-15 average for female participation: 58.1 percent; and respective rates for Spain, Italy and Greece: 47.5, 44.3 and 48.1 percent).

6 A small increase in employment (approximately 1 percent) was observed in 1998 reflecting a more services-oriented growth mix (European Commission 1999).

7 Unemployment slightly fell in 1999 (to 11.1 percent).

8 Similarly in Italy about 17 percent of the labor force (31 percent in the South) were employed in the black economy in 1998 (European Commission 1999).

9 Compared to the other South European countries, Greece remains a rather immature system of industrial relations (Kritsantonis 1992; Petmesidou 1994).

10 For instance, in the case of Italy, until the 1980s, Fabrini talks about a "non-state state," that is a state with weak economic management capacity, that lacks the ability to provide strong direction in social and economic reform (referred to by Della Sala 1997: 32).

11 For a long time South European social protection systems remained outside the scope of various comparative projects – with the exception of Italy, which is subsumed under the continental-corporatist model (see for instance Esping-Andersen 1990), or the state corporatist model (Korpi, in this volume). Yet, as also argued elsewhere (Petmesidou 1996a), some distinctive characteristics of South European social protection systems differentiate them even from the Bismarckian model with which they undoubtedly exhibit affinities. In addition to high fragmentation of income maintenance systems, other distinctive features are a dualistic structure counter-posing fragmentation in social security to universalism in health care (albeit still a weak variant of universalism, particularly in the case of Greece), the dominance of pensions in the social budget crowding out resources for other types of benefits like family and housing benefits or for the provision of services to families and the implementation of active labor market policies (Ferrera 1996).

12 As Regalia and Regini (1992: 466) stress, this change of emphasis was closely linked with a dominant strategy at that time that assigned crucial importance for national adjustment to the firms' ability to restructure and promote new forms of work organization and partnership in industrial districts.

13 The measures were targeted to the young and long-term unemployed, unemployed over 45 years of age, to the promotion of women employment in sectors in which they are underrepresented, as well as to the activation of disabled persons (Gutiérrez and Guillén 2000: 209–15).

14 General Confedaration of Portuguese Workers (usually referred to as *Indersindical*)

15 General Workers' Union.

16 A policy option of fixed-term and temporary contracts, similar to that adopted by Spanish authorities, was also introduced in Portugal much earlier than in Spain; yet the use of such contracts has not been as widespread as in Spain. At the end of the 1980s new legislation aimed at regulating the conditions under which such contracts could be used; in parallel, dismissals were made easier (European Commission 1996b).

17 A new medium-term pact signed in summer 1996 further enlarged agreement on the upgrading of human capital.

18 Changes in nominal and real wages were extensively influenced by government policies, a condition that affected unfavorably unit labor costs, price stability, availability of jobs and the general labor market situation.

19 Sometimes, though falsely, even Greece is referred to as an example of "a strong thrust towards the centralized bargaining of incomes policy and the signing of formal tripartite agreements" (Regini 1998: 10).

References

Argandona, A. (1997) "Spain and the European Social Charter: Social harmonization with unemployment and high wage growth," in Addison, J. T. and Siebert, W. S. (eds) *Labour Markets in Europe, Issues of Harmonization and Regulation*, London: Dryden.

Barreto, M. and Naumann, R. (1992) "Portugal: Industrial relations under democracy," in Ferner, A. and Hynman, R. (eds) *Changing Industrial Relations in Europe*, Oxford: Blackwell.

Beck, W., van der Maesen, L., and Walker, A. (eds) (1997) *The Social Quality of Europe*, The Hague: Kluwer.

Della Sala, V. (1997) "Hollowing out and hardening the state: European integration and the Italian economy," *West European Politics* 20, 1: 14–33.

EIRR (1999a) "The changing world of work," *European Industrial Relations Review*, 300: 1.

——— (1999b) "Basque country employment deal," *European Industrial Relations Review*, 301: 11.

Esping-Andersen, G. (1990) *The Three Worlds of Welfare Capitalism*, Cambridge: Polity Press.

——— (ed.) (1996) *Welfare States in Transition*, London: Sage.

——— (1999) *Social Foundations of Postindustrial Economies*, Oxford: Oxford University Press.

European Commission (1996a) *Labour Market Studies. Italy*, Luxembourg: European Communities.

——— (1996b) *Labour Market Studies. Portugal*, Luxembourg: European Communities.

——— (1996c) *Labour Market Studies. Greece*, Luxembourg: European Communities.

——— (1997) *Labour Market Studies. Spain*, Luxembourg: European Communities.

——— (1999) *Italy. National Employment Plan 1999*, Brussels: European Communities.

Eurostat (1999) *Employment and Unemployment*, Luxembourg: European Communities.

Ferrera, M. (1996) "The southern model of welfare in social Europe," *Journal of European Social Policy* 6, 1: 17–37.

Gregg, P. and Wadsworth, J. (1998) "Unemployment and households: Causes and consequences of employment polarisation among European countries," *MISEP Policies*, 63: 31–5.

Gutiérrez, R. and Guillén, A. M. (2000) "Protecting the long-term unemployed. The impact of targeting policies in Spain," *European Societies* 2, 2: 195–216.

Kritsantonis, N. (1992) "Greece: The maturing of the system," in Ferner, A. and Hynman, R. (eds) *Changing Industrial Relations in Europe*, Oxford: Blackwell.

Leibfried, S. (1994) "The social dimension of the European Union: En route to positively joint sovereignty?" *Journal of European Social Policy* 4, 4: 239–62.

Martinez Lucio, M. (1992) "Spain: Regulating employment and social fragmentation," in Ferner, A. and Hynman, R. (eds) *Changing Industrial Relations in Europe*, Oxford: Blackwell.

OECD (1996a) *Economic Surveys (1995–1996). Portugal*, Paris: OECD.

——— (1996b) *Economic Surveys (1995–1996). Spain*, Paris: OECD.

Petmesidou, M. (1994) *A State-of-the-Art Review of Studies on Workers' Participation in Greece* (Report in the context of the EPOC Project), Dublin: European Foundation for the Improvement of Living and Working Conditions.

——— (1996a) "Social protection in Southern Europe: Trends and prospects," *Journal of Area Studies*, 9: 95–125.

——— (1996b) "Social protection in Greece: A brief glimpse of a welfare state," *Social Policy and Administration* 30, 4: 324–47.

—— (1998) "Social change and risks of social exclusion in Greece. How do the middle classes fare?" in Berting, J., de Jong, M.-J., and Steijn, B. (eds) *Economic Restructuring and the Growing Uncertainty of the Middle Class*, The Hague: Kluwer.

—— (2000) "Social protection in Greece in the 1990s: Reforming the 'weak welfare state'," in Mitsos, A. and Mossialos, E. (eds) *Contemporary Greece and Europe*, Aldershot: Ashgate.

Petmesidou, M. and Tsoulouvis, L. (1994) "Aspects of the changing political economy of Europe," *Sociology* 28, 2: 499–519.

Pierson, P. and Leibfried, S. (1995) "Multitiered institutions and the making of social policy", in Leibfried, S. and Pierson, P. (eds) *European Social Policy*, Washington, DC.: The Brookings Institution.

Regalia, I. and Regini, M. (1992) "Italy: The dual character of industrial relations," in Ferner, A. and Hynman, R. (eds) *Changing Industrial Relations in Europe*, Oxford: Blackwell.

Regini, M. (1998) "Different trajectories in 1990s Europe: Deregulation vs. concertation," paper presented at the SASE 10th International Conference, Vienna.

Regini, M. and Regalia, I. (1997) "Employers, unions and the state: The resurgence of con-certation in Italy," *West European Politics* 20, 1: 210–30.

Rhodes, M. (1996) "Globalization and West European welfare states: A critical review of recent debates," *Journal of European Social Policy* 6, 4: 305–27.

—— (1997) "Southern European welfare states: Identity, problems and prospects for reform," in Rhodes, M. (ed.) *Southern European Welfare States. Between Crisis and Reform*, London: Frank Cass.

—— (1998) "Globalization, labour markets and welfare states: A future of competitive cor-poratism?" in Rhodes, M. and Mény, Y. (eds) *The Future of European Welfare: A New Social Contract?*, London: Macmillan.

Roca, J. (1991) "La Concertatión Social," in Miguélez, F. and Prieto, C. (eds) *Las Relaciones Laborales en España*, Madrid: Siglo Veintiuno.

Schneider, F. (1999) *The Shadow Economy* (unpublished report), Linz: Johannes Kepler University.

Segura, J., Durán, F., Toharia, L., and Bentolila, S. (1991) *Análisis de la Contratación Temporal en España*, Madrid: Ministerio de Trabajo y Seguridad Social.

Traxler, F. (1995) "Farewell to labour market associations? Organized versus disorganized decentralization as a map for industrial relations", in Crouch, C. and Traxler, F. (eds) *Organized Relations in Europe: What Future?*, Aldershot: Avebury.

Walters, W. (1997) "The active society: New designs for social policy," *Policy and Politics* 25, 3: 221–34.

Part II

Working on Europe
Constructing identities

5 State borders, border regions and the construction of European identity

Liam O'Dowd

Introduction

In the twentieth century Europe was a factory of state borders as its great multinational empires and many of its multinational states fragmented, often violently. The project of European integration may be seen partly as a response to this fragmentation and as an attempt to develop a more negotiated and consensual approach to border change in its geographical, functional and symbolic forms. The central argument of this chapter is that the study of what is happening to, and at, state borders is a *sine qua non* for an adequate understanding of the EU as an emergent transnational polity.[1]

In the last two decades, the borders and borderlands of Europe have attained a renewed salience arising from the "abolition" of internal EU borders in the "Single Market," the break-up of the Soviet bloc after 1989, the expansion of the external border of the EU and the growth of trans-frontier regionalisms and the rise of other, sub-national regionalisms in Western Europe. New borders have been created, old ones have re-emerged and existing borders have been problematized. While the social scientific literature on state borders and border regions is growing rapidly, sociologists have been slow to address border questions directly. They tend to delegate the task to political geographers, historians, political scientists and anthropologists – a strategy that has diminished the sociological contribution to understanding European integration and contemporary social transformation.

The chapter is divided into four sections. In the first, I briefly outline reasons why sociology has generally tended to either "normalize" or discount state borders thereby failing to problematize them for analytical purposes. I conclude the first section by attempting to locate a conceptual point of departure which is sensitive to the ambiguity and paradoxical nature of borders. In the second section, I locate the EC–EU in the context of the historically volatile nature of European borders. The third section examines the development of trans-frontier regionalism as one indicator of the way borders are being reconfigured within the EU. Finally, the chapter reflects on the new, more complex and specialized architecture of borders and its implications for the EU as a transnational polity. The chapter concludes that the EU's lack of stable political borders militates against the emergence of a coherent European identity. EU borders are differentiating rather than homogenizing and mark another stage in the chronically unsettled nature of the continent's borders and their problematical implications for the formation of a European identity. While the EU has encouraged a more consensual and negotiated approach to state borders, border policy continues to be relatively undemocratic with consequences for the EU as a transnational polity.

Borders in sociological analysis: normalizing or discounting

It may be taken as axiomatic that boundary creation, maintenance, and transcendence are integral features of human behavior for as long as human beings demand a measure of autonomy and self-direction. Boundaries are ubiquitous as social constructions, a necessary outcome of social organization, the division of labor, the maintenance of kinship and the promotion of collective identity within a bordered territory. Yet, all boundaries must be sufficiently fluid and permeable to accommodate survival and change (Duchacek 1986: 19). More specifically, for over two centuries of European history, territorial state borders have been central to accumulation of power, identity formation and to the process of social analysis itself.

However, two rather opposed tendencies in sociology have hindered the problematization of state borders for analytical purposes. One takes state borders for granted and in the process contributes to their normalization. The other assumes that they now count for little as they have become permeable to the point of insignificance. In crude terms, these positions correspond to either end of a modern–postmodern spectrum. The tendency to "normalize" borders is rooted in what Agnew terms the modern geopolitical imagination which is based on three assumptions that: (1) the world is divided into distinct sovereign states circumscribed by precisely defined geographical boundaries – in other words, the state-centric system traceable to the Treaty of Westphalia; (2) that the domestic and foreign are two distinct and separate realms; (3) that the boundaries of the state define those of the "society." On the other hand, postmodern approaches reject state-centric conceptualizations and point to deterritorialization, state failure and the emergence of a "borderless" global system of ever denser networks and flows (O Tuathail 1998: 17–18).

The tendency to normalize state borders is deeply rooted in sociology. The reasons may be traced to a number of sources: the dominant political ideologies which infuse contemporary sociological analysis, the affiliation of much sociology with large, long-established states such as the US, Britain and France where borders have long been taken for granted, and finally the settled conditions of most state borders in the period (1950–80) which marked the greatest institutional development of sociology as a discipline.

Historically, liberalism and socialism have heavily influenced sociology. Both ideologies combine universalistic programs with the normalization of existing state borders. Liberal democracy requires territorially bounded states for the rule of law and representative government to work. But the principle of self-determination provides no rules for where borders should be drawn. Nor does it provide guidelines on why there should be a multiplicity of states or the basis for belonging to one state rather than another (Anderson 1996: 8). Dahl (1989: 204) observes that "the majority principle depends on prior assumptions about the unit: that the unit in which it is to operate is itself legitimate and that the matters on which it is employed properly fall within the jurisdiction of the unit." As Eriksen (1999: 5) notes "majority voting presupposes agreement on political boundaries and power assignments, as it affects the sovereignty of states."

Hidden at the core of much liberal and sociological thought is a collective amnesia about the coercive or arbitrary establishment of most state borders. The liberal assumption then is that the legitimacy of these borders can be established *post-hoc* by struggles to extend democratic citizenship. The many varieties of socialism are more likely than liberalism to problematize state formation and to appeal for the transcendence of existing state borders in the name of universal rights and interests. In practice, however, most socialist and social democratic practice has been targeted on, and framed by, territorially bounded states. In the process, they have been border maintaining and normalizing.

Liberalism and socialism have been found in frequent alliance with different forms of nationalism. The latter has been the most durable and potent territorial ideology of the twentieth century. But appeals to nationhood, also conceal the arbitrary nature of established state borders (Habermas 1996: 288) and provide few guidelines for adjudicating competing demands for self-determination in the one territory. Many sociologists are also unwitting carriers of great state chauvinism, especially in long-established states such as the US, France and Britain where the state is often seen implicitly as a carrier of progressive or universalizing values in contrast to the allegedly reactionary and parochial nationalisms of more recent aspirants to statehood.

The empirical research agenda of the discipline has remained predominantly state-centered and state-funded. In this capacity, it has informed governments and serviced reformist movements framed by national states, thereby normalizing, often unwittingly, existing state borders. The latter are taken for granted even in comparative research where states remain the main units of analysis. For three decades after 1945, the Cold War had the effect of stabilizing existing borders while the development of the welfare state deepened their significance from within. This encouraged the identification of state and society within sociology. Even where sociologists engage in research funded by transnational entities such as the European Union, their contributions are frequently state-based.

The emergence of globalization as a major concern of sociology has definitively challenged the normalization of state borders but in so doing has encouraged a contrary position that territorial state borders count for little, or at the most that their significance is rapidly declining. Radical globalization theorists stress the extent to which economics, politics and cultural identities have escaped from bounded territories including states. They argue that the material value of territory is in secular decline, that state sovereignty is being eroded and that _territorial identities have lost their significance because concepts of time have become more important than concepts of space (Forsberg 1996: 365–6).

The metaphors of flows and networks are increasingly employed to describe the growing ease with which information, capital, goods, services and labor cross state boundaries (Castells 1998; Lash and Urry 1994; Heiskala in this volume). Increased permeability is associated with decreased significance. Students of globalization emphasize the transcendence of state borders in stressing the growth of transnational governance (Held *et al.* 1999), communities (Vertovec, 1998), social movements (Cohen 1998) and corporations (Sklair 1991). Appadurai (1995: 213) has suggested that one of the conditions of transnationalism is the "growing disjuncture between territory, subjectivity and collective social movement" and he notes the "steady erosion of the relationship, principally due to the force and form of electronic mediation, between spatial and virtual neighborhoods." New patterns of flows and networks here threaten to turn the map of the world into a "cartographic illusion."

A more qualified version of this argument is that borders have not so much disappeared, as proliferated, thereby reducing their significance. In this scenario, state borders lose their privileged position and are reduced to one type among many; the bundle of functions once associated with territorial state sovereignty is now seen to be dispersed to other territorial or non-territorial entities such as localities, cities, regions, transnational social movements, multinational corporations or even revitalized world religions. This approach holds out the prospect at least of studying how state borders are being reshaped, but it is prone to assume the relative decline in the significance of state borders in historical terms while downplaying factors which continue to sustain them, albeit in altered form.

The tendency to normalize or discount state borders marginalizes the study of state borders and obscures the paradoxes and ambiguities that they represent. Their typically coercive and non-democratic origins can facilitate the rule of law, liberal democracy and a range of citizenship rights. Boundaries and border zones perform dual functions, as barriers or buffers on the one hand, and as gateways, bridges or zones of interaction, on the other. They are manifestations of conquest and power as much as they are sites of voluntary, productive and enriching exchange with others. Borders stand for both denial and opportunity, for exclusion as well as inclusion, for coercive power as well as voluntary affiliation. They are constructed via narratives of integration and difference, implying processes of homogenization within the border and differentiation from the "other" outside (Paasi 1998). In William Connolly's (1994) terms, they provide the preconditions for social identity, for individual and collective action but close off possibilities which might otherwise flourish; they both foster and inhibit freedom, protect and violate life.

The volatility of European borders

The external and internal borders of Europe have continually changed and shifted over the centuries (Wintle 1996). As the source of the modern state system, nationalism and mass warfare, Europe is a particularly fertile producer of state borders and the paradoxes associated with them. One of the characteristics of Europe as a continent of old settlement, is the newness of its state borders. Foucher (1998: 235) estimates that more than 60 percent were created in the twentieth century. In geographical terms, of the forty-eight sovereign states in existence in Europe in 1993, thirty-six came into being in this century compared to twelve in the three previous centuries combined (Davies 1996) although this account underestimates the extent of border change in that it does not allow for adjustments to the borders of existing states. On one count only ten European states (of which by far the largest is Spain) had the same boundaries in 1989 as they had one hundred years earlier (Wallace 1992: 4) and Central and Eastern European countries have generated over eight thousand miles of new political borders since 1989 (Foucher 1998: 235).

Taking a much longer time span, the historian Norman Davies (1996) estimates that in 1493, at least thirty sovereign states could be identified among the hundreds of polities of the time. None of the thirty, he suggests, retained their sovereign existence throughout the subsequent five hundred years. War was an integral element in European state formation. As Tilly (1990) reminds us, war makes states as much as states make war. In his sweeping account of the many paths to state formation in Europe over the last thousand years, he shows the connection between war, the capacity to tax, and the beginnings of reciprocal relationships between rulers and ruled which lead to representative democracy in some states. The capacity to wage war, however, was intimately related to the capacity to tax and to control bounded territories incorporating people and resources, leading in turn to a felt necessity to delineate precise territorial borders. Internal pacification within these borders became the *sine qua non* of the effective mobilization for war against other states.

War also helped create a sense of collective identity in the face of the enemy. It helped construct nations as territorially bounded "communities of fate" for both states seeking nations and nations seeking states. The twentieth century was to confirm the relationship between war and the creation of national boundaries leading to the disintegration of all the major multinational empires (of which the USSR was the last). Three broad waves in the geographical reconstruction of borders may be identified in this century. These are associated with the First World War, the Second World War, and the post-1989 collapse of the Soviet bloc. The first two waves were associated with the two most bloody inter-state wars in history, prosecuted by the big states of Europe, the last with the outbreak of intra-state wars in Eastern Europe. The geographical volatility of state borders, however, was accompanied by major changes in the material and symbolic significance of state borders.

The period between 1918 and 1970 marked the high point of the "sovereign" national state in Europe shaped by war and inter-state conflict. Two distinct phases may be identified, however, in which war shaped state borders in two respects – altering their geographic allocation and strengthening them from within. The proliferation of new states after the Versailles Treaty was compounded between 1918 and 1939 by a retreat from the economic globalization and free trade of the nineteenth century and the promotion of national economic development behind high tariff barriers. The Second World War once again redrew borders, most radically those of Germany and Poland. Between 1945 and the early 1970s, there was a massive growth in the infrastructural power of states increasing their territorial boundedness (Mann 1993), a development common to both the welfare states of Western Europe and the state socialist countries of the East. But this was accompanied by a turn towards freer inter-state trade in the West and a growth in transnational governance, which included the founding of the EEC. Geopolitically, the East–West partition of Europe was to stabilize national borders for nearly forty years.

Whereas the location of the borders of the new Germany and the adjusted borders of Italy with France, Austria and Yugoslavia were demarcated by post-war arbitration dictated by the victorious states, the final resolution of the Saarland question in 1959 by plebiscite was a rare example, post-1945, of popular democratic input into the designation of state borders.[2] The latter was a pointer to alternative ways of creating borders and managing cross-border relationships – a key concern of the founders of the movement for European integration. The primary aim of the founders of the EEC was to remove inter-state war as a factor in Western European border change. But this meant accepting the role played by wars in creating existing borders while eschewing them as instruments of future border change. In practice, the stabilization of existing borders and the reconstruction of war-devastated national economies within these borders took precedence (Milward 1992).

Trans-frontier regionalism and European integration

The early protagonists of the EEC avoided politically sensitive questions relating to state borders and border regions while promoting economic cooperation across national boundaries. Nevertheless, as frequently noted, several of the most influential politicians in the formative years of the EEC had their origins in borderlands and had directly experienced the ways in which wars created borders.[3] The overall thrust of EEC policy was to reconstruct state capacity within existing borders while developing economic cooperation across them. However, from the 1950s onwards, a more explicit border policy advocating trans-frontier regionalism was in gestation, albeit initially outside the remit of the EEC.

Trans-frontier regionalism was influenced by the division of labor that developed in the 1950s between the institutions promoting European integration. It was the largely consultative Council of Europe that promoted the concept of trans-frontier regions initially in seeking to support the cooperative efforts of local, regional and municipal actors in the Rhine borderland. The Council of Europe concentrated on promoting positive cross-national cooperation by developing transnational models of political and legal cooperation. On the other hand, the much more powerful European Community concentrated on negative integration associated with removing barriers to transnational market formation. Yet, with hindsight it is clear that the Council of Europe prefigured many of the subsequent initiatives of the European Community. Trans-frontier regionalism proved to be one such instance.

To their most enthusiastic advocates, trans-frontier "regions" are central to European integration – an alternative to a Europe of sovereign states. For example, Ricq argues:

> Unlike the closed system of nation states . . . the trans-frontier regions, transforming themselves from regions of confrontation to regions of concentration, will see the first real signs of the surrender of sovereignty – Europe of the future will have to base itself on these regions in order to redesign itself and produce a better structure.
>
> (Quoted in Duchacek 1986: 25)

Later when the EC finally addressed the question of border regions in the wake of the Single Market Program, a Council of Europe report envisaged a new alliance between an EU with new competencies to integrate European economic space and regional and local bodies with a long-standing interest in trans-frontier cooperation (Mestre 1992).

In theory, at least, trans-frontier regions could be seen as providing for a re-design of territorial governance and a blurring of state boundaries. They promised a challenge to the principles of state sovereignty, exclusivity and territoriality which hindered closer European unity. At the very least they might serve as experimental laboratories for generating better insight into European integration and EU policy (van der Veen and Boot 1995: 90). In the early 1990s a Council of Europe report argued that the involvement of the EC and regional and local authorities would reduce the national states' monopoly of control in border regions constituting "the first step towards political union" and even representing "the cornerstone of the future European political community" (Mestre 1992: 14).

Even if the early political and theoretical claims for trans-frontier regions seem exaggerated, they did appear to promise an alternative to war and coercion as a means of constituting borders. They also envisaged a more practical, grassroots form of European integration than the elite bargains being continually negotiated at inter-governmental level in Rome, Paris and Brussels. Given their practical agenda and illustrative value, a closer examination of the history and characteristics of trans-frontier regions seems appropriate.

Three overlapping moments of trans-frontier regionalism may be identified that follow the trajectory of European integration overall:

1　The pioneering attempts in the Rhine Basin.
2　The stimulus to trans-frontier regionalism provided by the Single European Market and the direct EC/EU funding of cross-border projects. This sought to generalize trans-frontier regionalism from the Rhineland to all border regions of the now twelve-member Community.
3　The impact of the EU's expansion eastwards in the wake of the end of the Cold War and the upheavals in Eastern Europe. This was accompanied by an even wider application of trans-frontier regionalism as a prelude to the incorporation of post-socialist states into the EU.

The main thrust of cross-border regionalism has remained functional and mainly economic throughout. However, it has been shaped at each moment by the interaction between the existing geopolitical framework, the bordering states and the role of borderland residents and organizations.

The natural history of trans-frontier regionalism in many respects mirrors that of the European Union as a whole. Like the EU, its origins centered on the Rhineland and it developed against a background of the stabilization of Western European state borders, the creation of the European Coal and Steel Community and the Council of Europe. From the outset it prioritized functional forms of cross-border cooperation in terms of promoting economic and infrastructural development. As such, it has influenced all subsequent forms of EU sponsored cross-border development. However, the EC–EU reluctance to develop specific programs for cross-border regions until 1989 reflected the political sensitivity of borders and state sovereignty and the extent to which economic integration was insulated from "politics."

The Single European Market program initiated the second phase of trans-frontier regionalism and the introduction for the first time of an EC program specifically targeted at internal and external border regions. With the initiation of the INTERREG program, the EC commission became a major actor in cross-border regions. A triangular strategy, long advocated by the Council of Europe, could now be implemented involving European organizations, participating governments and regional and local authorities in border zones. INTERREG enabled the spread of trans-frontier regionalism to peripheral and "external" borders of the EC with little tradition of regional cross-border cooperation where "political sovereignty" and "security" had long taken precedence over issues of economic interdependence and development in border regions.

Finally, the changes in Eastern Europe and the proposed enlargement of the EU have re-problematized the links between economic and political integration. The extension of the market economy to the post-socialist states highlights the huge structural disparities on either side of the external border and provides a dynamic for a multi-faceted reconstitution of the boundary. The vehicles of this reconstitution include various manifestations of capitalism, from the use of cheap Polish labor, to the creation of huge border bazaars, to smuggling and other criminal activities (Kratke 1999; Stryjakiewicz and Kaczmarek 1997). Wallace (1999) has identified a new Central European buffer zone consisting of Poland, Hungary, the Czech and Slovak Republics that is characterized by particular forms of circulation of goods, capital influenced by the EU, the fall of state socialism and migration from other countries to the East and South-East. In the face of these developments the EU and its member states seek to police the border more closely and to control the border region more thoroughly to restrict illegal immigration, crime and potential for ethno-national conflict. The extent and timing of EU enlargement remains an open question and the rush to establish Euroregions is part of the unfinished business of constructing the external border of the EU, but it is only one part of a wider, and potentially more coercive reconstruction (Fure 1997).

From the Rhineland pioneers to the Eastern Euro-regions of the 1990s, there has been a dramatic increase in the number of regional, local and non-governmental bodies engaged in cross-border cooperation. Despite the functional and practical bias of these initiatives, perhaps their most striking impact has been symbolic. They have challenged the existing symbolic association of state borders with exclusive state sovereignty over sharply delineated territories.

In generating new relationships between supranational, national and local level institutions they seem to represent one possible future for the EU as a multi-level system of governance where authority is diffused among agencies of different sizes, scope and function (Risse-Kappen 1996: 68). For some observers they were symptomatic of an emerging neo-medievalism where the old hierarchical order of sovereign states is giving way to a "much more flexible, overlapping, intersecting and cross-cutting networks of social interaction that do not (necessarily) form a totality and whose socio-spatial dimension are not (necessarily) territorially fixed through state boundaries" (Mlinar 1995: 161). Trans-frontier networks seem to reflect what Anderson (1996: 149) sees as an emergent "mixture of old, new, and hybrid forms – territorial, trans-territorial and functional forms of association and authority coexisting and interacting."

Although most trans-frontier regions are created for pragmatic or instrumental reasons to access EU funding as a means of addressing shared environmental, planning or economic development problems, it may be argued that their real significance lies elsewhere. They may be seen as harbingers of what Risse-Kappen (1996: 70–1) calls cross-national policy communities, advocacy and discourse coalitions, and epistemic communities where the logic of communicative action, discourse and consensus creation may be just as important as the logic of instrumental action.

Structural weaknesses of trans-frontier regions

While trans-frontier regions may symbolize a more consensual and peaceful form of transnational integration, it is easy to exaggerate their structural importance. They fall far short of the expectations of their most enthusiastic advocates that they might constitute the territorial building blocks of European political union. Like EU institutions, they control remarkably few resources, despite their profusion. They comprise shifting and skeletal networks covering territorial areas with rather vague and elastic boundaries. Within these areas, the hierarchy of state institutions wields far more influence on daily life. The "infrastructural power" of national states, especially in its coercive and redistributive aspects, remains paramount. INTERREG, the main EU funded program for border areas, constitutes less than 1 percent of the EU Structural Fund expenditure (1994–99) (Williams 1996). The Structural Funds themselves count for less than half of the EU budget which itself is frozen at a level not above 1.3 percent of the GDP of member states.

The financial management and implementation of EU sponsored cross-border initiatives underpin rather than challenge the territorial state system. All monies are channeled through national governments that provide matching funds or oversee the provision of such funds by bodies outside of central governments. States develop single "operational programs" on their own side of the border, bringing forward projects themselves and eliciting proposals from local governments and non-governmental organizations.

Inter-governmental steering committees retain responsibility for coordinating and monitoring cross-border projects although applications are encouraged from bodies which have already forged cross-border links and which propose integrated cross-border projects. In many border regions, particularly those that are economically peripheral and part of centralized states, the states loom very large in a landscape characterized by a multiplicity of small and fragmented agencies. While there is much multi-level consultation with the EU and sub-state and non-governmental bodies, the states take the critical decisions to allocate the limited resources involved. There are exceptions where, as in Germany, regional authorities can act in lieu of the state but with its authorization. In general, trans-frontier regions are stronger where there is greater regional devolution as in Germany, Austria, Belgium and Switzerland (Mestre 1992).

Cross-border secretariats consisting of administrative and technical personnel may be set up to propose or implement particular projects. Their territorial remits span the border and are more precise than those of cross-border institutional networks. Yet, their existence is dependent on program funding and accordingly they are unable to provide continuity. Their importance, however, illustrates the bias towards bureaucracy and technocracy in trans-frontier regions. Electoral constituencies do not span borders limiting democratic involvement of elected representatives in cross-border networks. Instead, cross-border regions involve a series of flexible strategic alliances between local political, administrative and business elites. To this extent they are *fora* for limited forms of participatory democracy. The availability of funding brings into being new voluntary bodies and activates established bodies including municipal and regional authorities. It provides opportunities for such bodies to influence regional developments in border zones where historically the priorities of national governments have minimized local influence on cross-border regimes.

Trans-frontier regionalism reflects a move away from coercion to consensus and negotiation. Like the EU generally, trans-frontier regionalism has been premised on stabilizing existing state borders while modifying their functions and meanings. In this sense, it has had some effect in enhancing the consensual and negotiated aspects of borders at the expense of their coercive dimensions. But in highlighting border regions they expose the chronic lack of fit between nations and states and the arbitrary and coercive basis on many borders. They provide a glimpse of alternatives to existing states in re-forging links across historical, national, ethnic, religious and linguistic entities ruptured by the violent process of state formation. Cross-border regions on Germany's eastern frontier, and those involving the South Tyrol, the Irish and Basque border regions provide examples of cross-border regions seeking to re-forge old territorial and ethnic links.

Trans-frontier regions pose a very modest challenge to existing state sovereignty, however. Nevertheless, their significance is enhanced by the wider processes of fragmentation connected with the dilution of states' capacity to control economic, political and cultural activity within their territorial limits. Against this background the existing imperfect fit between nations and states comes under threat (Baumann 1992). As Rupnik (1994) suggests "balkanization" tendencies are present in Western Europe also with the growth of intra-state conflict at the expense of inter-state war. These trends involve the reconstruction of state borders as all manner of intra-state tensions emerge based on growing ethnic and cultural diversity and secessionist and regionalist pressures interacting with social inequalities. Intra-state conflicts are becoming far more common globally than traditional inter-state wars (Tilly 1990) and are much more significant for the future of state borders. The revitalization of some state nationalisms, the fortifying of the EU's external borders, and the emergence of strong "security" states, co-exist with trends toward more consensual, negotiated networking across state boundaries. The old ambiguities inherent in territorial boundaries are emerging in new forms. Trans-frontier regions symbolize how these ambiguities might be restructured to make the management of borders more consensual and democratic. They have the potential to mediate the chronic lack of fit between nations and states. However, their limited control over resources and their structural weaknesses undermine their potential role for democratizing border change and transnational integration generally.

Conclusions: the EU – what kind of borders, what kind of polity?

The evolution of border policy in the EU certainly provides greater scope for agencies other than central governments to contribute to the reconfiguration of borders and border regions. These include EU institutions, particularly the Commission, local, regional and municipal authorities, and a variety of non-governmental actors, chambers of commerce, universities, firms and voluntary organizations. This marks a move away from state monopoly, arbitration and coercive territorial strategies to a more consensual, negotiated and participatory approach. However, financial control remains clearly in the hands of national governments and the EU, through which money is channelled. The institutionalization of formal cross-border ties is often weak and transient. Trans-frontier regionalism remains largely focused on finding technocratic and bureaucratic solutions to particular problems such as physical infrastructure, ecological issues, and local labor market issues. Border reconfiguration in this respect remains, as throughout history, a matter for elites, although in this case involving local as well as national elites.[4]

EU attempts at framing a policy for borders also expose the great heterogeneity of border regions and border issues. This heterogeneity arises from different experiences of border formation and cross-border relationships – formal and informal, the relative economic and political power of contiguous states and the role, if any, played by ethno-national questions. The development of the EU has also greatly differentiated borders in terms of their specialized functions. This is not a new feature of European integration and may be traced to the variegated boundaries of transnational governance such as those of the Benelux, EEC, EFTA and NATO. Many of these selective, specialized borders are now internal to the EU and reflect the complicated architecture of the polity as a whole. Hence different combinations of state borders represent the Single Market, the Schengen Area, and the European Monetary Union.

The proliferation of functional, regional and ethnic borders within the EU cross-cuts and influences internal state borders. The outcome of this process remains uncertain, however. It may increase the sense of an overarching EU identity, especially within a strengthened and stable external border. Multiple and flexible borders might help underpin a form of European multiculturalism which favors free choice of identity, multiple affiliations and dynamic group formation. On the other hand, some states threatened by internal differentiation and internal conflicts may develop new forms of state nationalism and territorial control fueled by a scapegoating of immigrant groups, national minorities, or by growing opposition to "Brussels."

Culturally cohesive, smaller member states with a clearly defined role in the international division of labor such as Austria, Ireland, and Finland may flourish by "gradually replacing protective and redistributive with competitive and productive solidarity" (Streeck 1999: 5, see also Streeck, in this volume). In the process, they may fare better economically and politically than larger and more diverse states such as the UK, Germany and Italy. The latter have complex and often internally contradictory economic interests which encourage the emergence of strong regional entities trading on their competitive advantages. The bigger states not only have greater potential for regional fragmentation on economic grounds, some of them are faced also with intra-state conflicts based on ethnic, secessionist and anti-immigrant mobilizations.

The ongoing reconfiguration of state borders at present lacks sufficient integrative thrust to fully combat fragmenting pressures. Border issues, for example, are highly differentiated in terms of immigration, asylum-seekers, refugees and the control of more de-territorialized threats and global risks such as crime, terrorism and disease. Overall, the borders of the EU continue to change in terms of their geography, functions and symbolic meanings. The EU's internal borders, therefore, tend to differentiate, rather than homogenize, *vis-à-vis* "Others." The "enemies" or "dangers" facing individual states are quite diffuse and not easily amenable to territorial mobilization.

While the "unbundling" of border functions does reduce the prospects of cumulative divisions leading to inter-state conflict, it also privileges the role of technocratic, bureaucratic and business elites. They marginalize the role of elected representatives accountable to popular constituencies while reducing democratic accountability. This democratic deficit is not merely a consequence of a weak European Parliament or of a Brussels bureaucracy, it is deeply ingrained in the architecture of the EU and in the way it constructs its internal and external borders. The democratic deficit in border policy, however, has also much deeper historical roots in the coercive history of border formation and change.

The historical role of war in European state formation not only enhanced the role of state borders, it also helped build national allegiance, citizenship and popular democracy within these borders. The "long peace" since 1945, characterized by the absence of inter-state war in Western Europe, has reduced the role of war in bolstering the legitimacy of national governments and in sustaining national identities and solidarity. The result has not been to eliminate internal borders within the EU as the evidence from trans-frontier regions demonstrates, although they have become more flexible and specialized. Processes of deterritorialization co-exist with reterritorialization. The EU presents an opportunity structure for border building by proponents of regional autonomy or secession, but only a small number of such projects cross-cut existing national boundaries.

A critical speculative question is how this rather fragmented, diverse, and multi-bordered landscape will impact on the EU as a transnational polity. Here a key issue is the relationship between the internal and external borders of the EU. The latter remain fluid and continue to expand. On one level, the making of the external border may help affirm a European identity, at least for EU elites, as applicant countries are judged on their capacity to accept the *acquis communautaire*. The latter includes acceptance of the "market economy," electoral democracy and the "rule of law." A European identity may be further affirmed in the face of, what Volkov (1999) terms, deep-rooted Russian social practices rooted in personalism and patrimonialism, which subvert attempts at "Europeanization." Represented as such Russia is a candidate for the role of the leading European "Other" against which a deeper European identity might be forged *via* the EU. Such a prospect would be strengthened further by any future remilitarization of the continent.

However, Russia itself is internally diverse with other preoccupations along its diverse borders. The external border of the EU is itself divided into segments such as the Mediterranean, the Balkans, Central and Eastern Europe, each involving different kinds of interaction with a variety of "Others" with varying claims to be accepted as EU members. As Therborn (1995: 35) notes, the structural borders of "Europe" are sharply defined while the cultural borders are more fuzzy. The more the current EU incorporates states to its east and south-east, the greater the degree of socio-economic inequality internalized within its boundaries. This will threaten cohesion in the likely absence of strong redistributive policies at EU level.

Construction of the EU's external borders and identity must be distinguished, however, from historical border-making in Europe, which relied heavily on wars and other forms of collective coercion. The territorial enlargement of the EU does have a significant voluntarist and plebiscitary dimension lacking in border creation historically. States vote to join the EU and are queuing up to do so; they are neither coerced nor invaded. However, scrutinized more closely, practices of border construction and maintenance in the EU do retain many coercive and democratically unaccountable features to which a critical sociology of European integration must be alert.

The well-documented lack of popular identification with, or allegiance to, the EU has much to do with how its internal and external borders are being constructed. The EU impact on borders and border regions is growing but still remains heavily mediated by national states. The EU neither taxes nor conscripts for war against an extra-territorial "Other." By the same token its multi-level governance and differentiated borders provide little stimulus to mass participation or popular democracy. Its construction, even at its differentiated borders, is driven by elites and they remain its strongest advocates. The wider challenge for proponents of European unity is how to increase popular participation in the project of democratizing the EU and its changing borders.

Notes

1 The Indian sociologist, T. K. Oommen, has suggested that the "rise and fall, the construction and deconstruction of various types of boundaries is the very story of human civilisation and of contemporary social transformation" (quoted in Paasi 1998: 83). William Wallace (1992: 14), a leading analyst of European integration, argues that the question of boundaries is central to the study of political systems, legal jurisdictions and socio-economic interaction. Indeed all major political projects, not least those associated with European integration, have included images of frontiers and conceptions of territorial organization (Anderson 1996: 189).
2 The victorious states had arranged a number of plebiscites after the First World War through the Treaty of Versailles, largely to establish the borders of a defeated Germany. Examples included the votes in Silesia, Schleswig-Holstein and a belated plebiscite in Saarland, which voted to join the German Reich in 1935 (Davies 1996: 939).
3 Schuman, De Gasperi, and Spaak came from culturally mixed borderlands (Mayne 1996). De Gaulle, a key architect of the Franco-German alliance at the heart of the EEC, was a native of Lille. Like his German counterpart Adenauer, who was a native of Cologne, he was acutely aware of the problematical borderland between France and Germany. However, not all leaders born in borderlands favored peaceful cross-border cooperation, as the example of Hitler shows.
4 My own research on the Irish border region delineates the extent to which the impact of the EU has marked moves towards cross-border negotiation and cooperation in conditions of ethno-national conflict. But it also demonstrates the limits of such trends where two centralized states are involved with rather different policy agendas within the EU (O'Dowd 1994; O'Dowd et al. 1995; O'Dowd and Wilson 1996).

References

Anderson, J. (1996) "The shifting stage of the political: New medieval and postmodern territorialities?" Environment and Planning D, 14, 2: 133–53.
Anderson, J. and O'Dowd, L. (eds) (1999) "State borders and border regions," Special Issue, Regional Studies, 33, 7.
Anderson, M. (1997) Frontiers: Territory and State Formation in the Modern World, Cambridge: Polity Press.
Appadurai, A. (1995) "The production of locality," in R. Fardon (ed.) Counterworks: Managing the Diversity of Knowledge, London: Routledge.
Baumann, Z. (1992) "Soil, blood and identity," Sociological Review, 40, 2: 675–701.
Castells, M. (1998) The End of the Millennium, Oxford: Blackwell.
Cohen, R. (1998) "Transnational social movements: An assessment," paper presented to the Transnational Communities Programme Seminar, School of Geography, University of Oxford, 19 June.

Connolly, W. E. (1994) "Tocqueville, territory and violence," *Theory, Culture and Society*, 11: 19–40.

Dahl, R. (1989) *Democracy and its Critics*, New Haven: Yale University Press.

Davies, N. (1996) *Europe: A History*, Oxford: Oxford University Press.

Duchacek, I. (1986) "International competence of subnational governments: Borderlands and beyond," in O. Martinez (ed.) *Across Boundaries: Transborder Interaction in Comparative Perspective*, El Paso: Texan Western Press: 11–30.

Eriksen, E. O. (1999) "The question of deliberative supranationalism in the EU," *Arena Working Papers*, WP99/4.

Forsberg, T. (1996) "Beyond sovereignty, within territoriality: Mapping the space of late-modern (geo)politics," *Co-operation and Conflict*, 31, 4: 355–86.

Foucher, M. (1998) "The geopolitics of European frontiers," in M. Anderson and E. Bort (eds) *The Frontiers of Europe*, London: Pinter: 235–50.

Fure, J. (1997) "The German-Polish border region: A case of regional integration," ARENA Working Papers, WP.97/19.

Habermas, J. (1996) "The European nation-state – its achievements and its limits. On the past and future of sovereignty and citizenship," in G. Balakrishnan (ed.) *Mapping the Nation*, London: Verso.

Held, D., Goldblatt, D., McGrew, T., and Perraton, J. (1999) *Global Transformations: Politics, Economics and Culture*, Cambridge: Polity Press.

Kratke, S. (1999) "Regional integration or fragmentation?: The German-Polish border region in a new Europe," *Regional Studies*, 33, 7: 631–42.

Lash, S. and Urry, J. (1994) *Economies of Signs and Spaces*, London: Sage.

Mann, M. (1993) "Nation-states in Europe and other continents: Diversifying, developing, not dying," *Daedalus*, 122: 115–40.

Mayne, R. (1996) "Schuman, De Gasperi, Spaak – the European frontiersmen," in M. Bond, J. Smith, and W. Wallace (eds) *Eminent Europeans: Personalities who Shaped Contemporary Europe*, London: The Greycoat Press: 22–44

Mestre, C. (1992) *The Implications for Frontier Regions of the Completion of the Single Market*, Strasbourg: Council of Europe.

Milward, A. (1992) *The European Rescue of the Nation State*, London: Routledge.

Mlinar, Z. (1995) "Territorial dehierarchization in the emerging Europe," in J. Langer and W. Pollauer (eds) *Small States in the Emerging New Europe*, Klagenfurt: Verlag für Soziologie und Humanethologie Eisenstadt.

O'Dowd, L. (1994) "Negotiating the British-Irish border: Trans-frontier cooperation on the European periphery," Final Report to the ESRC, Grant Number R000 23 3053, April.

O'Dowd, L., Corrigan, J., and Moore, T. (1995) "Borders, national sovereignty and European integration," *International Journal of Urban and Regional Research* 19, 2: 272–85.

O'Dowd, L. and Wilson, T. (eds) (1996) *Borders, Nations and States: Frontiers of Sovereignty in the New Europe*, Aldershot: Avebury.

O Tuathail, G. (1998) "De-territorialised threats and global dangers: Geopolitics and risk society," in D. Newman (ed.) *Geopolitics, Special Issue, Boundaries, Territory and Postmodernity*, 2, 1: 17–31.

Paasi, A. (1996) *Territories, Boundaries and Consciousness: The Changing Geographies of the Finnish-Russian Border*, New York: John Wiley and Sons.

—— (1998) "Boundaries as social processes: Territoriality in the world of flows," in D. Newman (ed.) Boundaries, Territory and Postmodernity, Special Issue, *Geopolitics*, 2, 1: 69–88.

Risse-Kappen, T. (1996) "Exploring the nature of the beast: International relations theory and comparative policy analysis meet the European Union," *Journal of Common Market Studies*, 34, 1: 53–80.

Rupnik, J. (1994) "Europe's new frontiers: Remapping Europe," *Daedalus*, 123, 3: 91–114.

Sklair, L. (1991) *Sociology of the Global System*, Brighton: Harvester Press.

Streeck, W. (1999) "Competitive solidarity: Rethinking the European social model," MPIfG Working Paper 99/8, Max Planck Institute of the Studies of Societies.

Stryjakiewicz, T. and Kaczmarek, T. (1997) "Transborder cooperation and development in the conditions of great socio-economic disparities: The case of the Polish-German border region," paper presented to the EURRN "Regional Frontiers" conference, Frankfurt/Oder.

Therborn, G. (1995) *European Modernity and Beyond: The Trajectory of European Societies*, 1945–2000, London: Sage.

Tilly, C. (1990) *Coercion, Capital and European States AD 990–1990*, Oxford: Basil Blackwell.

van der Veen, A. and Boot, D.-J. (1995) "Cross-border cooperation and European regional policy," in H. Eskelinen and F. Snickars (eds) *Competitive European Peripheries*, Berlin: Springer: 75–94.

Vertovec, S. (1998) "Conceiving and researching transnationalism," Position paper on ESRC Research Programme on Transnational Communities, Institute of Social and Cultural Anthropology, University of Oxford (mimeo).

Volkov, V. (1999) "Practices, traditions, and the boundaries of European integration," paper presented to the 4th European Conference of Sociology, Amsterdam.

Wallace, C. (1999) "Crossing borders: Mobility of goods, capital and people in the Central European Region," in A. Brah, M. J. Hickman, and M. Mac an Ghaill (eds) *Global Futures: Migration, Environment and Globalisation*, London: Macmillan.

Wallace, W. (1992) *The Dynamics of European Integration*, London: Pinter.

Williams, R. H. (1996) *European Union Spatial Policy and Planning*, London: Paul Chapman.

Wintle, M. (1996) "Europe's image: Visual representations of Europe from earliest times to the twentieth century," in M. Wintle (ed.) *Culture and Identity in Europe*, Aldershot: Avebury.

6   Our time

Europe in the age of global networks and flowing identities

Risto Heiskala

In what follows I will discuss the articulation of Europe. I start with a discussion on the identity of Europe, go on with a discussion of globalization, and close with an attempt to tie these two themes together. I then raise, in a new context, Karl Polanyi's (1944) question: What kind of a time is our time? Throughout the chapter, specific emphasis is put on the EU, as this network state currently uniting fifteen and in the nearest future possibly twice as many European states as today is often what is referred to combined with the term "Europe", even if it would be a mistake to believe that these two are identical.

The articulation of Europe

Let us start with a look at the articulation of Europe. As an organizing device, I will use Weber's tripartition between culture, politics and economy. This distinction has recently been redeveloped by Michael Mann (1986, 1993a) who divides political regulation into two distinct classes of political and military power. This additional distinction is based on the claim that control of the state organization and diplomatic networks on the one hand and resources of organized violence on the other often do not overlap in history. As we will soon see, this distinction is well grounded in the analysis of contemporary Europe, and I will therefore pay attention to it when forms of political regulation are discussed.

In terms of *culture*, does a unified Europe exist? Certainly not. A look at a map presenting the major religions in Europe (Therborn 1995: 215) reveals the fact that our continent is rather systematically divided into three variants of Christianity. In the north we have the Protestant countries. Central and Southern Europe is Catholic, with the exception of Germany, the Netherlands and Switzerland which all are half Catholic and half Protestant countries. Orthodox Christianity prevails in the east, so that the dividing line goes roughly along the borders of the former Soviet Union, Romania and former Yugoslavia (the major exceptions being the Baltic countries in the north and Slovenia and Croatia in the south). In addition to these three variants of Christianity, Islam affects Europe at least in four ways. To begin with, there are Muslim countries at the borders of Europe in North Africa and the Middle East. Second, Turkey is a Muslim country. Third, in several European countries there are enclaves of millions of Muslim migrant workers (this is especially so in Germany, the Netherlands and the UK). Last but not least in the Balkans, in the areas of the former Yugoslavia and Albania we have a religious counterpart to the collision point of continental plates, which has made it into a scene of wars and ethnic cleansing today as well as earlier in this century. Finally, to complete the picture, we should still mention the tiny enclaves of other world religions in several European countries as well as Judaism, i.e., Israel in the Middle East and the Jewish communities or networks in Europe.

But it is not just religion that split Europe into different cultural regions. Nationalism in the populations of different European nation-states has still a considerable cultural impact. This is evident in the results of survey research, for example. Thus one study of the EU countries from the beginning of the 1990s reveals that only "less than 5 per cent of those asked said that they were first and foremost Europeans; 45 per cent said that they did not feel any European component to their identity at all. At the same time, 88 per cent closely identified with their nation or religion" (Reif 1993, quoted in Held *et al.* 1999: 375). And this is just a partial picture. In addition to religion and national identities, there are other factors such as languages and ethnic identities which further divide Europe (see Allardt 1979, 1981, for example).

Yet there are unifying mechanisms as well. Today, the media, interactive information technologies and tourism cross national and religious borders, making local self-evidences flow and possibly bringing forth what Parsons (1970) called "generalization of value commitments", i.e., the ability to understand other people's point of view and find similarities to one's own value position on a more abstract level. Even if this is seen to be too quick a conclusion these processes bring forth increased knowledge of alternative world-views and, together with the workings of transnational business organizations and international organizations, makes English as a second language the *lingua franca* of our time. In addition to this, there are modern educational institutions which, of course, have been a strong support for nationalism in every country but which are also today structured in rather similar ways in all European countries and are everywhere based on some version of the scientific world-view springing from the Enlightenment. Political institutions and their ideological legitimations based on democratic and rationalistic ideas dating back to the legacy of ancient Greeks and the Enlightenment are today shared, up to a point, with all European nation-states and all major religious groups. Finally, there is the ideology of Pan-Europeanism and Europe-wide co-operative networks and organizations such as the ESA (Mikkeli 1998; Droselle 1990). These ideological commitments and their institutional organizations are today supported by the EU bureaucracy which makes their ability to work significantly better than in the past.

To move on to economy, in terms of *economic integration*, how unified is Europe? As far as the states forming the core of the EU are concerned, quite unified, it must be said. In 1990 exports accounted for 28.3 per cent of the GNP of the then twelve EU states. Most of this was intra-EU trade as the share of exports to other EU states ranged from 54 per cent in Germany and Greece to 76 per cent in the

Netherlands in 1992, the other nine EU members being somewhere in between these relatively high figures (Therborn 1995: 198).[1]

In addition to the fact of economic integration, the EU is the only functioning customs union in the world which provides legal rules that guarantee a free flow of goods and services, and the EU Court backs the system and gives authoritative interpretations in cases of ambiguity or argument. The shared currency, the EURO, and the European Central Bank deepen the integration. This has sometimes evoked either enthusiastic or alarmed predictions of the emergence of a "Fortress Europe" which would close its borders and curl up into itself. I will take a closer look at this issue after discussing globalization, but it can be said here already that there are other free trade areas in the world[2] and the existence of WTO alone is enough to make such a prognosis exaggerated, as far as the sphere of economy is concerned (Held *et al*. 1999: 168).

In terms of *political regulation* there are signs of both unification and fragmentation. Political regulation is still very much concentrated to nation-states. Yet the strengthening and expansion of the EU cannot be bypassed because it is an institutional organization or a network state uniting fifteen of the European states (Austria, Belgium, Denmark, Finland, France, Germany, Greece, Italy, Ireland, Luxembourg, the Netherlands, Portugal, Spain, Sweden and the UK) as a loose but tightening federation with a free flow of goods and services, harmonized legal codes and attempts to somewhat centralized planning and decision making in internal as well as in foreign affairs – up to a point. Eleven of the fifteen member states even have a shared currency, the EURO (with the exception of Denmark, Greece, Sweden and the UK which will still take some time to follow the pioneers). In addition, the EU is negotiating with six more candidates on the possibility of their joining the Union (Czech Republic, Cyprus, Estonia, Hungary, Poland and Slovenia), and there are at least another six realistic candidates in queue waiting for the possibility to start membership negotiations with the Union (the six candidate states likeliest to make it are Bulgaria, Latvia, Lithuania, Malta, Romania and Slovak; and in spite of German resistance there is even the possibility of opening membership negotiations with Turkey, an Islamic country with little respect to its ethnic minorities). This is why the term "Europe" today has an actually existing referent in the social reality. It very much refers to the EU, even if it would be a mistake to believe that these two are identical.

After the Maastricht Treaty at the latest the EU has made the political system of Europe more multilayered. A sign of this is that, as pointed out by Ulrich Beck (1999a: 53), none of the current fifteen EU states could be accepted as members in the imaginary situation that they should have to apply for membership once again. This is so for the simple reason that more and more decisions are made autonomously by the Union and merely executed by the member states, and any state that has given up its sovereignty to such an extent is incapable of meeting the democratic requirements for membership. In other words, the EU is a significant factor in the emergence of a multilayered European pattern of political regulation, but there are others either overlapping or independent of the Union. To mention but three, we can point to the European Free Trade Association

(EFTA), the Council of Europe (CE) and the Organization of Security and Co-operation in Europe (OSCE).

If we take a look at military power, a curious pattern emerges. It shows that even with the existence of the West European Union (WEU) and proposals to make it a center in possession of some actual military power, the control of organized violence is currently fragmented in European nation-states, each of which has its own army. However, the superior military power with no imaginable enemy which could be equal to it in combat on the European continent is in fact no single national army but NATO. What is curious here is that the superior actor with an actual right to *veto* any plans for action as well as the main initiator of new policies in NATO is the US which is not a European state at all. Yet the US took the leading role and also provided a major part of the war equipment and personnel when NATO recently made its intervention in the crisis of Kosovo.

To draw an interim conclusion of these cultural, economic, political and military considerations, there seem to be factors bringing forth both European integration and fragmentation at the same time. However, we cannot make our prognosis on the basis of these considerations only. Our forecast for Europe is greatly affected by the way we interpret the relationship between Europe and the rest of the world. Therefore, some time must be spent on the theme of globalization before we are able to recall the question of the articulation of Europe.

The rise of global networks and the flow of local identities

The general definition of globalization given by Held, McGrew, Glodblatt and Perraton in their *Global Transformations* is that globalization "refers to the widening, deepening and speeding up of global interconnectedness" (Held *et al*. 1999: 14). It has been a process proceeding markedly fast in the 1980s and 1990s and especially so in the field of economy. Yet it would be a mistake to restrict our interpretation of the growth of global interconnectedness to the economic sphere. It would also be a mistake to restrict the interpretation only to the past two or three decades. Instead, Held and his co-authors outline processes of the growth of global interconnectedness in the spheres of political regulation, organized violence, economy, culture, migration and environmental risks. They distinguish between four periods of globalization. These are premodern globalization exemplified by the Roman Empire, the Catholic Church and the trade of luxury goods between Europe and Asia, for example; early modern globalization which took place roughly between 1500 and 1850 and was exemplified by the "discovery" and conquest of the New World, for example; modern globalization which took place in the period *circa* 1850–1945 and was exemplified by the colonialization of the entire globe as well as the development of the railway net and the steamboat; finally there is the period of contemporary globalization which started at the end of World War II and reached its accelerated form in the 1980s and 1990s. (Held *et al*. 1999: 415–35).

This fourfold division is without doubt important for an extensive study of the growth of global interconnectedness. As far as economic globalization is concerned, however, we may do well with a more simple division into two. Following this scheme the first significant period of economic globalization, based on the British Empire and the gold standard, took place at the end of the nineteenth century and the beginning of the twentieth (roughly between the 1870s and 1914). It was cut short by World War I. The war meant the beginning of the peak period of the heroic age of the European nation-state which lasted until the 1970s or so and effectively prevented the globalization of economy, among other things.[3] The current period of economic globalization is the reverse side of the erosion of this heroic age of the nation-state and the transformation of the role of the state in the global system.[4]

A claim has been made that contemporary economic globalization is nothing new in comparison to the first phase at the turn of this century (Hirst and Thompson 1996; Boyer and Drache 1996). The claim is justified as far as we measure economic globalization by the percentage rate of direct foreign investments in gross national product. Using this indicator the world economy seems to have been roughly speaking as integrated one hundred years ago as it is now. However, there are three reasons why this conclusion is erroneous. To begin with, GNPs have grown substantially in the past hundred years and, therefore, the absolute sums flowing across state-borders are now much bigger than at the turn of this century. Secondly, international trade today is so extensive that one-fifth of the goods and services which ever enter into statistics moved across state borders in 1995 (Martin and Schumann 1996). Last, but certainly not least, the sales of the foreign subsidiaries of multinational corporations (6,022 billion dollars in 1995) were in 1995 twice as much as world total export and growing faster than this equally growing figure (Väyrynen *et al.* 1999).

The dimensions of current globalization, then, are something unforeseen even if we do not think of anything else but the economy. What is also new is, as Held and his co-authors have pointed out, that, irrespective of the US's strong position in the global system, "the contemporary epoch is historically unique in so far as patterns of globalization, unlike earlier periods, are no longer associated with, or reliant on, the expansionary logic or coercive institutions of empire" (Held *et al.* 1999: 425) such as the Roman or the British Empire. Instead, they obey the logic of decentralized networks.

According to Manuel Castells, "a network is a set of interconnected nodes. . . . Networks are open structures, able to expand without limits, integrating new nodes as long as they are able to communicate within the network, namely as long as they share the same communication codes (for example, values or performance goals). A network-based social structure is a highly dynamic, open system, susceptible to innovating without threatening its balance" (Castells 1996: 470). Networks are mechanisms of communication. They were originally developed in situations of co-presence but the emergence of modern information technologies makes it possible for networks of virtual communication to extend on a global scale. That is, in addition to other effects, they make economic globalization possible.

Compared to an "empire", for example, "network" may sound rather nice and democratic but there are nodes in the net and it is these nodes that, according to Castells, make the global net of information, money and goods a mechanism of power. "The inclusion/exclusion in networks, and the architecture of relationships between networks, enacted by light-speed operating information technologies, configurate dominant processes and functions in our societies. . . . Switches connecting the networks (for example, financial flows taking control of media empires that influence political process) are the privileged instruments of power. Thus, the switchers are the power holders" (Castells 1996: 470–1).

In terms of the labour market, class distinctions are, according to Castells, increasingly being replaced by a threefold division into what he terms networkers, flextimers and the jobless. The networkers are the rather small elite located in such nodes of communications where several important communications routes intersect. They control the system even if their mutual interest struggles prevent the rise of one unified point of view or party. Instead, the system is in a state of constant rearticulation shaped by the logic of capitalist society, i.e., the necessity of valorization. The flextimers are those whose contracts are for fixed periods. They must always hope for an extension and be afraid of cuts in their projects as they go on with their daily work constantly hunting for a better appointment. Finally, the jobless are those who are not needed.

Castells develops this distinction in the context of studying the labor market. Yet in the global network society it can be generalized to cover the distribution and control of other valuable things as well. In relation to these too, there are networkers, those who are forced to pursue flexible standards and those who are excluded because they are not needed. This clearly is a distinction between different regions of the world, where areas such as almost the whole of Africa are excluded while the networkers of the US, the EU and Japan (or East Asia more generally) direct the workings of the world economy and most of the other regions get the position of flextimers. But as such this is too simple a description of the nature of network society. As information technologies make the networks at least potentially and in some cases actually global, there are networkers, flextimers and those who are not needed in every part of the world as the unemployed and badly housed people in all the rich centers of the world economy know.

This gives birth to a new pattern of political struggle. The global network of capitalist economy has cut all or most of the ties it had to the culture of its places of emergence. It is driven on solely by the abstract need for valorization which has neither a fatherland nor any respect for Mother Earth. Therefore the changes in the states of the global network of capitalist economy threaten to make people's lives in local contexts impossible or difficult. Every now and then in one place or another, economic conditions change in ways which are unbearable for people whose identities are tied to local forms of life now made impossible or very difficult to pursue. This is when, according to Castells, identity movements arise.

The pattern is always the same. Changes in the states of the global net make local identities menaced. Not always but often people react with social counter movements which have cultural value commitments and identity patterns in their core. These can be backwards looking movements such as nationalist movements, movements for the restitution of the patriarchal family, or fundamentalist religious movements. But they need not be. They can equally well be such radical movements as feminism and the environmental movement.

The current information society makes it possible for these movements to employ similar strategies of building and maintaining networks as corporations do. Therefore, at least a potentially global specter of resistances emerges. This is where we are today: on the one side there is the globally networked capitalist economy, on the other, the patchwork quilt of at least potentially globally networked resistances based on locally cherished cultural identities, which are made flow and felt to be threatened by the dynamism of the capitalist net. In between there are modes of juridical and political regulation channeling the ways the economy is allowed to work. In the heroic age of the nation-state this political regulation worked predominantly through different nation-states. Today, a more multilayered system with global, international, regional, national and area-based directives is emerging and it is this multilayered system of political regulation where struggles over what direction globalization will take are fought.

Our time

Let us now take another look at the articulation of Europe, this time in the global context.

In terms of economy, the past two or three decades have meant a major step towards a transnationally networked global economy. This economical net today has nodes everywhere but the nodes overlap, interact and are densest in the three centers of current world economy: the US, the EU and Japan (or East Asia more generally). Two figures presented by Manuel Castells (1996: 100–1) give us an idea of what is going on.

Figure 6.1 is about the structure of world trade in 1991. It records the percentages of total trade between the three centers as well as between each of the centers and its satellites. In the case of the EC (turned into EU after the Maastricht Treaty), Asia, Latin America and Africa intra-regional percentages are given as well. In the case of the US and Japan, however, the figure conceals part of their strength as domestic markets are invisible in world trade and only European integration already referred to above can be seen. Even so, we can note the triangular structure and the relatively weak position of the satellites, with the partial exceptions of Canada and Asia.

Figure 6.2 shows the structure of world direct investment in 1989–91 (average). It gives us an idea of the workings of multinational corporations, as a great deal of direct foreign investments flow to or from the subsidiaries and subcontractors of MNCs. The figure is rather similar and complementary to that given by Figure 6.1 on world trade and, instead of going into details here, I will draw your attention to three crucial facts apparent in the two figures.

First, the global network of capitalist economy seems to be concentrated in three centers. Second, there are significant flows not only in each of the centers and between its satellites but also between the centers. Therefore, rather than

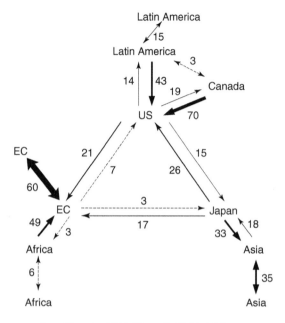

Figure 6.1 Structure of world trade, 1991 (Castells 1996, 100).

Figures are percentages of total trade (exports plus imports). Weight of lines between trading partners indicates intensity of exchanges.

Source: International Monetary Fund, *Direction of Trade Statistics Yearbook, 1992*, Washington, DC: IMF, 1992; elaborated by Stallings (1993). (Reprinted with the permission of Cambridge University Press.)

three fortresses waging trade wars, one flexible network of capitalist world economy seems to be emerging. Third, there are peripheries and areas which are not needed in the world. The figures indicate that almost the whole of Africa, for example, is currently such an area. Yet it would be a simplification to stick to the rich North poor South divide as the developing countries today are split into two radically different groups. One group is actually not developing at all. This group includes most African countries and many Asian countries, for example. The other group, however, is experiencing a developmental boom. This is what happened to the OPEC countries after the oil crisis and a similar if not even more radical process is now under way in the East Asian "Tigers". (For more on this developmental split into two groups see Held *et al.* 1999.)

Using the vocabulary of Immanuel Wallerstein's world-system analysis (Wallerstein 1974, 1980, 1989 and Shannon 1996) a system with three inter-related centers, their satellites as semi-peripheries and the rest of the world as periphery is emerging. However, Manuel Castells brings an important conceptual contribution to this scheme by laying emphasis on the flexible and decentralized nature of current economic networks. Global virtuality created by information technologies such as the telephone, fax, e-mail and Internet make it possible to

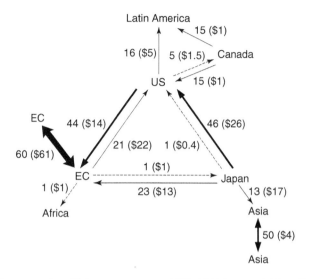

Figure 6.2 Structure of world direct investment, 1989–1991 (average) (Castells 1996, 101).

Figures are percentages of total direct investment; those in parentheses are absolute values in US$ bn. Weight of lines between trading partners indicates intensity of exchanges.

Sources: For US: *Survey of Current Business*, August 1992; for Japan: Ministry of Finance, unpublished data; for Europe: UNTNC: *World Investment Report, 1992, Survey of Current Business* (inflow to US), and IMF, *Balance of Payments Yearbook, 1992*. Other figures are estimates. Data elaborated by Stallings (1993). (Reprinted with permission of Cambridge University Press.)

split the various tasks of economic organizations so that each will be executed in those parts of the world where it can be done the most effectively and at the lowest possible cost. Therefore, there are networkers in all parts of the globe even if their majority can be found in the three centers. A reverse side of this global-ization of the net is that flextimers and those who are not needed can also be found everywhere. That is, living in one of the centers does not protect people from the impact of the capitalist net which turns most of them into flextimers and makes many unneeded under the pressure of competition from less affluent areas of the world, where labor costs of manual work especially are cheaper.

Our time thus seems to be the time of the emergence of one global economical network and this is especially so since the collapse of the Soviet Union opened the last closed gates of the previously socialist world to market economy. Europe is part of this global network of capitalist economy as one of its three centers. It is articulated as an identity of its own, as the relatively high figures of intra-EU trade prove, but its economic borders are not closed and there have been no signs of such a development commencing even in the future.

In a way we are today in a new global context in a situation resembling the one Karl Polanyi in 1944 called the "great transformation". With this term he referred to the breakthrough of capitalist market economy first in England, then in continental Europe and the US and finally in the rest of the world. He understood the core of this transformation to be a cultural switch or change of frame into one which interpreted the world through the three basic factors of production known to the economists, i.e., land, labor and capital. In other words, stripped of the jargon of the economists the great transformation turned nature, human beings and the token of transactions into goods which could and should be given a price (i.e., land rent, wages, profit) and sold. This subjected the factors of production – or, in other words, us and the world we live in – to the logic of the market instead of cultural value commitments. Or that was what would have happened should the most radical formulation of the idea of market society have been successful. This radical version said that the market and only the market should rule, and the state and similar external interventions to the workings of the market should be minimized. An unrestricted market society, however, was for Polanyi a self-destructive system incapable of avoiding implosion. This is so because it would have meant that the "satanic mills" of the market would have ground the workers, their communities and natural environment to pieces. Therefore, radical marketization of the world faced countermovements everywhere. Finally, three solutions to the problem of political regulation and free market emerged. These were fascism, socialism and New Deal policies leading to the democratic welfare state. Fascism and socialism subjected the market to centralized planning. The welfare state let the market be free but channeled and complemented its workings by laws, directives, plans and subventions (Polanyi 1944; Heiskala 1996).

Fascism, socialism and the welfare state were all nationalist projects irrespective of what lip-service the socialists and others gave to internationalism. Today, each of the solutions has come to a dead end of its own. Fascism met its fate in Nürnberg. Socialism died in 1989–91 when the Soviet Union collapsed and Russia lost its grip on its satellites. The welfare state began to face problems growing more and more difficult after the oil crisis of 1973 which also meant the end of the period of long economic growth after World War II and attempts to find a new pattern for growth. The current globalization of the economy is very much a result of these attempts to find a new orientation that would make growth possible and probable (Castells 1996).

One of Polanyi's central points was that even though the protagonists of the market society turned their rhetoric against the state as soon as the structures and legislation for the marketization of their country were brought up it would have been impossible to establish a society organized by the capitalist economy without the support and active role of the state. Today we can make an analogous observation. It would have been impossible to establish globalized economical structures or the net without the support and active role of the states which have deliberately given up part of their sovereignty by such treaties as founding the WTO, for example. The reason they have done this is their attempts to promote economic growth which would be channeled to their populations. The reverse side is that they have had to give up some tasks characteristic of the heroic age of the nation-state, make their strategies more internationally co-operative and accept the fact that globalization might hit part of their population very hard in a situation where possibilities for subvention seem to be reduced (Kosonen 1994).

This has already led us from the economy to the field of political regulation and it has become obvious that the question cannot be set dualistically by asking which is stronger, economy or the state? What has made the globalization of the economy possible is not the decline of state power as is sometimes claimed. Instead of an erosion of the state and political regulation we are dealing with the transformation of the pattern of political regulation.

Here we should distinguish the pattern itself and its content at a given time. As Held *et al.* (1999) make clear, a multilayered pattern of political regulation binding individual states more closely to international co-operation and restricting their sovereign power to take action has been emerging from the second half of the nineteenth century at the latest. One indicator for this is the growth of intergovernmental organizations (IGO) and international non-governmental organizations (INGO) recorded in Figure 6.3 (Held *et al.* 1999: 54). Another is the existence of certain rather powerful international organizations such as the UN, WTO and the EU as well as international conferences on central global problems such as the Rio Conference on the Environment and the Cairo Conference on Population Control.

A multilayered system of political regulation, then, has emerged. This is most evident to the EU member states as the Union figures in their politics on a daily basis. But it is not just the Union but an extensive and steadily growing net of international treaties and organizations that any nation-state today regularly interacts with and must take into account in its action plans. The fact of the existence of a multilayered system, however, should not be confused with the existence of a clear direction or a single center where decisions are made. In principle the UN is such a center but in practice its power is very limited, which is apparent, among other things, in the fact that it does not have its own army.

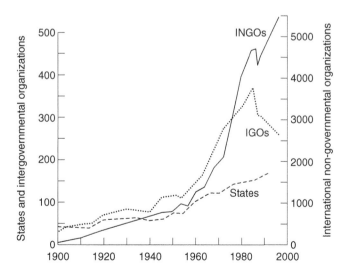

Figure 6.3 States, IGOs and INGOs in the twentieth century (Held *et al.* 1999).

Sources: Union of International Associations, 1996

Instead, military power is fragmented to different nation-states, each of which has an army, and when international interventions take place they are implemented by NATO and other military organizations based on the leading role of the US. These interventions are sometimes approved by the Security Council of the UN and sometimes not, but irrespective of this they take place whenever the US finds it beneficial to its interests or some more high-minded goals. This is especially embarrassing to the EU as it has sought ways of raising its capacity to be an actor in foreign policy but has, in the case of the powder barrel of former Yugoslavia, had to admit that it is not ready to take action foreign policy even in cases where an alarming crisis takes place in its own back yard. Therefore, the US and NATO have been the actors.

To turn to the content of the pattern, it can be said that a multilayered system of political regulation exists but it is not integrated around one center or plan. The most obvious substantial factors are sectoral co-operation in different fields, the military supremacy of the US, and successful attempts to remove hindrances to market exchanges and capital flows across state borders. The free market policy has been apparent in the EU, a customs union, as well as the emergence of free-trade areas such as NAFTA (between the US, Canada and Mexico) and APEC or ASEAN (Asia Pasific) and finally the WTO.

The policy of making markets free has so far largely taken place in a form where there have been very few subventions to those whose conditions of life the workings of free market make worse. Similarly, there have been only limited attempts to create a set of norms directing the hazards the production and consumption of goods is allowed to cause to the environment and workers. In spite of this current trend there is no reason why political regulation could not affect these issues and make global or regional restrictions to the ways in which the economic net is allowed to treat people and nature. I will here briefly outline four alternative scenarios for the future, taking the EU and its possible strategies as a point of departure.

1   *Globally free market, no subventions, no protection.* Michel Mann (1993b) once wrote that even if Marx and Engels were mistaken in understanding the modern state in general as a joint venture of capitalists this interpretation fits the EC very well. Today's EU is already beyond this point, as there are directives dealing with the quality and environmental aspects of goods as well as some directives on social policy. Yet it is important to remember that this is where the EU started from and there is a tendency to fall back on this strategy.

2   *Globally free market, subventions for EU citizens, protection in labour market competition.* This is the current line of the EU, as there are some subventions on the level of the Union (especially so in agriculture) and plenty of subventions on the level of different member states (Kosonen 1994). Protection in labour market competition is apparent in the relatively strict policy of granting work permits and immigrant visas for people coming from non-EU countries. Commitment to the globally free market policy, however, makes the latitude of this strategy restricted, as there is no way to prevent companies moving their assembly lines to non-EU countries with reduced labour costs.

3   *Global trade war, free EU home market.* This is not a scenario in sight but it is
a theoretical possibility, as the EU is a region large enough to cope with
reduced transactions with the rest of the world. Alternatives for internal
policy range from the no subventions, no protection line to the subventions
and protection strategy.
4   *Globally free market, subventions and protection for all on a global scale.* This is
the most ambitious strategic line for long-term policy. Almost everybody
agrees with it as long as it does not cost anything. Beyond that, there are no
actual signs of implementing this policy in the EU, but there are political
actors and movements for such a strategy (the current German Minister of
Foreign Affairs, Joschka Fischer 1997 and Beck 1997, for example).

Which one of these scenarios will come true will be decided by future political
actors. Who these actors will be and what kind of a policy they will pursue
depends on the political climate which again depends on cultural factors to which
I will now turn.

There is no such thing as global civil society and there is no European civil society either (Beck 1997). No European TV channel, no European newspaper or
weekly magazine, no Europe-wide political mobilization, as the EU Parliament
election campaign takes place in every member state separately with national candidates and national campaign themes, and the rest of the EU works as a
co-operation between governments and not with citizens. Turnout percentages in
EU Parliamentary elections are low and at the beginning of the 1990s only 5 per
cent of those polled identified themselves first and foremost as Europeans (Reif
1993). Yet Europeans today know more about each other than in any other period
in history. The media, new information technologies, transnationalization of
working environments, tourism and efforts of the EU bureaucracy to integrate
educational institutions and culture are all bringing forth increased knowledge of
alternative world-views and ways of life. To adapt the optimistic view of Talcott
Parsons (1970) tailored to the analysis of integration problems in the US melting
pot, this could be a basis for a process of "generalization of value commitments",
i.e., an improved ability to understand others' points of view and find similarities
with one's own value position on a more abstract level. All three European variants of Christianity are, after all, based on the Bible, Judaism shares half of the
Bible with Christianity and is the original intellectual context from which
Christianity springs, and even Islam is partly based on the same sources as
Christianity. Moreover, all five are monotheistic and rationalistic religions with a
tendency to push their followers to abstract contemplation and some degree of
asceticism. Nationalism makes borders by definition, but its message is the same
everywhere: our national heritage is valuable and makes us distinctive. Is it actually such a big step to start to apply this scheme to Europe instead of or in addition
to one's country of origin? Personally I do not find it difficult at all but then
again I am part of a community of priests worried about integration problems and
anomie or conflicts which may threaten the balance, i.e., the transnational network of sociologists. It may well be that the parish finds the new doctrine more

difficult to swallow than the pastor. But even if this is so there is a more modest interpretation. Its code word is "reflexive modernization" (Beck *et al.* 1994) and it suggests that rather than a melting pot we are entering into a "salad bowl", where different species lie abreast without losing their identities in the co-existence. This brings forth a risk of conflict, but as modern communication and transportation technologies make us all relatively knowledgeable of and potentially tolerant towards other world-views and ways of life there is also a possibility for peaceful co-existence and fair compromises (Beck 1999b; Giddens 1994). This could provide a basis for European identity as a reflexive project.

European identity on a more abstract level is a possibility which both the Parsonian and the reflexive modernization paradigm open, even though both admit the possibility of fragmentation and conflicts as well. A related cultural issue is the prediction by Manuel Castells of the rise of identity movements based on local culture and brought up by the threats caused by the global economic network to local cultural identities and ways of life. Here too a possibility of integration as well as fragmentation emerges. Information technologies make the movements able to network on a potentially global scale and as their opponent, the global network economy is already globally networked, this strategy will certainly occur to these movements. But nothing guarantees that different resistances can actually find enough common ground to work together. This may happen in some cases such as Greenpeace, the environmental movement, more widely, or feminism; but it is difficult to believe that these movements could find anything in common with the National Rifle Association in the US or nationalist reactionaries or pro-family movements. The network of resistances is therefore a chance for all movements to find congenial companions, not one front. Yet it makes political action such as purchasing boycotts and simultaneous demonstrations possible on the European as well as on the global scale. Another factor which works towards Europeanization and even globalization of political movements is the tripartition into networkers, those who are forced to pursue flexible standards and those who are left out of the game. This is so because members of those three groups can be found everywhere and in trying to push through reforms which would benefit them (or struggle against reforms which are against their interests) they are forced to network, because their opponent is already globally networked. This is why we are going to, in the nearest future, witness the Europeanization and possibly even globalization of the strategies of labour unions and other interest groups.

What conclusions should we draw from all this? Is there a unified European identity emerging and how will it be related to the rest of the world on the one hand and the cultural and political dividing lines within Europe on the other? I will close with three comments.

1   *Economically* Europe is strongly integrated as far as the EU is concerned. (The average share of intra-EU trade for an EU member state is about 60 per cent.) This does not, however, mean that the EU would be curling up into itself. In addition to internal integration it is integrating with the two other

centers of the world economy, the US and Japan (or East Asia more generally), and there are no actual signs of trade war in sight.

2   *Politically* a multilayered system of regulation has emerged. The EU is one of
the strongest actors in this political system and its influence on its member
states is significant. It is constantly negotiating with new membership candidates. In addition to new members the future agenda includes harmonization
of taxation, strengthening of the Union's ability to take action in foreign
policy and the issue of integrating armed forces under at least a partial control of the WEU. However, there are no guarantees that any of these attempts
to make the Union stronger will be successful in the near future. Furthermore,
it is an open question what kind of an economic and social policy the Union
will be pursuing in the future.

3   *Culturally* Europe is fragmented but there are unifying factors as well. It is possible that a European identity pattern is in the process of emerging. Yet if this
is so it will not replace people's other cultural identities but complement them.
The probability of its emergence is highest in such social groups as might, in
addition to a European identity, also develop even fragments of global or cosmopolitan identity, i.e., among well educated networkers and flextimers.

Notes

1   To be more accurate, the share of export to other EU states was more than 50 percent
but less than 60 percent in Germany (54), Greece (54), Denmark (55), the UK (56)
and Italy (58). It was 63 percent in France and more than 70 percent in Spain (71),
Ireland (74), Portugal (75), Belgium-Luxembourg (75) and the Netherlands (76)
(Therborn 1995: 198).

2   In addition to Europe, of course, there are the free trade areas of the Americas
(NAFTA between the US, Canada and Mexico) and Asia-Pacific (APEC or ASEAN).

3   The heroic period itself had already started in the eighteenth century as European
proto-nations began to develop towards the current nation-state with centralized organizations and cultural bases (Mann 1993, for example).

4   As we will be able to observe later on, the erosion of the heroic age is not the same as
a significant decline in state power. What it is, however, is the transformation of its cultural role and strategic position in relation to other political actors and the economy.

References

Allardt, E. (1979) *Implications of the Ethnic Revival in Modern, Industrialized Society. A
Comparative Study of the Linguistic Minorities in Western Europe*, Helsinki: Societas
Scientarum Fennica.
—— (1981) *Språkgränser och samhällsstruktur: finlandssvenskarna i ett jämförande perspektiv*,
Stockholm: AWE/Gebers.
Beck, U. (1997) *Was ist Globalisierung? Irrtümer des Globalismus – Antworten auf
Globalisierung*, Frankfurt am Main: Suhrkamp.
—— (1999a) "Democracy beyond the nation-state. A cosmopolitan manifesto", *Dissent*,
Winter: 53–5.
—— (1999b) "The cosmopolitan perspective: On the sociology of the second age of moder-
nity", *British Journal of Sociology* (in print).

Beck, U., Giddens, A., and Lash, S. (1994) *Reflexive Modernization. Politics, Tradition and Aesthetics in the Modern Social Order*, Cambridge: Polity Press.

Boyer, R. and Drache, D. (eds) (1996) *States Against Markets*, London: Routledge.

Castells, M. (1996) *The Information Age: Economy, Society and Culture. Volume I: The Rise of the Network Society*, Oxford: Blackwell.

Droselle, J.-B. (1990) *Europe: A History of Its Peoples*, London: Viking.

Fischer, J. (1997) *Für einen neuen Gesellschaftsvertrag: Eine politische Antwort auf die globale Revolution*, Köln: Kiepenheuer & Witsch.

Giddens, A. (1994) *Beyond Left and Right: The Future of Radical Politics*, Cambridge: Polity Press.

Heiskala, R. (1996) *Kohti keinotekoista yhteiskuntaa*, Helsinki: Gaudeamus.

Held, D., McGrew, A., Goldblatt, D., and Perraton, J. (1999) *Global Transformations: Politics, Economics and Culture*, Cambridge: Polity Press.

Hirst, P. and Thompson, G. (1996) *Globalization in Question: The International Economy and the Possibilities of Governance*, Cambridge: Polity Press.

Kosonen, P. (1994) *European Integration: A Welfare State Perspective*, Helsinki: Helsingin yliopiston oikeussosiologian julkaisuja No. 8.

Mann, M. (1986) *The Sources of Social Power. Vol. I: A History of Power from the Beginning to A.D. 1760*, Cambridge: Cambridge University Press.

—— (1993a) *The Sources of Social Power. Vol. II: The Rise of Classes and Nation-States, 1760–1914*, Cambridge: Cambridge University Press.

—— (1993b) "Nation-states in Europe and other continents: Diversifying, developing, not dying", *Daedalus* 122: 115–40.

Martin, H.-P. and Schumann, H. (1996) *Die Globalisierungsfalle*, Reinbek bei Hamburg: Rowohlt.

Mikkeli, H. (1998) *Europe as an Idea and an Identity*, London: Macmillan.

Parsons, T. (1970) "On building social system theory: A personal history", *Daedalus* 99: 826–81.

Polanyi, K. (1944) *The Great Transformation: The Political and Economic Origins of Our Time*, Boston: Beacon Press.

Reif, K. (1993) "Cultural convergence and cultural diversity as factors in European identity", in Garcia, S. (ed.) *European Identity and the Search for Legitimacy*, London: Pinter.

Shannon, T. R. (1996) *An Introduction to the World-System Perspective. Second Edition*, Boulder: Westview Press.

Therborn, G. (1995) *European Modernity and Beyond: The Trajectory of European Societies, 1945–2000*, London: Sage.

Väyrynen, R. *et al.* (1999) *Suomi avoimessa maailmassa. Globalisaatio ja sen vaikutukset*, Helsinki: Sitra/Taloustieto.

Wallerstein, I. (1974) *The Modern World-System: Capitalist Agriculture and the Origins of the European World-Economy in the Sixteenth Century*, New York: Academic Press.

—— (1980) *The Modern World-System, 2: Mercantilism and the Consolidation of the European World-Economy*, New York: Academic Press.

—— (1989) *The Modern World-System, 3: The Second Era of Great Expansion of the Capitalist World-Economy*, San Diego: Academic Press.

Weber, M. (1922/1968) *Economy and Society. An Outline of Interpretative Sociology*, Berkeley: University of California Press.

7 Contradictory trends in constructing European citizenship

Beyond the gender gap

Chiara Saraceno

Europe and European citizenship: contested concepts or contested practices?

There is a growing body of literature addressing the contradictions, ambivalence and difficulties implicit in the twin issues represented by the construction of Europe (as a clearly defined supranational body, at least institutionally) and of European citizenship. The latter is seen as an embedded dimension with specific contents in terms of rights and duties, substantially adding to national citizenship in each EU member country, e.g. Habermas 1992; Weiler 1998; Delanty 1998; Rusconi 1998; Emerson 1998). Though adopting different perspectives and approaches, the literature points to the intrinsic tensions between nation-state and supra-state polity (as well as the contrasting conceptions of Europe as supranational body), and between national citizenship and European citizenship. It also underlines the contrast between the instrumental view of the Union and a view which sees the Union as a society consisting of its own citizens, not by the member countries' citizens.

Two kinds of questions are raised. The first concerns the kind of political body the present "non-identified political object", to use Schmitter's (1996) words, could become. The second concerns the future of European, and also national citizenship, in contemporary society where plural, not monolithic identities and loyalties are increasingly the norm.

A further body of literature, which possibly has a wider audience among non academics and non experts, suggests that the difficulties raised by European citizenship may be due to the lack of democracy within the European Union itself and the institutions of which it consists. From this perspective, the problem of European citizenship lies not so much in its multi-layered and contested nature, but in the democratic shortcomings which undermine its base. This particular critique has been popular among feminist analysts (e.g. Meehan 1993; Kravaritou 1997; Varkas 1997; Saraceno 1997a; Liebert 1997, 1999).

The two strands of analysis are, of course, not mutually exclusive. On the contrary, the lack of democracy is embedded to a large extent in the unsolved contradictions and ambivalence implicit in European institutional policy-making. But these problems are not easily solved through institutional tinkering. They require complex rethinking and negotiations, not only about the role and position of Europe *vis-à-vis* nation-states, but also the role of the European Parliament *vis-à-vis* the Commission and the Council of Ministers, the power relations between the various national and European institutions, as well as between these and other supranational bodies (as the Serb-Kossov war has clearly illustrated). They also require the development of consensus on the basic aim of European integration, and hence European citizenship. As many commentators have in fact observed, the values and ideals behind the setting up of the Community in the post-war period (peace, prosperity and supranationalism – see Weiler 1998), for various reasons no longer have the same appeal. As a consequence, the European Union seems to have become an end in itself, rather than a means, and at the same time, the meaning of "Europe" is exploding in numerous directions (Emerson 1998).

Rather than interpreting this phenomenon simply as a weakening of past ideals, it can be seen as a result of the (largely) successful construction of the European Union. The concrete existence of the Union, its institutions, practices and discourses are now part of the context in which the Union itself, and more broadly Europe, is being perceived and constructed. On the other hand, the weakening of the founding values could also be seen as a critical self-appraisal, as the inequities and exclusions which were previously shrouded are now more exposed. The contrasting, and sometimes even contentious, meanings attached to the idea of the European Union and European citizenship could be the mature, self-critical (even if sometimes cynical) "offspring" of those ideals. This is made possible by the very processes developed to interpret and achieve the ideals, as well as the various actors – including states, governments, institutions, also lobbies, networks and movements, down to the self-consciousness of individual citizens in the various nation-states – which have taken part in these processes and have, to some extent, been created by them. This renders both the goal of European integration and the content of European citizenship an open-ended project, the outcome of which is necessarily unknown.

European policy-making as European citizenship building: a trend reversal?

As I share the idea that both Europe and European citizenship are less a set of given contents than an ongoing and open construction (Emerson 1998; Weiler 1998), in these brief comments I wish to examine one of the actors in the process of construction: the European institutions themselves and, more specifically, their discourses and policy-making. I wish to argue that there is a growing tension – not just a gap or a delay – in present trends in European policy. In particular, there is a contrast between the apparent strengthening of the foundation and scope of European citizenship enshrined in both the Maastricht and Amsterdam Treaties (as well as in a number of directives and recommendations) and the actual effects of policy-making (the definition of priorities and requisites imposed on member states by the Union, especially in the economic and monetary area).

This is almost exactly the opposite of the way the Community and the Commission worked up to the 1980s. Until then, the Community's sphere of action and competence was progressively enlarged by various directives and the sentences of the European Court. For example, the social rights it granted and protected practically forced, one might say, the boundaries of workers' rights to include citizenship rights. Also for women, the Community advanced from the mere, though important, principle of equal treatment to promoting positive action, and acknowledging that, in order to promote equity in the labor market, it is necessary to tackle the division of labor within the family and the (passive and active) caring needs of individuals and family members. At the same time, it recognized the need to include women in decision-making processes, not only as an end in itself, but as a means of developing a more democratic political decision-making process.

Looking at this development, it could be suggested that at the Community level the reduction of European citizenship to a (very reduced) social dimension was perceived as not only overly limited, but inefficient first for women, and only subsequently for men too. In this perspective, one might say that in its discursive shifts the Commission acknowledged the feminist critique standard concepts of citizenship, including Marshall's, despite its possibly being the most encompassing. As many feminist analysts have pointed out with regard to national citizenship (e.g. Williams 1989; Zincone 1992; Lister 1997; Leira 1992), Marshall's three-tiered citizenship paradigm in the case of women appears at the same time particularly insightful and less firmly coherent than for men. Access to social rights and social provisions, as well as to education, is, in fact, for women a crucial resource for developing that kind of autonomy which is necessary to be able to make use of civil and political rights, including the right to work and the right to participate in decision-making processes. Yet, women have often been granted social rights more easily than civil and political ones; the latter two do not derive automatically from the former. Of course, denial of civil and political rights both in European nation-states and in the European Union itself is no longer based on legal grounds. It is more a *de facto* process, often hidden under women's "unwillingness" to be present in crucial areas of activity, or to compete. Thus the problem of the significance of European citizenship beyond the three "founding freedoms" emerges more clearly, and sooner, when addressed from women's point of view, forcing a breakdown of conceptual as well as competence boundaries.

Since the late 1980s, however, despite the strengthening of the institutional framework of the Union (and the building of a kind of political body which, among other things, bestows citizenship on member countries' citizens), the actual policy-making practices seem to point to a reduction in the scope of the Union's direct activity and involvement (e.g. the insistence on the subsidiarity principle), particularly in the area of social rights. There seems to be a similar spillover effect of the Union's economic policies on national social citizenship rights.

This tension between institutional and symbolic enlargement of European citizenship and "reductionist" practices should not, however, be seen exclusively in negative terms. Rather, it is shaping the symbolic, regulatory and communication space in which the different social actors develop their views and practices on citizenship and stake their claims at the national and European level. This may contribute to the development of common cross-country features – in the way issues are defined, processes are interpreted, alliances are sought and built up – but also cross-country differences, given the diverse national traditions and embodiments of citizenship, i.e. the different standpoints, experience and understanding of what citizenship is about. This includes different gender cultures and relations, specific ways in which gender is included in the fabric of citizenship and, more particularly, ways in which women's gender interests are acknowledged and constructed (e.g. as mothers, wives, workers, legal individuals and so forth – see O'Connor *et al.* 1999).

I develop my argument on the basis of three examples: the tension between the constitutionalization of equality rights and the dominance of economic criteria in the making of the Union, with its consequences on the resources allocated to social provisions; what I call the paradoxes of mainstreaming, that is the coexistence of an increasing demand for gender parity at all levels and the acknowledgement of the partial failure of positive action; the growing fragmentation and also obfuscation of decision-making processes as a consequence of the principle of subsidiarity and social partnership – and therefore also of the construction of a European civil society. The first two, in particular, concern women's status and options within European citizenship and gender equity. Gender (in)equity, as well as nation-specific differences in gender concepts and relations are at the core of most current debates on national and European citizenship, both from a contemporary and historical perspective. At the same time, a gender perspective helps to de-construct the assumptions, actors and relationships involved in citizenship discourse and to illuminate the dilemmas it generates (e.g. autonomy versus interdependence, community versus individualism, rights versus duties, commonality versus differences).

The constitutionalization of equality rights and weakening of the resources to implement them

With the Amsterdam Treaty, respect for human rights and fundamental freedoms became a fundamental principle of the European Union. The Treaty includes specific mention of action to promote equality between men and women, beyond the area of equal pay. The European Court will have the power to judge whether actions and practices by the various member states and EU institutions are compatible with those principles. Thus, in principle, gender equality has been inscribed as a human right and fundamental freedom. It has also, together with other fundamental rights and freedoms, been constitutionalized within the European Union, not only as an intention, but in practice. In fact, the idea has been introduced that in order to evaluate equity and the respect for human rights, it is necessary to look at the effects of the relative norms and practices, not only at their formal content. In principle, therefore, the Union and the Court have an ample range of actions and responsibility, insofar as virtually all norms and practices are open to scrutiny if there are sufficient grounds for suspecting that their effects may be discriminatory.

As a consequence, a highly problematic arena has been opened up. The various actors may negotiate conflicting and contentious views about what should be included in the list of fundamental freedoms (e.g. abortion? fertility by any means and in any condition? family-friendly working schedules?) and which indicators should be used to evaluate the implementation of fundamental rights and their compatibility with specific practices and norms. Precisely for this reason, to limit ourselves to exposing the purely symbolic, rhetorical value of this grand affirmation of principles would be too simplistic, although the role of symbols and their capacity to furnish codes of interpretation and self-representation should not be underestimated. As the record of the Court on gender equity issues testifies, the opening up of a symbolic arena supported by judicial power helps shape perceptions and define interest groups – even if sometimes in a counterfactual way (Meehan 1993; Barbera 1999).

Turning to the actual process of European integration, culminating in the Maastricht and Amsterdam Treaties and monetary union, a reverse trend seems to be emerging. The strong emphasis on the monetary and economic dimension, including budget requisites to enter the inner circle of the monetary union, is now weakening the very conditions which render full participation and sharing in national citizenship possible for a large part of the population. These conditions, i.e. social rights, are particularly crucial for women. However, the degree to which they are weakened depends on specific features of the national economies and social citizenship, including the welfare and social policy regime.[1]

Here, I am not thinking primarily of pension rights, but of income support, child care services, services for the handicapped and the frail elderly, and so forth. I do not argue that all welfare models or regimes are equally defendable, and even less that in the past they all supported gender (and also class) equity, granting everyone the social rights necessary to develop their own capacities. On the contrary, as feminist analyses have shown, European national welfare states have in many instances strengthened, or helped to crystallize, gender and generation asymmetries, as well as class ones. They have not always been able to offset social inequalities in the ability to satisfy fundamental needs – as the many typologies of welfare states developed by social and political analysts have attempted to document. It is also true that the need to fulfill the fiscal and budgetary requisites of the Maastricht Treaty has led to cuts in deficit spending and the revision of social expenditure, opening up room for debate not only on "overspending", but also the inequities and inefficiencies implicit in specific redistributive models. Yet, certainly in Italy, as well as in other countries, the priority given to financial requirements at the national and Union level, has not been coherent with the founding principles of the Union, particularly with the promotion of gender equality. Cuts and "restructuring" in social spending lead to some kind of "re-familization" and/or commodification of caring needs – both at the symbolic and the practical level – and at the same time to the de-familization of social security and social assistance provisions. Thus family responsibilities in providing care –

either directly or through the market – are being re-enforced as a means of containing the otherwise growing demand for personal social services (e.g. OECD 1994; Lewis 1998). Increasing recourse to means testing not only erodes individual entitlements, shifting the boundaries between social security and social assistance, it also has gender specific consequences, insofar as lack of income, for married and cohabitant women especially, may be more easily "hidden" due to their supposed attachment to a "family income" which they may in fact have no control over (see also Sainsbury 1996). At the same time, measures which supported and acknowledged the traditional gender division of labor – e.g. survivors' pensions, income support for poor mothers – are being revised. Thus, for instance, in Italy entitlement to a survivor's pension is now becoming means-tested. Both in the UK and the Netherlands, previously generous (though stereotypically gendered) regulations concerning the availability for work of lone mothers receiving income support have been tightened (Scheiwe 1994). Particularly in the UK, lone mothers on benefit have become a target of social criticism and turned into the symbol of welfare dependency. Finally, increasing concern with the cost of public social services translates either into a mere reduction of publicly funded services or into some kind of "payment for care". The latter is at best an ambivalent, or ambiguous way of acknowledging the competing demands for income and care, in its impact on the gender division of labor within families and on class differences between women (e.g. Fagnani and Rassat 1997; Ungerson 1997; Waerness 1998; Leira 1999).

All these shifts in policies are far from being gender and class-neutral: elderly women expecting a survivor's pension, single mothers counting on income support, working class families and mothers with small children – may all find it increasingly difficult to meet their needs, while being identified as profiteers. Although the forms of this restructuring (e.g. payment for care rather than simply the reduction of publicly funded services), the rationale offered for them (e.g. the need to foster independence in single mothers, rather than the need to strengthen kin and family solidarity) and their outcomes may differ widely, depending on the social policy regime and gender and family cultures which they affect (see Saraceno 1997b; Lewis 1998).

As well as the restructuring of social expenditure, there is another phenomenon which needs to be made more coherent with the founding principles of the Union. Many of the labor market policies encouraged by the Union tend to weaken, if not undermine, those social rights which were better protected within and by the Union in the past, especially workers' rights. Increased flexibility in labor contracts, the spread of so-called atypical contracts and so forth, have meant that a growing percentage of workers are now not covered by the traditional guarantees. Within this phenomenon, we are witnessing an increasing feminization of a casualized workforce and of the lower strata of workers (Allen *et al.* 1999; Crouch 1999). Despite this, no common regulation for minimum protection has yet been developed at the European level. The result is an increase in the already wide national differences in last resort or basic income support systems and the guarantee of minimum resources (see Saraceno 1998; Guibentif and Bouget 1997; Gough *et al.* 1997).

In this connection, one is struck by the lack of communicability between the different "European discourses" – on European integration and what makes the Union a Union – and by their quite different binding force on member countries' behavior. This difference cuts across the economic, political and social differences. The impossibility, at least until now, of developing consensus on a set of binding social requisites (like those in the economic field), be they a maximum unemployment rate, a minimum schooling level, or a minimum social protection package, is a telling testimony to this. In my opinion, this difficulty is due not only to powerful business lobbies or government resistance to outside regulations modifying the cost of labor or social expenditure budget. It also depends on the interests and self-perceptions incorporated in the various national approaches to social citizenship which, as it has been noted, embody and differentiate what citizenship is about in industrial democracies. The recent Communication from the Commission, "Towards a more inclusive Europe" (March 1, 2000), followed by the agreement reached in the Lisbon summit, might point to a fresh move in the direction of developing some kind of European social benchmarking (an expression used in the Communication). Also the decision by the Commission not to develop another "top down" anti-poverty program to be added to the existing national programs, but to fund inter-country cooperation in developing common standards may be read within this perspective; although it is also the consequence of the national governments' resistance – in the name of the principle of subsidiarity – to having a European program in the field of social policy.

The paradoxes of mainstreaming

The new keyword for gender equity and equality is "mainstreaming". In the history of feminism, mainstreaming has always been presented as a less radical, less innovative approach or goal than that advocating difference or separatism. It has been interpreted as the attempt to insert women in existing institutions and areas of activity, as well as including gender in prevalent scientific paradigms, possibly changing them from within, but not radically overturning or rejecting them on the ground of their being gender blind or straightforwardly sexist. In this sense, mainstreaming is perceived as a sort of "middle of the road" approach, which leaves things (as well as theories) substantially unchanged. Although one could point to the subversive hypothesis which lies behind the goal of mainstreaming: that by their presence women can change both the rules of the game and the conceptual and explanatory framework, I do not want to enter this debate here. I only point to the fact that, in the language of the Commission, mainstreaming is taken to mean a demand for no less than the universal introduction of women as concrete, individual, actors (actresses?) in all areas of decision-making, and that a gender perspective should be adopted in all sectors and levels of the Union and Union-making process, not only in *ad hoc* initiatives. It does not "merely" ask for 50 per cent representation, but it requires that women be present in all bodies and decision-making processes. It also holds that women's experience, outlook and competencies should be allowed to modify the entire social set up and the processes which shape it. No small objective!

However, this move from support for positive actions to the goal of main-streaming is more the result of an *impasse* in the progress towards gender equality than the outcome of previous progress. Positive actions, even when individually effective, have not succeeded in changing the balance of gender-specific power relations or discrimination mechanisms, whether in the labor market, the politi-cal arena, or in processes of economic decision-making. They have largely remained *ad hoc* experiences.[2] Moreover, their legitimization has become increas-ingly problematic even within the arena of the European Court decisions which in the past were a crucial means in legitimizing them. After the notorious decision by the Court on the Kalanke case in 1995, it has become somewhat uncertain what exactly the ground of equal opportunity actions is.[3] The under-representa-tion of women in the various fields, says the sentence, cannot be addressed by direct positive action, aiming at redressing the consequences of past discrimina-tion from "the top down", so to say, that is by institutional means; it may be only addressed at the level of society as a whole, i.e. the patterns of organization of labor and organization of the family, of cultural prejudices and processes of socialization and so forth. It is, therefore, outside the range both of the Court and of Community law. The same Court of Justice had, in fact, previously explicitly made clear that the 76/207 on equal treatment does not aim to regulate issues con-cerning the organization of the family or change the allocation of responsibilities within the couple (see sentence July 25, 1991).

Thus, although positive actions may continue to be developed on a case by case basis, they can no longer be assumed as the main road to equality, on legal or cul-tural grounds, since they are liable to become a contested field, even among women themselves, as testified by the debates on the issue of quotas developing in most European countries as well as in the United States.

With "mainstreaming", the focus of the EU discourse is moving from actions "for women" (e.g. NOW programs and the like) to having a gender sensitive focus on all policies and areas of action. Yet, in order to achieve mainstreaming, women as individuals, sharing differentiated, if not conflictual, women's agendas, need to be present in the most relevant decision-making and agenda-setting processes. This is exactly where women are most conspicuous by their absence and where assumptions concerning gender interests and relations are least explicit and most taken for granted.

This unsatisfactory outcome of positive action could also be considered a spe-cific, albeit not exclusive, responsibility of the Commission, insofar as it has failed to put it on the "general" agenda or to modify the relationship between symbolic and practical priorities, between general policies and *ad hoc* ones, i.e. positive actions. Thus "conciliating" paid work and family life (in the beginning, it was tellingly called "re-conciliating") has remained a sectoral objective aimed mainly at women, notwithstanding the wording of the two Delors White Papers – *Competition and Growth* and *European Social Policy*. On the contrary, the "flexibi-lization" of labor contracts and modes of work, or the fulfilling of Maastricht requirements are considered "general" objectives. No explicit or meaningful link is made between the two. The two areas, as well as the two "European vocabulaires" – one concerning gender equity and the other the crucial requisites of the common European labour market and financial budget – therefore remain not only reciprocally impermeable, but could be played against each other.

Mainstreaming requires that women be present in substantial numbers in all relevant areas, and that gender perspectives be adequately developed and shared among all decision-makers (women and men): two conditions which are far from being fulfilled. The limits of mainstreaming thus derive more from the paradoxical nature of its conditions than on its not being radical enough. Moreover, as comparative research has indicated, there is relative autonomy between the most relevant areas of gender (in)equality: a strong presence of women in the area of political decision-making, as in the Scandinavian countries, does not necessarily translate into comparable equality in the area of economic decision-making (Fornengo and Guadagnini 1999).[4] In fact, politics seems to have been more permeable to mainstreaming than economics, as far as participation in the decision-making process is concerned, although to very different degrees in the various countries. Thus we may witness the emergence of a gender gap not only within the two main areas of decision-making at the national and European level, but also between them. At the same time, at least at the national level, there is no clear causal link between an increase in women's participation in politics and the development of woman-friendly policies (Siim 1994). This further shakes the implicit assumptions of mainstreaming, and even empowering. While it is easy conceptually, if not practically, to set the goal of mainstreaming women, i.e. inserting women in decision-making positions and processes, it is much less easy to mainstream women's interests or a gender perspective. As a number of feminist scholars have argued, women's (like men's) interests cannot be defined in an objective or self-evident way; rather, they are historically, culturally and also class related. Thus, the contents – rather than the areas – of mainstreaming are open to conflicting definitions.

Hence, though the symbolic power of mainstreaming as a password should not be ignored, its meaning and use may differ widely between countries, as well as across the political spectrum. It may even help to shape and render explicit differences between women, as well as between women and men, and between men, with regard to what gender interests are and the best way of addressing them (see also O'Connor *et al.* 1999). This might well be an unforeseen, but not necessarily negative, effect of mainstreaming and of having constitutionalized gender equality. Gender issues have become part of the European public agenda, and therefore the controversies which surround them, as well as the implicit assumptions concerning them, can no longer be kept from the public discourse.

Fragmentation and displacement of decision-making

Analyses of the effects of the growing importance of supranational bodies and the reorganization of traditional decision-making processes in the era of globalization point out that this phenomenon has various implications. It tends to weaken the arenas in which interdependent actors could traditionally express their interests, but creates new public arenas in which they can negotiate, as in the case of trade unions and entrepreneurs. It also weakens, or reduces, the role of the nation-state, while increasing that of regions and metropolitan cities (Mendras 1997).

Here I wish to identify those phenomena which particularly affect the democratic process and therefore the civil and political rights of citizens. The most relevant, in my view, among those specifically encouraged and promoted by the Union itself, are: (1) the systematic recourse to the subsidiarity principle; (2) the strengthening of various forms of social partnership; (3) the systematic recourse to forms of concerted decision-making processes ("concertation") which involve various social actors outside the institutional bodies.

All these phenomena can be seen as ways of broadening social participation by citizens beyond the institutional sites and bodies, of valorizing the competencies of those who would otherwise remain outside relevant decision-making processes, of activating and giving responsibility to the various actors in civil society and local communities. To some degree, these phenomena may be interpreted as strengthening opportunities for an actor-rich civil society at the local, state and European level. With regard to the last policy, in particular, the formal and informal acknowledgement by the Commission and positive incentives to the creation of interest groups, networks and lobbies, has helped to create (for the moment in a top-down way) a sort of "European civil society" which spills over also into national and local civil societies.[5] More generally, they are part of the recent transformations in the EU governance, particularly after Maastricht (Liebert 1999).

It could also be argued that these phenomena create more opportunities for women to make their voice heard, both individually – as experts – and in an organized way, than was normally possible through the traditional channels of political participation in most European countries. Yet, these same phenomena can also be seen as an example of the worst aspect of democratic deficit – lack of transparency and allocation of power to non-representative bodies. I will mention three aspects in particular which could be problematic from the point of view of democracy.

First, "social concertation" *de facto* weakens the role of parliamentary decision-making, as it allocates political negotiating power to bodies – trade unions, entrepreneurs' associations, churches, charities, associations of various kinds – which have not received a mandate to negotiate on all the matters they are in fact called upon to do so.[6] Enlarging the number of interest groups and associations invited to sit at the concertation table does not solve this problem – it may simply transform parliamentary democracy into a sort of corporate democracy. Second, these groups and associations may be, and often are, less democratic than parliamentary bodies with respect to their forms of representation and agenda setting. This phenomenon may be strengthened by their growing political and international importance, as their visibility in the public arena adds to the attraction of their leadership positions. This has marginalizing effects for women. Even within volunteer associations, it has been noticed that although women make up a substantial part of the rank and file or the intermediate organizational positions, the reverse is more likely to be true at the top level.

These phenomena may have different impacts on the various countries due to specific traditions in policy-making and in dealing with social partnerships, as well as the different way gender relations have developed. But an aspect which should not be overlooked is that in countries where women have succeeded in achieving a near to equal quota in formal politics, they may now discover that the increasing recourse to concertation processes strengthens extra-parliamentary bodies and hence the strongly masculine control on decision-making processes in the European Union as well as in their own countries.

Third, the subsidiarity principle is far from being unambiguous. While in matters concerning everyday life and social rights, it appears to acknowledge the role of national states as against the EU, of local as against central government, intermediate social bodies and organized civil society as against state or public intervention, and families as against communities, it also seems to declare the irrelevance of these same issues from the point of view of European integration and European citizenship. In countries where social rights are little and/or unevenly acknowledged, such an approach can weaken demands for reform, particularly when it conflicts with the desire for greater local autonomy and power. The emphasis on civil society and its formal and informal institutions, including the family, also seems to ignore the fact that not all citizens have the resources to organize themselves or collect adequate information to sustain action, and that communities, churches, families and so forth may have very asymmetrical internal power relations. "To be sent back" to one's own community, family, network of private associations may well be, for some citizens and in some circumstances, quite a let down and not improve their capacities and rights.

Concluding remarks

The ambivalence I have sketched above is real. The development or interpretation of the processes of European unification is not at all straightforward. What will happen in the future will depend on the interactions and reactions of the various actors: those who are acknowledged, and those who are not, or not yet enough, as well as those who will constitute themselves in the wake of these and other processes. This means that there is space for social actors to negotiate the meaning of these processes and to influence the direction they take. In other words, it is precisely the ambiguity of the indications coming from what we could call the "dual register" of the process of European unification – simultaneously widening and restricting the opportunities – which calls for a conscious mobilization of social actors and actresses to interpret and construct the political agenda, identify the rules of each specific arena, and possibly draw up specific, well spelled out objectives to be discussed and evaluated through agreed-upon indicators, in the same way as the economic ones.

In this process, it is possible not only that the gender imbalances in the process of European citizenship-making will be revealed, but that the diversity of interests between European women will become a much more explicit issue than it is at present. This is already apparent in the much weaker support given to the expanding role of the EU by Scandinavian women compared to Scandinavian men, as well as other European women, particularly those living in more gender unbalanced countries. They in fact suspect that they will lose in Europe what they have earned in their own country. The persistent gender imbalance in the European Parliament testifies that this fear has real grounds, further strengthened by the virtual absence of women – including Nordic women – in the European economic institutions. Thus, it is not paradoxical that Scandinavian citizens, and particularly women, resist the extension of the Union's range of action in the social sphere, while this is perceived by women in other countries as a way of giving their national claims a more solid basis. The proposed enlargement of the Union will multiply these divergent interests. This might further weaken the basis for a widespread legitimization of the EU as a common polity.

The "gender lens" thus renders clearer at least three of the ambivalent features which characterize theories as well as perceptions of citizenship in Europe: its being nation (and some time even local) specific but at the same time increasingly defined also by supranational rules and conditions (e.g. also Roth 2000); its being a multi-layered (well beyond Marshall's three dimensions) and dynamic phenomenon, therefore always the result of situated provisional balances between different dimensions and contents; its being both an institutional, principle-based, framework and a contested and negotiated arena between various actors and institutions. But precisely because of the sharpness with which these phenomena appear in the case of women and of the gender dimensions of citizenship, the ambivalence and contradictions themselves within the European space, the emergence to visibility of different gender and women's interests, may help render more fluid, more negotiable, more open to scrutiny and redefinition the hidden or open agendas which formally or informally shape gender experiences and relations at the national and European level. In this perspective, the role both of European institutions and the creation of what I have called a "European civil society" may become a crucial arena in which new points of view may be elaborated and issues redefined (see also Liebert 1999). If some kind of benchmarking in the area of gender equality were ever developed, it would be first of all a means to compare and assess not only and primarily degrees of equality, but meanings and means to achieve it, beyond a simplistic best practice approach oblivious of the contextual nature of any social practice. At the same time, alliances may be created which "mainstream" women's interests and a gender perspective in other fields than those traditionally focused on – and vice versa. The "unforeseen" alliances in the protest against WTO, whatever one may think of the protest itself, testify how new problems are not only creating new actors, but also re-arranging old ones.

Notes

1 On the distinction between these two terms see Shaver 1990; O'Connor *et al.* 1999: 12. On gender social policy regimes see also Lewis 1992, 1997, Ostner and Lewis 1995.
2 This seems to be also the conclusion of March 1, 2000 Commission's report on the implementation at the national and EU levels of the 1996 directive on a more balanced presence of women and men in decision-making process.
3 Mr Kalanke made recourse to the European Court because the Land of Bremen had decided to promote Ms Glissman instead of him. The two candidates had identical qualifications and the Land had taken its decision on the basis of an equal opportunity law which stipulated that, in hiring and promoting, when candidates had identical qualifications but were of different sex, preference should be given to women candidates, if in that area women were under-represented. The Court declared that the German law was discriminatory and therefore Mr Kalanke rightfully considered himself discriminated against on the basis of gender.
4 This study is based on the data and material collected by the "European Network on Women in Decision Making" as part of a Commission sponsored research project.
5 For example, in order to participate in European networks, formerly dispersed groups at the national level may coordinate themselves, develop a common language and even choose to present themselves to local or central governments as a unified actor when seen as appropriate to do so.
6 This is a criticism leveled against the role of concertation in Italy, where extra-parliamentary agreements can involve child allowances, the National Health System, the state university system, the funding of research and so forth.

References

Allen, J., Cars, G., and Madanipour, A. (1999) "Introduction," in Madanipou, A., Cars, G., and Allen, J. (eds) *Social Exclusion in European Cities*, London: Jessica Kingsley Publishers: 7–24.

Barbera, M. (1999) "L'eccezione e la regola, ovvero l'eguaglianza come apologia dello status quo," in B. Beccalli (ed.) *Donne in quota*, Milan, Feltrinelli: 91–129.

Crouch, C. (1999) *Social Change in Western Europe*, Oxford: Oxford University Press.

Delanty, G. (1998) "L'identità europea come costruzione sociale," in L. Passerini (ed.) *Identità culturale europea*, Florence: La Nuova Italia: 47–66.

Emerson, M. (1998) *Redrawing the Map of Europe*, London: Macmillan.

Fagnani, J. and Rassat, E. (1997) "Garde d'enfant et/ou femme à tout faire? Les employées des familles bénéficiaires de l'AGED," no. 49, septembre.

Fornengo, G. and Guadagnini, M. (1999) *Un soffitto di cristallo? Le donne nelle posizioni decisionali in Europa*, Ivrea: Fondazione Adriano Olivetti.

Gough, I., Bradshaw, J., Ditch, J., Eardle, T., and Whiteford, P. (1997) "Social assistance in OECD countries," *Journal of Social Policy* 7, 1, February: 17–44.

Guibentif, P. and Bouget, D. (1997) *Minimum Income Policies in the European Union*, Uniao das Mutualidades Portuguesas: Lisbon.

Habermas, J. (1992) "Citizenship and national identity: Some reflections on the future of Europe," *Praxis International* 12: 1–19.

Kravaritou, Y. (1997) "La cittadinanza europea e le donne," in Bimbi, F. and Del Re, A. (eds) *Genere e democrazia*, Torino: Rosenberg & Sellier.

Leira, A. (1999) "Introduction," to Id (ed.) *Family Change, Practices, Policies and Values*, Stamford, Conn.: JAI Press: ix–xxii.

—— (1992) *Welfare States and Working Mothers*, Cambridge: Cambridge University Press.

Lewis, J. (ed.) (1998) Gender, Social Care and Welfare State Restructuring in Europe, London: Ashgate.

—— (1997) "Gender and welfare regimes: Further thoughts," Social Politics 4: 160–77.

—— (1992) "Gender and the development of welfare regimes," Journal of European Social policy, 2, 3: 159–73.

Liebert, U. (1999) "Gender politics in the European Union," European Societies 1, 2: 197–240.

—— (1997) The Gendering of Euro-Skepticism: Public Discourses and Support to the EU in a Cross-National Comparison, Institute for European Studies, Cornell University, Working Paper no. 97.2.

Lister, R. (1997) Citizenship. Feminist Perspectives, London: Macmillan.

Meehan, E. (1993) Citizenship and the European Community, London: Sage.

Mendras, H. (1997) L'Europe des Européens. Sociologie de l'Europe Occidentale, Paris: Gallimard.

O'Connor, J. S., Orloff, A. S., and Shaver, S. (1999) States, Markets, Families, Cambridge: Cambridge University Press.

OECD (1994) Caring for Frail Elderly People, Social Policy Studies 14, OECD, Paris.

Ostner, I. and Lewis, J. (1995) "Gender and the evolution of European social policies," in Leibfried, S. and Pierson, P. (eds) European Social Policy: Between Fragmentation and Integration, Washington DC: Brookings: 159–93.

Roth, R. (2000) "Chances of new local policies in European cities – time of civil society," in Jyvrvela, M. and Ward, D. (eds) From Social Exclusion to Participation, Action Research Community Work, University of Jyäskylä, Working paper no. 106: 19–39.

Rusconi, G. E. (1998) "Cittadinanza e costituzione," in L. Passerini (ed.) Identità culturale europea, Florence: La Nuova Italia: 133–56.

Sainsbury, D. (1996) Gender, Equality and Welfare States, Cambridge: Cambridge University Press.

Saraceno, C. (ed.) (1998) ESOPO – Evaluation of Social Policies at the Local Urban Level. Income Support for the Able Bodied, Final Report to the DG XII, Turin.

Saraceno, C. (1997a) "Family change, family policies and the restructuring of welfare," in Family, Market and Community, Social Policy Studies, no. 21, OECD, Paris: 81–100.

—— (1997b) "Gender and Europe: National differences, resources and impediments for the construction of a common interest for European women," in Klausen, J. and Tilly, L. Markets, States and Social Citizenship: European Economic and Political Integration. 1900–1995, New York: Rowman & Littlefields: 249–66.

Scheiwe, K. (1994) "Labour market, welfare state and family institutions: The links to mothers' poverty risks," Journal of European Social Policy 4, 3: 201–34.

Schmitter, P. (1996) "Some alternative futures for the European polity and their implications for European public policy," in Meny, Y., Miller, P., and Quermonne, J. (eds) Adjusting to Europe. The Impact of the European Union on National Institutions and Policies, London: Routledge.

Shaver, S. (1990): Gender, Social Policy Regimes and the Welfare State, SPRC Discussion Paper no. 16, Social Policy Research Center, University of New South Wales, Sydney 1990.

Siim, B. (1994) "Engendering democracy: Social citizenship and political participation for women in Scandinavia," in Social Politics 3: 286–305.

Ungerson, C. (1997) "Social politics and the commodification of care," Social Politics 4, 3: 362—82.

Varkas, E. (1997) "Una cittadinanza in quanto donna?" Elementi del debattito europeo: parità versus uguaglianza, in F. Bimbi and A. Del Re (eds) Genere e democrazia, Torino: Rosenberg & Sellier.

Waerness, K. (1998) "The Changing 'Welfare Mix' in Childcare and in Care for the Elderly," in Lewis, J. (ed.) (1998) *Gender, Social Care and Welfare State Restructuring in Europe*, London: Ashgate: 207–28.

Weiler, J. H. (1998) "Excursus 1: Gli ideali dell'integrazione europea" and "Excursus 4: La cittadinanza europea," in Biagiotti, V. B. and Weiler, J. H. (eds) *L'Unione Europea*, Bologna: Il Mulino: 24–42 and 666–75.

Williams, F. (1989) *Social Policy. A Critical Introduction: Issues of Race, Gender and Class*, Cambridge: Polity Press.

Women of Europe. Supplements (1992) "The Position of Women on the Labour Market. Trends and Developments in the Twelve Member States of the European Community, 1983–1990," no. 36.

Zincone, G. (1992) *Da sudditi a cittadini*, Bologna: Il Mulino.

Part III

Working on Europe
Perspectives and institutions

8 Missing a European public sphere[1]

Jürgen Gerhards

In December 1999 the European Council resolved to take up membership negotiations with Bulgaria, Latvia, Lithuania, Malta, Romania, Slovakia, and Turkey
after already having taken them up with Estonia, Poland, Slovenia, Hungary, the
Czech Republic and Cyprus in 1998. As a result, the EU is to be expanded by thir-
teen countries. If one proceeds from the premise that the difficulties of integration
are proportionate to the differences between EU countries on the one hand and
candidates for accession on the other, then one can expect that eastward enlargement of the EU will not be an easy task. Not only is there a smoldering foreign
policy and military conflict between Greece and Turkey, not only are the democratic traditions quite different in these countries, above all there are great
economical differences between some candidates (e.g. Romania and Bulgaria)
and the present EU countries with consequences in terms of, among others, possible migration movements and transfer payments.

But the European Council not only resolved an enlargement of the European
Union but also speeded up the internal consolidation of integration. The size and
composition of the European Commission, the vote distribution in the Council,
and the range of voting with a qualified majority are to be changed and expanded.
The consolidation is supposed to increase the EU's ability to function; that means
in essence further allocation of competences to the level of the EU at the cost of
sovereignty of the member states. In the future, the citizens of the member countries will be even more directly subject to the EU's decisions and less to those of
their respective nation-states. The EU is thus increasingly a supranational regime
whose decisions will directly affect the citizens' lives.

It is astonishing, in view of the dramatic changes and potential conflicts in connection with the EU's planned eastward enlargement and internal consolidation,
how little the public sphere reacted to the resolutions of the European Council.
Indeed, the media reported about it comprehensively as about every other
European summit meeting but there were and there are no broad debates about
the pros and cons of an enlargement and consolidation, about possible conflicts,
decision blockades in the Council, migration movements, etc. The media's attention quickly turned to new subjects when the summit meeting was over. It is by
example of the Helsinki resolutions that this article discusses the near absence of
a European public sphere.

The theoretical approach that I have chosen in order to analyze the absence of a European public sphere is a macro-sociological perspective that is treated in the literature under the term of globalization. I will analyze the development of the public sphere in conjunction with the development of other subsystems of a society, especially the economic and the political system. The line of argument will be laid out in the following steps. In a first step, I define the terms globalization and transnationalization. I then confine myself in the following empirical sections to analyzing the fields of economy, politics, and the public sphere of the Federal Republic of Germany, because only for these fields is empirical data available. I will analyze in the second section to what extent the economy has been transnationalized over time (1950–96). In the third section I pursue the question whether politics have been transnationalized over time and – in respect to politics and economy – whether the markets have run away from political control The results will show that there indeed has been a moderate process of transnationalization of the economy, but this turns out to be primarily a process of Europeanization that is accompanied by a parallel process of Europeanization of the political system. In the fourth section I pursue the question to which extent the public sphere has become transnationalized or Europeanized and Europeanized politics have run away from being controlled by a still nationally based public sphere. The results will show that the development of a European public sphere really does lag behind the process of a Europeanized political system. I examine the causes of the empirically diagnosed lag of a European public sphere in the fifth section in order to draw a conclusion in the sixth section.

1. What does globalization or transnationalization mean?

Globalization refers to the idea that we live in a globalized world or are on the way towards a globalized society. The boom of the concept of globalization is – as so often with fashionable concepts – connected with the diagnosis of a crisis. The potential crisis that is ascribed to the processes of globalization results mainly from assumed control problems of the political system. While politics – and with that political control – is still based on and limited by the borders of the nation-state, economics as well as other parts of society have liberated themselves from the confines of the nation-state and have become globalized. The previously existing congruence between economic borders of trade and the political borders of regulations has dissolved. Enterprises invest where conditions for high returns are the best but pay taxes where the tax rate is the lowest; stock holders are supposedly withdrawing more and more from politics that are bound to national borders.

In spite of the wide circulation of the term globalization there is no consensus about what is to be understood by it. I think the following specifications of the term make sense.

1   The term globalization will be substituted in the following text by that of transnationalization (de Swaan 1995); other authors speak of denationalization of a society (Zürn 1998; Beisheim *et al.* 1999). This change of terms has

the advantage of defining a starting point for developments – namely societies constituted as nation-states – and at the same time leaving the reference point of the development open: the term transnationalization does not conceptually prejudge whether societies are empirically globalizing, Europeanizing, or Americanizing themselves.

2   Furthermore, I will work on the principle that nationally constituted societies can be best comprehended in their internal structures as consisting of various fields or subsystems: economics, politics, public sphere, science, and art, among others, each forms a different subsystem in a nationally constituted society. When examining a society's transnationalization with the concept of differentiation into various subsystems, it allows us to distinguish various grades and levels of each subsystem's transnationalization and to examine their relationships to one another.

3   Transnationalization is defined as a relational concept in accordance with the early work of Karl Deutsch (1959) that relates the interactions or transactions within a nation-state to interactions and transactions with units from the outside. Defining the term in such a way takes the fact into account that in addition to transnational communication internal (national) communication can have increased as well, which would not be taken into consideration in an absolute measurement of transnationalization processes.

In sum, transnationalization is defined as the ratio between outer interaction and internal interaction of a social subsystem of a society. The process category transnationalization of a society would mean that the subsystems of a nation-state have increasingly become transnational in the sense that the shares of border-crossing interactions have increased, whereby it is an open question what the reference point of the development is. I have oriented my empirical analyses in the following sections by this definition, but I limit the analysis to the three subsystems – politics, economy, and the public sphere – in the Federal Republic of Germany and ask to what degree they have been transnationalized and how the relationships to one another can be qualified.

2. Level and development of transnationalization of the economy in the Federal Republic of Germany

Together with Jörg Rössel I have attempted to specify empirically the degree and the development of transnationalization processes of some subsystems of German society – art, science, economics, and politics – of the last forty years (cf. Gerhards and Rössel 1999). Here I will concentrate on the field of economics and the transactions that cross the border of the nationally constituted society of Germany from without (to within). Similar to other subsystems, the field of economics is differentiated into different sub-fields. Therefore it seems appropriate to speak of an inner differentiation of the economic system and to distinguish between labor market, market for goods and services, investment market and stock market.

The development of the different subsystems of the economic system and their level of transnationalization can be seen in Figure 8.1.[2] The level of transnationalization can vary from 0 percent to 100 percent. At 0 percent the respective subsystem remains completely closed nationally, there are no interactions to the external world, and at 100 percent there is a complete transnationalization.

The investment market shows the lowest level of transnationalization. We have calculated the transnationalization of production by the percentage of foreign direct investments in relation to total investments in Germany. At the time of the last survey in 1996 the percentage was 2.21. Conversely, almost 98 percent of the direct investments were domestic ones. For the labor market we calculated the percentage of foreign workers in relation to the total employees in Germany from 1955 to 1996. The percentage of foreign workers came to 5.72 at the time of the last survey in 1996. The labor market also remains limited within the nation-state. The level of transnationalization is higher for goods and services. For goods and services we calculated the percentage of the total imports in relation to the gross national product. In 1995 this quota came to 24.6 percent. In order to measure the transnationalization processes in the financial market, we calculated the share of foreign stocks sold in Germany to the total sales of stocks in Germany. The percentage of foreign stocks in relation to total stocks sold in Germany was 51.9 percent in 1996.

Figure 8.1 makes two analyses possible. On the one hand, one can compare different markets to one another. This comparison demonstrates that different segments of an economic system may have quite a varied level of transnationalization. The markets for labor and direct investments (transfer of companies) are

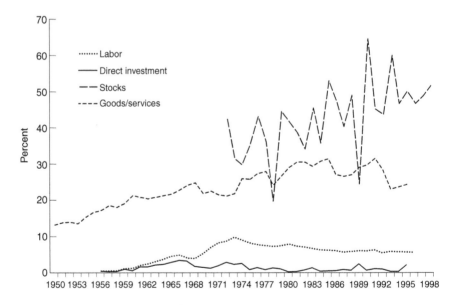

Figure 8.1 Transnationalization of the economy.

at the lower end of the scale, markets for goods and services in the middle, the financial markets at the upper end. Except for the stock market, one cannot very well speak of a transnationalization of the economy since the majority of the interactions remain limited within the nation-state. On the other hand, Figure 8.1 shows us the development of each economic segment over time. If one compares only the beginning and ending points then one can see that the German economy has indeed – with the exception of foreign direct investments – become increasingly transnationalized. As a rule, the process unfolds – with the exception of the financial market that always shows a high volatility – rather slowly and steadily, the rates of increase in all three segments are relatively small. As compared with the public debate about transnationalization the real development is actually rather slow and continuous, but still moving in the direction of an increasing transnationalization.

The fact that border-crossing interactions and transactions take place does not say anything about where these transactions come from, and where they go to. Where do the goods and services, the workers, the investments, the stocks, etc. come from that are imported? We examined the various transnational communications and transactions of the different sub-fields of the economic system as to how they were concentrated, first, on the EU countries and second, on Europe as a whole (for exact data cf. Gerhards and Rössel 1999). Approximately one-third of the foreign nationals in the work force come from EU countries, 87.8 percent come from Europe as a whole, including Turkey that is a candidate for membership in the EU. Almost two-thirds of the imported goods and services come from EU countries, and 71.6 percent come from Europe as a whole. And even when observing foreign direct investments in Germany, nearly half come from EU countries and almost two-thirds from Europe. Of the German direct investments abroad almost two-thirds go to the EU or somewhat more than two-thirds to the whole of Europe. We see that there is indeed a process of economic transnationalization which is, for the most part, a process of Europeanization with a strong concentration on the EU (cf. Hirst and Thompson 1998).

I draw the following interim conclusion: (1). The time comparison shows us that the markets for goods and services, stocks and partially also the labor market are moving in the direction of an increasing transnationalization; however, this process is rather slow and continuous and not quick and erratic, in contrast to the political and scientific debates on globalization. (2) Economic transnationalization means not globalization but rather Europeanization.

3. Transnationalization of the political system

The crisis diagnosis, which is connected to the globalization thesis, presumes that the transnationalization processes dodge the controlling powers of society's politics insofar as political control must stop at the nation-state's border whereas the interactions of other subsystems proceed increasingly across borders. A possible answer to the political control dilemma caused by the transnationalization of the economy is that the political system transnationalizes itself and that the authority for collectively binding decisions is shifted to a higher level of transnational institutions. The odds for political control of transnational interactions would become increasingly favorable provided that the political system transnationalizes, namely in the direction of a Europeanization because this is really where the transnationalization of the economy has moved to. A Europeanization of politics could thus absorb a large part of transnationalization and thereby reestablish the congruence between the economic and the political system.

This is what appears to be happening with the increasing integration of the European Union. The members of the EU have handed over a part of their national sovereignty to the EU: the nation-states and their citizens are immediately affected by its resolutions; European law supersedes national law; the Commission supervises the implementation of its resolutions and the European Court of Justice can install sanctions upon member countries for non-compliance (Lepsius 1990).

One can attempt to determine empirically the extent of the nation-states' delegation of sovereignty to the EU. If one wishes to stick with the principle of a relational measurement one must relate the European decisions to the national political decisions. Marianne Beisheim *et al.* (1999) surveyed various indices of transnationalization of different fields.

For the political system they calculated the ratio of national decisions to European decisions. Figure 8.2 illustrates the ratio of laws and resolutions passed by the Council of the European Union to the laws passed by the German Parliament (Bundestag) over time. Unfortunately, the time series of the surveyed data only extends back to 1989.

Figure 8.2 shows that the ratio between decisions by the nation-state and EU-decisions has changed in favor of the EU over time which is an indication of the shift of political sovereignty from the nation-state to the EU. Apart from the increase in the proportion of European decisions in relation to decisions on the nation-state level there is an extension of the EU through the creation of a new system of political institutions.[3]

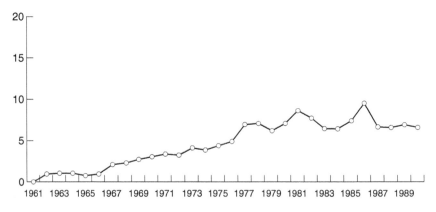

Figure 8.2 Transnationalization of the political system (laws and resolutions passed by the European Council in relation to the laws passed by the German Parliament).

Are politics therefore overcome by the supposed globalization processes of the economy? The empirical results show that the political system has been transnationalized in the same direction as the economy, indeed politics have decisively contributed to the Europeanization of the economy. Transnationalization is foremostly a Europeanization of both domains. Control problems can be resolved by this congruence between politics and economy, or at least the conditions for such a solution have been created.

4. Transnationalization of the public sphere

Before I present empirical data on the transnationalization of the public sphere I must draw attention to some theoretical remarks on the relationship between the public sphere and the political system. A democratic political system means that the production of collectively binding decisions is linked to the citizens' interests. In a representative democracy such a coupling occurs, as is generally known, first and foremost by elections. The citizens of a certain territory elect at periodic intervals persons who take up governing positions and who are authorized to make and enforce generally binding decisions for them. However, these elected persons can also be dismissed from their governing positions at the next election if the citizens do not feel adequately represented.

In order for citizens to be able to make or revise an election decision they must have the chance to acquire adequate information on their representatives and their competitors as well as their actions and platforms. Correspondingly, Robert Dahl (1989: 111 f.) calls the chance to acquire adequate information one of the criteria for a democratic process and terms it "enlightened understanding". It is exactly this function of imparting adequate information that is, among others, the role of a political public sphere. A great number of studies have shown us that, above all, the mass media are the central institutions of information supplies between citizens and politics and that the citizens make adequate use of this possibility: over 80 percent of German citizens get their daily information on politics via one of the media of television, radio, and newspapers, many use several media daily to get their political information (cf. Berg and Kiefer 1996: 183). The mass media are therefore the citizens' most important sources of information on politics.

On the level of the nation-state there exists a congruence between citizens, decision makers, and the public sphere. There is a congruence between the decision makers and citizens insofar as those who can elect the governing powers are also those that are subject to the decisions made by those governing powers. There is a congruence between the public sphere and politics insofar as the media spreads information on the decision makers and their competitors and the citizens can form their opinions based on this information.

This congruence may have begun to sway with the transnationalization of the political system (in the sense of shifting power from the nation-states to the EU) which can become manifest in a democracy deficit on the one hand and a deficit of the public sphere on the other. The *democracy deficit* of the EU is to be found in the fact the addressees of decisions by the EU are not identical to the "demos" that has elected the decision makers: the European Council as an assembly of the member-countries' heads of government and the Council of the European Union consisting of the member countries' ministers have not been elected by the European people directly but have been indirectly legitimized via national elections. This is discussed commonly in the literature as the EU's democracy deficit (for a systematic summary see Benz 1998).

A *deficit of the public sphere* exists when more and more political decisions are not made by the nation-states but by the EU, but public debate is about national issues and does not, or only to a limited degree, inform about European decisions and discussions. The consequence would be that the citizens are not adequately informed about the discussions and decisions that they are directly affected by. An "enlightened understanding" in Dahl's sense would therefore be unlikely. In the following, I will concentrate on this deficit of the public sphere.

That political decisions have shifted from the nation-state to the European level was described in the previous section. Whether the public sphere in Germany has been Europeanized in its reporting is an empirically open question. One can imagine two different models of a European public sphere: the model of a cross-national European public sphere on the one hand and the concept of the Europeanization of national public spheres on the other (cf. Gerhards 1993).[4] In the following I will only discuss the concept of a Europeanizing of national public spheres. Empirically it is quite improbable that a cross-national European public sphere will develop (cf. Gerhards 2000).

Up to now, we have not collected any time-series data on media coverage that could help to describe the rate of transnationalization and Europeanization of the public sphere; but thankfully we can fall back on data that Hans Mathias Kepplinger gathered (Kepplinger 1998).[5] Kepplinger reconstructed the reports on politics in the quality newspapers *Frankfurter Allgemeine Zeitung*, *Süddeutsche Zeitung*, and *WELT* from 1951 to 1995. Kepplinger differentiates in his analysis various themes to report on. The following thematic fields were aggregated into three upper categories: (1) national German affairs (including those concerning East German–West German relations); (2) themes from the field of European relations; and (3) themes from the field of other international relations. Figure 8.3 shows the development of these three thematic fields over time.

On average, 60.4 percent of the subjects that were reported on in the analyzed media had to do with German internal affairs, so 39.6 percent were transnational subjects. This very high level of transnationalization of media coverage is due to the fact that only quality newspapers were analyzed; their transnational orientation is much higher than that of average newspapers (cf. Deutsch 1959).

If one examines in a first step the share of German themes to transnational themes (European *and* non-European subjects) then one cannot make out a clear direction of change. In the period from 1960 to 1985 the proportion of transnational themes does increase so that one can speak of a slight increase in the transnationalization of the West German public sphere, but from 1986 on (more exactly: 1989 with the Wall coming down and the reunification in the following year) there was a strong increase in national themes at the expense of

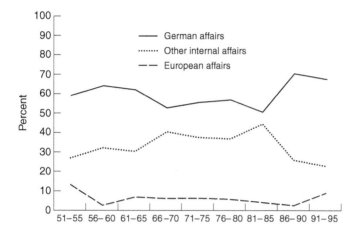

Figure 8.3 Europe in the mass media.

transnational themes. In fact, the fixation of the public sphere on national issues reached an as yet untold high-point in German history.[6] At least after 1986 the West German public sphere's attention developed in the opposite direction as the economy and the political system did, i.e. the public sphere became fixed on internal matters while the economic actions and political decisions transnationalized.

This change looks slightly different if one compares the European themes to other transnational themes and internal German affairs. The European themes are the ones of all three thematic fields which got the least media attention. Their average proportion value was 6.9 percent over the years. The media's attention decreased continuously in the period 1961–90, in order to return lately to the value of the period of 1961–65. So, while political decisions became increasingly transnationalized and above all Europeanized, the public sphere has continued to lag behind this development and still lingers within the nation-state. Hence, the data gathered by Hans Mathias Kepplinger does not show a Europeanization of Germany's national public sphere. However, one must bear in mind that Kepplinger's content analysis was not laid out for the questions analyzed here so that my interpretations are to be taken with caution. More precise studies are necessary in order to examine whether the conclusions drawn here can be confirmed empirically.

5. Possible reasons for the absence of a European public sphere

If the preliminary impression should be confirmed that the national public sphere has remained fixed mainly on national issues and has not become Europeanized, then the question arises as to the reasons for these findings. The media's attention to issues generally depends on three factors: the motivation for public relations work and activities by collective actors; the news value of the information; and finally journalistic activities. In reference to all of these factors one can diagnose deficits with regard to the reporting on European issues.

1   The Commission's orientation towards the media is rather weak due to structural reasons. The commissioners are not elected by Europe's citizens; they primarily need backing by their respective national governments that nominated them, and do not require to be supported by citizen voters. Therefore the necessity to acquire approval from the citizens via the media is not given, and the Commission's structurally caused abstinence from the public sphere is the result. In addition, the Commission develops the propositions in the law-making process in closed session, the public being excluded. The propositions are represented – following the collegial principle – by the Commission as a whole. The exclusion of the public as well as the collegial principle of the Commission are factors that hardly favor the Commission's publicity orientation. Finally, the Commission's public relations are not homogenized and synchronized enough and are partially also not organized professionally (Gramberger and Lehmann 1995; Meyer 1999). Christoph Olaf Meyer recounts that while the budget for public relations tripled from 34.9 million to 102.5 million Euro in the years 1992 to 1998 the structural deficits in public relations work that are based on its fragmented structure were not eliminated. There is a similar diagnosis with regard to professionalism in the Commission's public relations activities (Gramberger and Lehmann: 1995; Gramberger 1997).

It is true that the institutionalized counterweight to the Commission and the Council of European Union, the European Parliament, has a stronger publicity orientation, but it is only equipped with weak power resources to make decisions and decision intentions of the Council and the Commission to publicly debated issues. It is true that the European Parliament's rights have been extended but it still remains a relatively weak institution in comparison to the Commission and the Council.

2   The European Union has been described by various authors as being a dynamic multi-level system (cf. Jachtenfuchs and Kohler-Koch 1996). By this the authors mean that there is a pluralization of control levels that extends from the local level via the nation-states up to the different institutions of the EU. Intertwining relations such as these do not easily reveal a distinct actor who alone is competent for making decisions and to whom responsibility can be attributed (Lepsius 1997). Therefore, the important personalization of politics for media resonance is hampered. In addition, the very complex decision-making processes of the EU that are ruled by an administrative rationale (Bach 1999) are hardly transparent and are lacking in many news-relevant factors on which the media orient the selection of their information. So ultimately the EU remains without profile and overly complex and this impedes media reports on it.

3   Finally, reporting on issues depends on journalistic activities. To my knowl-
    edge there is no empirical data available at this time as to whether these are
    different or weaker in Brussels than in Berlin or other capitals (for England cf.
    Morgan 1995). For the beginning of the 1990s I found in a small field study
    that the German media institutions were quite weakly represented in Brussels
    (Gerhards 1993) and respectively the journalists' research activities were
    very limited with regard to personnel.

6. Conclusion and prospects

The empirical analyses have shown that the markets for goods and services, stocks
and partially also the labor market demonstrate as a rule slowly moving trends
towards an increase in transnationalization. These transnationalization processes
in the economic system are not globalization processes but primarily
Europeanization processes. One can also find transnationalization processes in the
field of politics; moreover, the empirical findings show that politics has been
transnationalized in the same direction as the economy. The European unification
process means a continuous shift of national sovereignty to the institutions of the
EU. This congruence between politics and economy creates at least the conditions
to resolve a political control of economic problems. The public sphere has developed in a different way. Even though the empirical data situation is more scant
here, the findings show that the public sphere is still nationally bound: the media
does not increasingly report on Europe over time. There is an incongruence
between a Europeanization of political decisions on the one hand and media coverage of European politics on the other. The public sphere lags behind the
transnationalization of the political system; it remains nationally bound while politics has been Europeanized.

Our empirical analyses of the public sphere end in 1995. Since then the focus
on European themes may have changed. Even the ratification of the Maastricht
Treaty had an enormous response in the media in those countries in which the
people were directly polled – as opposed to Germany. The Commission intensified
its public relations activities in the 1990s, especially after 1994; this is shown on
the one hand by the amount of budgetary means that were spent on information
politics (Gramberger 1997: 270) and on the other hand by the professionalization
of its public relations activities. Besides the Maastricht crisis it was the introduction of a new currency (EURO) in eleven states on one hand and the reproaches
of fraud and mismanagement against the European Commission led by President
Santer on the other, which have led to high rates of media coverage. What structural conditions triggered this media coverage and what can we learn from this for
the future development of the public sphere?

The fact that there was a wide public debate on the Maastricht Treaty in those
countries in which a referendum was held shows to what extent the democracy
deficit of the EU and the deficit of the public sphere are interdependent. At
those times when the citizens had greater opportunities to decide on European
matters the public debate on Europe was also much wider. Therefore one can

assume that a stronger democratization of the EU would lead to a Europeanization of the public sphere at the same time.[7] An extension of the citizens' decision power will force the political actors to legitimize their actions via the media. Similar to the extension and strengthening of the public sphere during the process of democratization of the nation-states one can expect that the democratization of the EU would speed up the development of a European public sphere. And democratization of the EU is on the EU's future agenda. Should this succeed then one can expect an intensifying of public debate on Europe in the media.

How the Santer Commission was forced to resign by public pressure in March 1999 is insofar an instructive case because other structural parameters create the media coverage. Christoph Olaf Meyer (2000) reconstructed the case. The media coverage resulted above all from changes in the cooperation between journalists in Brussels. The Commission's offenses were put on the agenda by the alliance of a multinational group of journalists who researched in terms of investigative journalism the disappearance of EU funds in Luxembourg, exchanging information, coordinating their publications in their respective native newspapers, therefore determining the coverage of the media, triggering intermedia-agenda-setting-effects, and protecting themselves from sanctions from their editorial departments and the Commission by forming a social group. In addition, there was close cooperation between the journalists and some of the representatives of the European Parliament which increased the pressure on the Commission. Whether this special type of alliance of the structurally "weak" (of journalists from different countries on the one hand and members of parliament on the other) will be durable and whether it will contribute to a Europeanization of the public sphere remains to be seen.

Notes

1   This article is an abridged and revised version of an article published in German (cf. Gerhards 2000) and was translated by Catya de Laczkovich. In the first part, I refer to data and analyses that I gathered and analyzed with Jörg Rössel (cf. Gerhards and Rössel 1999). I wish to thank Hans Mathias Kepplinger for providing me with the data on the development of media coverage in Germany.
2   The figures are taken from the statistical yearbooks, the capital market statistics and the monthly reports of the German Federal Bank.
3   Wolfgang Wessels (1997: 267) calculated various indices to measure the EU's increase in competence.
4   For further differentiation see van de Steeg 1999.
5   Holger Sievert (1998) presents the best overview on the current state of research in his dissertation. Unfortunately, the data that Sievert gathered does not allow for an analysis of the development of the media's attention on Europe.
5   The increase in domestic political themes in the period 1986–90 refers primarily to the years 1989 and 1990.
7   This is not a normative statement but a hypothesis. That a democratization of the EU will again be subject to prerequisites and many resulting problems is shown by, among others, Peter Graf Kielmannsegg (1996), Joseph Weiler (1991), and Fritz Scharpf (1998).

Bibliography

Bach, M. (1999) *Die Bürokratisierung Europas: Verwaltungseliten, Experten und politische Legitimation in Europa*, Frankfurt am Main: Campus.

Beck, U. (1997) *Was ist Globalisierung? Irrtümer des Globalismus – Antworten auf Globalisierung*, Frankfurt am Main: Suhrkamp.

Beisheim, M., Dreher, S., Walter, G., Zangl, B. and Zürn, M. (1999) *Im Zeitalter der Globalisierung? Thesen und Daten zur gesellschaftlichen und politischen Denationalisierung*, Baden-Baden: Nomos.

Beisheim, M., Dreher, S., Walter, G. and Zürn, M. (1997) "Globalisierung – Rhetorik oder Realität? Zum Stand der Denationalisierung in der G-7 und in der Bundesrepublik," 96–108, in W. Fricke (ed.) *Jahrbuch Arbeit und Technik*, Bonn: Dietz.

Benz, A. (1998) "Ansatzpunkte für ein europäisches Demokratiekonzept," 345–69, in B. Kohler-Koch (ed.) *Regieren in entgrenzten Räumen*, Sonderheft 29 der PVS, Opladen: Westdeutscher Verlag.

Berg, K. and Kiefer, M.-L. (1996) *Massenkommunikation V. Eine Langzeitstudie zur Mediennutzung 1964–1995*, Baden-Baden: Nomos.

Dahl, R. A. (1989) *Democracy and its Critics*, New Haven, London: Yale University Press.

Deutsch, K. W. (1959) "The Propensity to International Transactions," *Political Studies* 7, 137–54.

Eder, K., Hellmann, K.-U., and Schmidt, Th. (1998) "Regieren in Europa jenseits der öffentlichen Kommunikation? Eine Untersuchung zur Rolle von politischer Öffentlichkeit in Europa," 321–44, in B. Kohler-Koch (ed.) *Regieren in entgrenzten Räumen*, Sonderheft 29 der PVS, Opladen: Westdeutscher Verlag.

Gerhards, J. (1993) "Westeuropäische Integration und die Schwierigkeiten der Entstehung einer europäischen Öffentlichkeit," *Zeitschrift für Soziologie* 22, 96–110.

—— (2000) "Europäisierung von Ökonomie und Politik und die Trägheit der Entstehung einer europäischen Öffentlichkeit", in M. Bach (ed.) *Die Europäisierung nationaler Gesellschaften*, Sonderheft der Kölner Zeitschrift für Soziologie und Sozialpsychologie, Opladen: Westdeutscher Verlag.

Gerhards, J. and Rössel, J. (1999) "Zur Transnationalisierung der Gesellschaft der Bundesrepublik. Entwicklungen, Ursachen und mögliche Folgen für die europäische Integration," *Zeitschrift für Soziologie* 28, 325–44.

Gramberger, M. R. (1997) *Die Öffentlichkeitsarbeit der Europäischen Kommission 1952–1996. PR zur Legitimation von Integration?*, Baden-Baden: Nomos.

Gramberger, M. R. und Lehmann, I. (1995) "UN und EU: Machtlos im Kreuzfeuer der Politik? Informationspolitik zweier internationaler Organisationen im Vergleich," *Publizistik* 40, 186–204.

Grimm, D. (1995) *Braucht Europa eine Verfassung?*, München: Carl Friedrich von Siemens Stiftung.

Habermas, J. (1996) "Braucht Europa eine Verfassung? Eine Bemerkung zu Dieter Grimm," 185–91, in *Die Einbeziehung des Anderen*, Frankfurt am Main: Suhrkamp.

—— (1998) "Die postnationale Konstellation und die Zukunft der Demokratie" *Blätter für deutsche und internationale Politik*, 7, 804–17.

Held, D. (1995) *Democracy and the Global Order. From the Modern State to Cosmopolitan Governance*, Stanford: Stanford University Press.

Hirst, P. and Thompson, G. (1998) "Globalisierung? Internationale Wirtschaftsbeziehungen, Nationalökonomien und die Formierung von Handelsblöcken," 85–133, in U. Beck (ed.) *Politik der Globalisierung*, Frankfurt am Main: Suhrkamp.

Jachtenfuchs, M. and Kohler-Koch, B. (1996) "Einleitung: Regieren im dynamischen Mehrebenensystem," 15–44, in B. Kohler-Koch (ed.) Europäische Integration, Opladen: Westdeutscher Verlag.

Kepplinger, H. M. (1998) Die Demontage der Politik in der Informationsgesellschaft, Freiburg und München: Alber.

Kielmannsegg, P. Graf (1996) "Integration und Demokratie," 47–71, in M. Jachtenfuchs and B. Kohler-Koch (ed.) Europäische Integration, Opladen: Leske + Budrich.

Lepsius, M. R. (1990) "Der europäische Nationalstaat: Erbe oder Zukunft," 256–68, in Interessen, Ideen, Institutionen, Opladen: Westdeutscher Verlag.

—— (1997) "Bildet sich eine kulturelle Identität in der Europäischen Union?," Blätter für deutsche und internationale Politik, 8, 948–55.

Meyer, Chr. O. (1999) "Political Legitimacy and the Invisibility of Politics: Exploring the European Union's Communication Deficit," Journal of Common Market Studies 37, 617–39.

—— (2000) "Die Europäisierung politischer Öffentlichkeit: Länderübergreifender investigativer Journalismus und der Rücktritt der EU-Kommission," Paper presented to the Congress "Transnationale Kommunikation in Europa," Berlin, 29.10.1999.

Morgan, D. (1995) "British Media and European Union News. The Brussels News Beat and its Problems," European Journal of Communication 10, 321–41.

Münch, R. (1993) Das Projekt Europa. Zwischen Nationalstaat, regionaler Autonomie und Weltgesellschaft, Frankfurt am Main: Suhrkamp.

Perraton, J., Goldblatt, D., Held, D. and McGrew, A. (1998) "Die Globalisierung der Wirtschaft," 134–68, in U. Beck (ed.) Politik der Globalisierung, Frankfurt am Main: Suhrkamp.

Scharpf, F. W. (1998) "Demokratie in der transnationalen Politik," 228–53, in U. Beck (ed.) Politik der Globalisierung, Frankfurt am Main: Suhrkamp.

Sievert, H. (1998) Europäischer Journalismus, Opladen: Westdeutscher Verlag.

Swaan, A. de (1995) "Die soziologische Untersuchung der transnationalen Gesellschaft," Journal für Sozialforschung 35, 107–20.

Tumber, H. (1995) "Marketing Maastricht: The EU and News Management," Media, Culture and Society 17, 511–19.

van de Steeg, M. (1999) "A Case for a European Public Sphere. An Analysis of the Dutch and Spanish Newspaper Debates on EU Enlargement with the Central Eastern European Countries to Suggest Elements of a Transnational European Public Sphere." Paper presented to the Congress "Transnationale Kommunikation in Europa," Berlin, 29.10.1999.

Weiler, J. H. H. (1991) "Problems of Legitimacy in Post 1992 Europe," Außenwirtschaft 46, 411–56.

Wessels, W. (1997) "An Ever Closer Fusion? A Dynamic Macropolitical View on Integration Processes," Journal of Common Market Studies 35, 267–99.

Zürn, M. (1998) Regieren jenseits des Nationalstaates. Globalisierung und Denationalisierung als Chance, Frankfurt am Main: Suhrkamp.

9 Micro-foundations of postindustrial transformation

Gösta Esping-Andersen

The problem

To economists, a general equilibrium is theorized independently of time and place, whereas to most sociologists an equilibrium would only make sense in terms of a specific social era. When sociologists have attempted to emulate economists, they have usually gone wrong. Modernization theory and functionalist sociology of stratification are examples of ambitious, and ultimately unsuccessful, general equilibrium theorizing in the sense that both posited trans-historical laws of motion that overpower all else forever. But when sociologists have focused on temporal equilibria, they have often made insightful contributions that aid hypothesis development and invite empirical scrutiny. Postwar leitmotifs such as the "era of welfare capitalism," "industrialism," Lipset's (1960) "democratic class struggle," or the era of "Fordism" all contributed to the making of exciting research agendas. Unlike Parsons' (1951) AGIL scheme or Davis and Moore's (1945) principles of stratification, these were typically not meant as theories of eternity but as a way to synthesize the essence of an epoch. Good sociology is sensitive to variation rather than constants, and so it did not take long before we discovered varieties of Fordism or of welfare capitalism.

Our equilibria come and go and let us, for the moment, agree that we are presently poised in a no-man's land, passing from one stable societal order into another. The equilibrium we have left behind is exceedingly familiar to us all. We could give it a label pregnant with commonly shared meaning, like welfare capitalism, and its constituent prototypes, like the Parsonian nuclear family, the organizational man, or the standard production worker, were credible representatives of the norm. Our problem begins when the cornerstones of that order no longer stand, when the Parsonian nuclear family is no more typical, when the standard production worker has become minoritarian, and when the housewife has become a threatened species. At this point we have empirically recognized the end of an equilibrium, and we then face the challenge of how to identify and conceptualize the evolving new order. This new order is virtually impossible to encapsulate and label, because not even its precise contours are yet manifest. We see the emergence of unaccustomed rules, impulses, and dynamics, but that is all they are so far: unaccustomed.

In such a situation sociology is easily at a loss. The outcome may be unclear but, worse, even the process that takes us there is difficult to pin down. We are wandering in dense fog. To be sure, we are not the first sociologists condemned to grope their way through dense fog. In their day, Durkheim and Weber struggled with an equally dimly visible industrial capitalist order in the making.[1]

How do we actually know whether or not a societal rupture is in the making? As a first answer, I would suggest that we re-read sociology textbooks of the 1960s. Can we recognize Parsons' family in today's society? Do Blau and Duncan's mobility tables adequately portray the world of stratification that we are now grappling with? Is the youthful street corner gang of William Foote White what we now find in Los Angeles, Birmingham and Milano? The words we use in sociology today may be the very same as before, but their content is now radically altered. If the textbooks of Golden Age capitalism are now obsolete, so is probably also our understanding of society.

Let us focus on two institutions that indisputably are in flux: work and family. Most postindustrial theorizing has concentrated on working life, on the tertiarization of employment and production. With few exceptions, demographics and family change have been treated as something exogenous to whatever postindustrial society might be.[2] One overriding point I wish to make is that the two are part of the very same dialectic.

Family and family formation

Sociologically speaking, the family must be a fruitful place to begin. It is the central institution that connects individual and society, work and leisure, market and state. And, after all, this is normally where society is being reproduced. The typical family of welfare capitalism, at least according to the textbook, was effectively nuclearized, based on a male breadwinner and, in the majority of cases, on a full-time housewife. Retirement had become institutionalized and so grandparents lived separately; children were likely to leave the nest with the onset of adulthood. Indeed, we can here also identify a typical family *formation* pattern, namely early marriage and young ages at first childbirth. "Normal" families would have three children and they looked by and large stable.

The majority of contemporary families appear "a-typical." Today's entering female cohorts rarely abandon employment with childbirth; the housewife has for all practical purposes already disappeared in Scandinavia, and is in the process of doing so everywhere in the advanced world. There is no longer a prototype household, but the vast majority deviate significantly from the Parsonian norm: two-career couples, single parents, singles, and more or less stable cohabitation arrangements. There are few children, but those few that do find their way into society may have, *de facto*, not four but eight or possibly twelve grandparents, all depending on the frequency of marital dissolution. The divorce rate is close to 50 percent in the United States, the United Kingdom, and Sweden.[3] It is perhaps in the dynamics of family formation that we most clearly see historical flux. In an ongoing life-history study of Italy, we find that age of marriage was extremely predictable for women in the "Fordist era": virtually all married within one year of age 25–26. When we examine the cohort of their daughters, women coming of age in the 1980s, marriage behavior suddenly appears purely stochastic, particularly among those with more education and career ambitions. Basically, there is an almost equal chance that first marriage occurs at age 25 as at age 33, and the same goes for first child birth.[4]

Some call this the individualization of the life course, and there certainly is some truth to this. Perhaps a core feature of the "postindustrial" order to come will be extreme individualism. But we can also interpret the data differently: the kinds of exigencies that must be managed in people's life courses have grown and managing them has become more complicated. People encounter incompatibilities that once hardly existed. Young female cohorts today manage their education, family, fertility, and work careers all in conjunction, one with another. Hence, an alternative way of identifying an emerging new societal equilibrium is that it seems to be powerfully driven by women's altered *economic* role. Women clearly do not abandon family altogether. In fact, the "family" is not a vanishing institution, but it is being revolutionized in content and form. Pinpointing the root causes of this is not hard. There is a virtual consensus that it is driven by women's rising education, quest for independence and their occupational aspirations; by technological progress ranging from the pill to household time-saving machinery; by the rise of the service economy; and by the welfare state. In brief, *a large array of societal institutions are interacting in unfamiliar ways*. The central point here is that "a-typical" family forms and "a-typical" employment patterns are evolving in tandem, and the likely end-result is a novel nexus between the two: a new political economy if you like.

The family–work nexus

The motivations and incentives that drive our work life, like money, prestige, power, or self-realization, have probably not changed much. But the sociological reality that identical motives engender appears as revolutionary as does the family. The Fordist male of welfare capitalism, the erstwhile standard production worker, would begin his career around age 16, retire at age 65 and then, two years later, literally drop dead. It is not an exaggeration to claim that it was *this* male who embodied the creation of Fordist society. He usually came from agriculture, had little education, but profited from high industrialism, meaning a stable albeit dreary job that paid a solid family wage. Productivity growth and high demand for his products meant that he could anticipate sustained real wage growth. Hence, the standard male was, for the first time in history, capable of emulating erstwhile bourgeois standards, such as homeownership, an automobile, and full-time housewifery.

The passage towards the welfare capitalist era was, in a sense, spearheaded by the "new male" responding to perennial motives, but in a new context. The prototypical woman receded into the family. But here is where good sociology must identify variance: our Fordist male and his housewife became the "middle class" norm exactly at the moment when the old middle class began to leave it. The Ozzies and Harriets of America, the millions of Parsonian families everywhere, secured that the epoch became truly "Fordist" because they where the working class attaining bourgeois behavioral norms. Unfortunately for Ozzie and Harriet, the bourgeoisie was already busy undoing the past and carving out novel norms. The most visible among these was the rapid growth of wives' sustained dedication to careers; the revolution in women's educational attainment began among the daughters of the upper strata.

When we examine cohort-specific life histories over the past decades, we are struck by one great difference: men continue to behave more or less as they always did. Some changes occur at the margins, but we see few ruptures. Women, on the other hand, are in the midst of rupturing most of those behavioral norms that reigned in the past. And the ruptures are especially dramatic and visible among women with education. Hence, to venture a somewhat hazardous hypothesis, *it would seem that the passage towards "postindustrialism" is, this time around, being spearheaded by the "new woman," also responding to perennial motives, but in a new context.*

Yes, males appear to be quite passive in the contemporary passage towards a new equilibrium. They make pretty much the same kinds of life course decisions that they always did; they pace and sequence events and transitions much as their fathers did. Certainly, men spend more years in school and, perhaps, longer time getting a stable job. But most of what happens among men is a question of delayed timing. As always, they tend to marry or form families pretty much in connection with steady employment. The only radical departure from past norms is that men now seem eager to exit the labor force at the earliest moment possible (now at 59 on average in Europe), all-the-while that they now live ten years longer. Men are hardly creating new patterns and logics of social behavior.

The data suggest that, indeed, it is women who are creating the new frontiers of social life. The great contemporary surge in educational attainment is mainly a female phenomenon. In most European countries today, women's attainment exceeds that of men'. And, in contrast to men, women increasingly attempt to remain employed as much as possible, often against heavy odds; often renouncing children. Not only are women delaying marriage and births so as to time family formation with education and career objectives, but it is women who, in the first place, are creating the new dominant household models – be it the double-income, the single person, or the lone parent variety. Above all, it is these very same women who, in large measure, are creating the new "postindustrial" employment structure – at least as far as personal and social services are concerned.

You could at one time make a good living if you were a unionized steel worker; a good living today requires social skills and strong cognitive capacities. This is true for the conventional male labor market, but is probably even truer for the expanding services. And since conventional lower-skilled male jobs are in decline, a good living increasingly requires that wives also work. Whether women work to offset husbands' declining earnings capacity or to pursue independent career goals, the net result is similar. They create a new economy simply by leaving housewifery. In part, added household revenues imply greater purchasing power and this favors service consumption, like more entertainment. In part, the decline in housewife time means that households are forced to externalize erstwhile labor intensive domestic activities, like caring for children and the elderly, or preparing food and ironing shirts. Working mothers create a potentially massive labor market for personal and social services in which more women will find employment opportunities. In just about all advanced economies, services account for almost all net job growth over the past decades. And, women's employment growth accounts for the lion's share of this expansion.

The traditional steel worker's pay was directly linked to productivity improvements. But distributional claims become much more complicated in an economy dominated by services for which we often do not have a clear measure of productivity. What does it mean to be productive in a postindustrial setting? Are we, as Fred Block (1990) asserts, in a neo-physiocratic world where we easily recognize that the vanishing metal worker is productive, but not the daycare worker or home-helper? If conventional notions of productivity and just rewards have become inoperable, how is wealth being produced?

In the servicing economy most production is concomitantly consumption. This is the very essence of servicing. The product disappears the moment it is produced, leaving hardly any trace except perhaps a fatter belly, a cleaner car, shorter hair or a better conscience. Is a fatter belly value added? But the very fact that production coincides with consumption implies that traditional principles of pay and performance assessment must be replaced by new ones. It is principally the customer, and less a supervisor, who evaluates the quality of a service. Hence, work hierarchies are bound to change, as are reward systems. The same manicure or hamburger serving may result in drastically different remuneration, partially owing to the social skills of the server. A service worker's pay may still depend on the manager's assessment, but the manager must take his or her clues from customers, and not from higher up echelons in the organization.

A new social stratification order

Most sociologists are unlikely to accept that a new social order is in the making unless it also clearly manifests a rupture in the system of social stratification or, if you like, a new class structure. Although the precise nature of the postwar stratification system was fiercely debated, most would probably agree that Lipset's (1960) concept of the democratic class struggle contained a strong grain of truth. His basic notion was this: classes as social collectivities had not disappeared, but the cleavage that produced naked zero-sum conflict had been evened out; the basic correlates of class had weakened. In any case, it was the industrial working class that occupied center-stage in the stratification order of welfare capitalism. Heroic to some and problematic to others, this working class hardly merits much attention anymore. Can we identify emerging new cleavages? Based on what? Expertise? Having a job? Gender? Age?

Sociology is certainly not unaware that something is unfolding. Indeed, all the above dimensions have been proposed as the new dividing line of a postindustrial class structure. Daniel Bell (1976) and many others emphasize expertise as the source of emerging cleavages; the knowledge class is their primary manifestation. Van Parijs (1987) and Claus Offe (1985) see an emerging abyss between insiders and outsiders; if jobs become a scarce good, privilege means having one. Many feminists highlight gender as a seminal new axis of inequalities. Some claim that *chrono-politics* are displacing class politics (see, for example, Hernes, 1987).

Still, a prior question that any new stratification model must resolve is whether or not the household remains the basic unit of class. The very fact that debate on this issue has been raging over the past decades testifies to its ambiguity.[5] And as all readily agree, the basic issue has to do with what is happening to families, and to what extent women's economic behavior is being dislodged from that of their male partners. This is not the moment to propose yet another class scenario for the future to come, but if I were to follow-up on the empirics described earlier, there are a few hypotheses that do present themselves. Take, firstly, Hakim's (1997) argument that women are essentially bi-modal in terms of their life-time economic role: on one side, those inherently dedicated to careers; on the other side, those who may or may not be employed, but whose basic drive remains that of family. Without doubt this bi-modal breakdown is changing rapidly, with an ever larger share falling in the former group. If more and more women now tailor their family formation process to their career exigencies, clearly they become independent class actors. Yet, this does not necessarily imply that the household – and thus usually the male – ceases to be the effective unit of class definition. But it would if additional changes occur. One would be if, increasingly, women represent the dominant source of household income, a situation that is still minoritarian.

Another would be if increasing marital instability produces such a flux that people shift between household types many times throughout life. What, for example, would we do with a working woman who remains single into her 30s, then marries a husband in a superior class position, divorces and remains single again for a period, re-marries now with a husband of identical status and, then spends her final years in employment as a widow? Or, a typical situation today: husband is retired at age 55; wife, who is five years younger, maintains the household for the next ten years? A great part of the answer to such evolving biographies has to do with marital homogamy. It makes sense to assume that women's class position is derivative of their husbands' as long as many women's main chance of upward mobility occurs via marriage. But what if women, as now is the norm, are more educated than men? Marital homogamy is apparently increasing in all advanced societies because of women's education and careers, but this same process is likely to diminish the marriage market for the most educated women, simply because they outnumber available equivalent males.

But there is a third realistic scenario that emerges from household data, namely growing *inter-household* differentiation and polarization. As the Parsonian family explodes into myriad diverse forms, and as households' welfare and resources increasingly rely on women's earnings, homogamy will almost certainly produce polarization: at one end, dual-career couples, in the middle the conventional one-earner model which finds itself in evermore reduced circumstances, and at the other extreme phenomena such as no-work households and single parents. Just like male knowledge workers marry female knowledge workers, so the weak marry the weak, and the losers the losers. In many OECD countries today, working-age, no-work couple households account for up to 10 percent of all. If women and family change are the building blocks of the new society to come, it would not be a surprise if emerging cleavages reflect the dynamics of household change.

But the dynamics are not such that we can easily identify linear trends. It may be that Goldthorpe's conventional view is being gradually undone by women's changing employment and family priorities. At the same time, Goldthorpe's position may be reinforced if homogamy and household concentrations of winners and losers both solidify.

Conceptualizing the emerging new equilibrium

Sociology has made little progress in identifying the larger *Gestalt* of the new order. What we mainly have are an assortment of "post-something" applied to phenomena we *do* know, like postindustrial, postmaterialist, postmodern, or post-productivist. This is a far cry from analysis. In the fog of change in which Marx or Weber found themselves a hundred years ago, emerged powerful questions and hypotheses about bureaucratization, about class polarization, or about anomie. Do we now have anything even remotely similar? I think most of us, and certainly myself, gathered here in Amsterdam only a few months before the new millennium arrives, would shamefacedly admit that, no, we are not making much progress with the grand questions of our times. Why not? My view is that we have lost the methodological capacity to penetrate dense fog.

When I was a student, the sociology that mattered was to be found in, say, five journals plus a modest pile of authoritative books. I have no clue how many journals are now *sine qua non*, and there is probably no sociologist able to read all the books that, to his or her colleagues, matter hugely. This ocean of words testifies to the fact that we are more sociologists and, possibly, also more productive. But it also reflects the growth of endless new disciplinary tentacles. In search of more clarity, a huge number of sociologists abandon the core of their discipline, and often their discipline altogether – possibly because the core of sociology is, indeed, stale and tired. As a consequence, we see the proliferation of sociology courses that mainly dedicate themselves to postmodern de-construction with Foucault and Derrida as the guiding lights. And, we are going micro in a big way: we seem to be navel-gazing, obsessed with ourselves, with our anxieties and ambiguous identities, our gender, our sexual inclinations. We worry a great deal about the meaning (and lack thereof) of words, language or symbols. The discipline has evidently begun to resign itself to the sorry truth that there are no grand questions, and that society is no longer driven by any particular logic or innate force. Social life has become one great stochastic happening.

We also see many sociologists now becoming "deep historians." Of course, good sociology is always anchored in history, but what is more worrisome are those, just like many postmodernists, who go native; who pride themselves that they have shed their disciplinary mantle by embracing linguistics, philosophy or history as their genuine expertise. Unfortunately, linguists will always be better at language; historians better at history.

And then we see a third influential current: those seeking comfort in the hard and inescapable over-determinism of path dependencies. Once the rails have been put down, nothing short of revolution will stop the train from plowing ever forward along its preordained path. Those sociologists dedicated to path dependencies do serve a crucial corrective function because they invite us to shun exaggerated visions of dramatic rupture, cataclysmic change.

The sociologists of rupture

Besides the many other sociological currents, too many even to contemplate, there exists however one that seriously believes that we are moving from one to another social order, lock-stock-and-barrel. Manuel Castell's (1996; 1997, 1998) three volume opus on the information society may not be everybody's idea of best-practice sociology, but it is nonetheless being portrayed as the seminal contemporary equivalent to Max Weber or Adam Smith.[6]

I am not convinced that Castells has opted for the soundest methodology possible. He works in the tradition of beginning with an imagined *Gestalt*, a pre-assembled jig-saw puzzle, and then the task is to assemble all the bits and pieces so as to fit them into a preconceived vision. Here is a prototype of Tilly's (1984) "encompassing comparison." It is certainly possible that Castells will be proven right. We shall not know until, perhaps, many of us are already safely dead and buried. Nonetheless, to come to grips with the emerging society, my personal sociological instinct tells me to pursue a radically different methodology, one based on directed empiricism and variation finding to use, once again, Tilly's vocabulary. Indeed, strong *a priori* theory may be harmful if it preordains the kinds of facts we look at and the nature of their inter-connections. I would prefer an empiricism based on weak theory or, better, loose hypotheses. I would not begin with *Gestalt* at all, but instead with a well-known and fundamental sociological institution – like the family.

The family is a good choice for directed empiricism because it connects individual incentives and normative behavior, rational choice with received culture, institutional constraints and the winds of global change. For these reasons, the family is a potentially good methodological choice because it should provide a maximum amount of data on the *mechanisms* involved in change. Above all, the focus of directed empiricism should be on identifying the mechanisms that link cause to effect. In the world of our textbook heroes of the past, the family had become the site of care, intimacy and consumption; the nest that allowed males to become maximally commodified. In hindsight, the postwar Parsonian family was the equilibrium point of the industrial political economy. But, as I noted, barely a generation later this equilibrium exists no more. The economic role of families now is not only to be a bulwark of male commodification; for most families, the one-earner model is sub-optimal for all its members: children are more likely to grow up poor; marital instability means that women need economic independence; women *want* independence regardless; the collectivity would lose a massive reservoir of human capital if women remained housewives; and as I have attempted to argue, society would stagnate because the revolution in women's behavior is its primary font of change.

If the main consumption desires of the Parsonian family were refrigerators, automobiles and televisions, the new families are more inclined towards services. Families cannot build their own refrigerators, but they can in principle wash their own dishes and care for their own children. The revolution that comes with women's labor supply today is that self-servicing is no longer feasible. So, the emerging family creates the emerging service economy, be it at the high end of psychoanalysis and marriage councilors, or at the low end of home-help services and fast-food outlets. All those myriad micro-decisions that households make just in order to pass from one day to the next, add up to a tidal wave of social transformation: unpaid housework becomes service jobs, potentially polarized between lousy and good jobs, low and high wages, and the upshot is the evolution of new cleavages. *Homo economicus* created industrialism, but the emerging service economy is being created by *femina economica*. And in the process, the family's integrative capacities change. Here, then, is a hypothesis about the mechanisms at work. It may be right or wrong, but the only way to tell is to broaden and intensify our empirical scrutiny.

Arlie Hochschild (1998) may be on to something in her terrifying depiction of the workplace as a primary locus of people's sociability, all-the-while that family life is being colonized by work. If having children becomes incompatible with household welfare optimization, fertility rates collapse; if all the members of most families are usually at work, in kindergartens or in school, communities empty out during day-time. During evenings and weekends, communities will increasingly do what one does in corporations.

Tracing trends in family behavior surely does not answer all questions we might raise about the postindustrial society to come. Yet, the point is that focusing our headlights on the empirics of one social institution reveals – potentially – new core dilemmas and interactions across others. Generalizing from my admittedly limited effort, there emerges one potentially promising research strategy: shun *Gestalts* and Derrida and revert to what are the true strengths, the basic *raison d'être*, of sociology, namely to scrutinize empirical variation and trends. For illustration, I chose to scrutinize the family but could equally well have settled on leisure, on the labor market, or on religion. Trying to fit the family or religion into an imagined future *Gestalt* of the societal totality will yield very little and, I believe, deconstructing language or doing exegesis on Derrida, will yield even less. Just plainly monitoring what is happening to the family, and then hypothesizing about its consequences and correlates might, with luck, some imagination, and lots of diligence, result in a workable and – hopefully – controversial new ideal type – a leitmotif of the "welfare capitalism" kind. The "service economy," let alone "postindustrial society" are exceedingly vague concepts and I, for one, am unable to flesh them out. But once I began to examine the family, basically on a hunch, I also began to understand much more clearly what precisely are some of the most fundamental driving forces in the evolving service economy. Gradually, then, postindustrial society is becoming something concrete, visible and, I think, sociological. This was perhaps not their real intention, but the feminists should be thanked for their persuasive call for more attention to the family and gender.

Notes

1 Many of the points raised in this presentation are more fully developed in Esping-Andersen (2000).
2 The classical example of the "work" centered analysis of postindustrialism is Bell (1976). Among those who treat family change as endogenous to postindustrialism are Block (1990), Gershuny (1978), and Clement and Myles (1994). See also Esping-Andersen (1999).
3 This is about a three- or four-fold increase over the 1960s. Italy's divorce rate is among the lowest, but if we add divorce and legal separations, Italy arrives at 25 percent (1994), again a three-fold increase since 1970 (Maggioni, 1997: Table 1).
4 I am here citing unpublished results. See, however, Barbieri *et al.* (1999).
5 Goldthorpe (1983) is of course the primary exponent of the conventional view. For an overview, see Sorensen (1994).
6 See, for example, the review by Giddens (1996).

References

Barbieri, P., Bison, I., and Esping-Andersen, G. (1999) "Italy. A Postindustrial Laggard or an Historical U-Turn?" Paper presented at the ECPR workshop, Mannheim, September 7–8.

Bell, D. (1976) *The Coming of Postindustrial Society*, New York: Basic Books.

Block, F. (1990) *Postindustrial Possibilities*, Berkeley: University of California Press.

Castells, M. (1996, 1997, 1998) *The Information Age: Economy, Society, and Culture*, Three Volumes, Oxford: Blackwell.

Clement, W. and Myles, J. (1994) *Relations of Ruling*, Montreal: McGill-Queen's University Press.

Davis, K. and Moore, W. (1945) "Some principles of stratification," *American Sociological Review*, 10: 242–49.

Esping-Andersen, G. (1999) *Social Foundations of Postindustrial Economies*, Oxford: Oxford University Press.

——(2000) "Two societies, one sociology, and no theory," *British Journal of Sociology*, 1: 59–77.

Gershuny, J. (1978) *After Industrial Society: The Emerging Self-servicing Economy*, London: Macmillan.

Giddens, A. (1996) "Review of the information age," *The Times Higher Education Supplement*, December 18.

Goldthorpe, J. (1983) "Women and class analysis: In defence of the conventional view," *Sociology*, 17: 465–88.

Hakim, K. (1997) *Key Issues in Women's Work*, London: Athlone.

Hernes, H. (1987) *Welfare State and Women Power*, Oslo: Norwegian University Press.

Hochschild, A. (1998) *The Time Bind,* New York: Metropolitan Books.

Lipset, S. M. (1960) *Political Man,* New York: Doubleday Anchor.

Maggioni, G. (1997) "Le separazioni e i divorzi," in Barbagli, M. and Saraceno, C. (eds) *Lo Stato delle Famiglie in Italia,* Bologna: Il Mulino: 232–47.

Offe, C. (1985) *Disorganized Capitalism. Contemporary Transformation of Work and Politics,* Cambridge, MA: MIT Press.

Parsons, T. (1951) *The Social System,* Glencoe, Ill: The Free Press.

Sorensen, A. (1994) "Women, family and class," *Annual Review of Sociology,* 20: 27–47.

Tilly, C. (1984) *Big Structures, Large Processes, Huge Comparisons,* New York: Russell Sage Foundation.

Van Parijs, P. (1987) "A Revolution in Class Theory," *Politics and Society,* 15: 453–82.

10 The language constellation of the European Union

Abram de Swaan

Taken as a whole, the five thousand different languages spoken throughout the world constitute a single system. This evolving global constellation of languages takes its coherence from multilingualism. Multilingual speakers ensure the cohesion of the human race by linking different linguistic groups, either directly when polyglot speakers meet, or indirectly through translation by a third party.

The global constellation of languages in its entirety is structured in a simple and solid fashion – a rather rare phenomenon in the human sciences – since the languages of the world, or rather the corresponding linguistic groups, are connected in an hierarchical manner.

The global constellation of languages can be represented as tree-structure, a sort of flow-chart on four levels. The first level is that of the local languages, notably languages with an oral tradition in which knowledge is preserved not in writing, but through memory; these languages which are mostly ignored by official administrations and by the media are rarely spoken or taught at school. However, in the current scheme, a cluster of them is linked each time to a central language through the conduit provided by multilingual individuals. These peripheral linguistic groups are linked only tenuously with one another because of the rarity of people competent in more than one of them. However, they all include within their ranks some multilingual individuals who, through their knowledge of the central language, connect them with the central linguistic group. The peripheral languages can thus be compared to satellites revolving around the planet of the central language. In this way, the speakers of Frisian, Papiamento, Limburgish and Sranan Tongo, for example, only rarely speak each other's language, and if they know a second language, it tends to be Dutch, which is both the central language and the language of the state.

The central language often functions as a national language, and generally also as an official state language. If at the first level there are several thousand oral languages, "languages of memory", each one used by less than a million people (the greater majority of them are spoken only by a few thousand people at most), at the second level only a hundred central languages, spoken by millions or indeed tens of millions of people can be identified. The conservation and use of almost every central language are ensured by the state which guarantees that they are taught at school, used in parliament, in the courts of justice, the corridors of bureaucracy and in the press and the electronic non-print media. They are both written and printed languages, regulated by a standardized grammar, syntax, vocabulary, orthography and pronunciation.

A cluster of these "planetary" languages, surrounded by their "satellite" languages, is in turn connected to its "supercentral" language, a "solar" language so to speak, further extending the astronomical metaphor. In each such group of central languages a number of bilingual persons have learned the same "supercentral" language allowing them to communicate among themselves and with the native speakers of the language. At this third level, on the "solar" plane, a dozen languages can be counted, most of them spoken by hundreds of millions of people, and in the case of Chinese and (most likely) English, by more than a billion.

Nonetheless, there is one, unique language which in its turn functions as an intermediary between the various supercentral languages, and which links the speakers of Arabic and Chinese, or of Spanish, Russian and French, or Malay, Swahili, Portuguese and Hindi. At this level, astronomy can no longer furnish terms to describe the pivot of these solar languages, the axis of the linguistic galaxy. This "hypercentral" language, connecting the supercentral languages together, unifying the whole global constellation of languages, is – at present – English. This has not always been so, but such is the case in the world of today.

The notion of a world-wide global constellation of language groups allows on the one hand to analyze transnational society at the level of the linguistic rivalries and accommodations which represent an essential aspect of the current discourse on globalization. On the other hand, this concept will help to understand specific, regional language conflicts within their global context.

The global language constellation constitutes one component of the world system, one that so far has been entirely overlooked in the literature, which usually focuses on the political, economic, cultural and ecological aspects of the system. The present analysis of the language constellation is based on the political economy and the political sociology of language.

The concept of society constitutes the very basis of sociology, even if in this discipline which has prospered under the aegis of the national state, the notion of society refers almost exclusively to a national framework.

A sociology which aspires to transcend national frontiers must redefine its objectives in relation to related disciplines, opting for a concept of transnational society which transcends national borders. The sociology of transnational society concerns itself with research into transnational links, that is the connections linking people across national borders, either directly from person to person or indirectly, through the intervention of corporations, markets, states or international organizations.

The sociology of transnational society must, therefore, study the cross-border circulation of people, commodities and services, capital and information. These exchanges proceed through language, they must be verbalized and translated, i.e. they need to be encoded in one language and next recoded in another. Furthermore, these languages do not enter the game as a transparent and neutral medium – on the contrary, they help to determine available connections, set priorities, and affect the very information that is exchanged in the process.[1]

The global language constellation must be understood within the framework of transnational society and its clearly hierarchical structure corresponds to the structure of the global system – a system constituted by a "core", a "periphery" and a "semi-periphery" to quote Immanuel Wallerstein's famous triad.[2] One of the most striking characteristics of this global system corresponds precisely to the structure of the world language constellation: exchanges between peripheral economies occur only via the mediation of core markets, just as peripheral languages, in the absence of direct mutual links, communicate indirectly, through the medium of the central language. Parallels go much further. According to the model, peripheral economies export only raw materials for further treatment in semi-peripheral countries and for the subsequent transformation into mass consumption goods in the core economies of the world system. The Beninese philosopher Paulin Hountondji has characterized scientific relations between "developing" countries and "developed" countries in similar fashion. Data collected on the ground by local assistants for researchers from the core countries are next analyzed within the universities of the core area and only then fetch their full academic value in publications for the most prestigious international journals.[3] Similarly, music, sculpture and painting from distant cultures are imported into the core countries, judged in accordance with Western aesthetic criteria and commercialised through channels provided by the Western market. Whatever is expressed in the native languages of those countries remains unnoticed outside their linguistic area, unless in highly exceptional cases it is translated, and even then it must first be selected by "gatekeepers" in the core countries, who will then distribute it as they see fit (as Pascale Casanova has demonstrated for the literature of peripheral countries, relayed, if at all, via core cities such as Paris).[4] The distribution of ideas and texts moves from the centre to the periphery, from the most widely spoken languages to those used by a more limited number. The vast majority of texts produced in languages spoken by smaller groups remains unread and ignored. This is what the Dutch sociologist, Johan Goudsblom, has rightly called the "one-way mirror effect", small nations follow what happens in larger ones, while themselves remaining largely unnoticed.[5] These observations demonstrate how the hierarchical schema, far from being merely a formal construction, corresponds, on the contrary, to the everyday realities of cultural priority.

During the Modern Era, one institution has transformed language use more than any other – the state. The state has succeeded in fashioning language after its own image. In the West, when people say "language" they have already thought "state". From the beginning, states have imposed a single language, or rather a single dialect that superseded the other idioms of the realm. Once a specific language was chosen, it was standardized and codified for the whole territory, for all domains and *ad eternam*. The official language comes to resemble the state, covering the same territory, sharply demarcated from its neighbours by the same frontiers and equally regulated as the state itself. In Europe, on behalf of the state, linguists and academicians codified their respective languages in an official grammar, fixated the vocabulary in dictionaries and acted as guardians of its purity by policing its usage. Hence, in contrast to many non-Western languages which for lack of state intervention remain quite "fluid", the official languages of European states are "robust".[6] In Europe, states exact a civic loyalty towards their language which has been elevated to the status of a national treasure. France may be the most telling example of these practices. The language is transformed through its usage by government agencies and courts of law, and increasingly by the ever-expanding bureaucracy and by an army with universal conscription. But it is the school, especially the primary school, compulsory for all young citizens, which has most profoundly modified the transmission and usage of language among the population. Without doubt the state's interference in language management is an essential element in nation-building. It is yet again the state which, by imposing a single language, has relegated all other dialects to an inferior status and often hastened their extinction. At present, however, most linguists have come to defend linguistic diversity as vigorously as their predecessors zealously insisted on national language unification, less than half a century ago. But a dilemma remains: on the one hand, the wealth of an infinitely varied and variable linguistic heritage, reinforcing the cultural identities and customs of regional and ethnic communities; on the other hand, the necessity for effective communication across cultural, ethnic, religious and political borders, that is at the national, and, as the case may be, at the transnational level.

Some foreign languages are in fact compulsory subjects in school. English nowadays almost always is. As a second foreign language, only a few alternatives are available to students, either because they have been prescribed by the government, or because schools expect there to be demand for them. In Europe, formal secondary education provides the lion's share of language instruction. Apparently, individual governments almost entirely ignored the aggregate effects of these curriculum decisions upon all-European communication. As a result, and in a blind process, every national education system gravitated towards English as the first foreign language, while each government continued to defend publicly the necessity of a multiplicity of languages for communication at the European level. France alone pursued an explicit international language policy, which has been rendered ineffectual by the combined decisions (or rather "non-decisions") of the other European governments, in the end forcing the French to adapt to the predominance of English in Europe.

The relatively autonomous dynamic of a language constellation also results from the interplay of individual expectations. If people anticipate that a language will become current, they will not hesitate to adopt it themselves, but if, on the other hand, they suspect that in their environment one language will be abandoned for another, they themselves will use it less, will neglect to teach it to their children and will favour the new language. Nowadays, these expectations may affect not only regional or national languages but also those spoken on a continental or even global scale, as the current fate of French beyond France demonstrates.

Suppose that a person might choose the language which seems most useful, which offers the greatest possibilities of communication, either directly or through the mediation of an interpreter or translator. The choice will depend on two characteristics of the languages under consideration. A language is more likely to be selected, the more *prevalent* it is in the relevant language constellation (the larger the number of persons it allows to communicate with directly) and the more *central* it is (the greater the proportion of *multilingual* speakers who have it in their repertoire). The constellation might be global, continental or regional, as the case may be. These notions can now be formalized.

The utility of a language for a speaker (i) in a constellation or sub-constellation (S) can be expressed in terms of its "communication value", Q_i, indicating its potential to link this speaker with other speakers in S. The "prevalence" (p_i) of language i, refers to the number of speakers (P_i) that are competent in i, divided by all the speakers (N^S) in constellation S. The "centrality" (c_i) refers to the number (C_i) of multilingual speakers who *also* speak the language i, divided by all the multilingual speakers (M^S) in constellation S. The communication or Q-value equals the product of the prevalence (p_i) and the centrality (c_i) of language i in constellation S.

The formula can be written as follows:

$$Q_i = p_i \cdot c_i = \frac{P_i}{N^S} \cdot \frac{C_i}{M^S}$$

The current scarcity and unreliability of statistics on language competencies do not permit a more elaborate measure. A simpler measure would lack validity. Elsewhere I have published the Q-values of the official languages of the member states in the European Union (Community) since 1975.[7] As might be expected, English obtained the highest score. Although German was much more current as a mother-tongue, the large number of multilingual speakers competent in English gave it the greatest prevalence and, necessarily, the largest centrality. The case of French is of special interest since it had a weaker prevalence than German (and certainly than English), but nevertheless it obtained a higher Q-value than German because so many more Europeans had learned French as a foreign language.

Apparently, the measure reflects the rough assessments, based on the rather vague estimates that people make when considering which foreign language to learn. In fact, these estimates also reflect the anticipated decisions of others or, in other words, the future state of the constellation. When these expectations reinforce one another, they result in a stampede towards the language which is expected to win, and will in fact win because of those very expectations.

This touches upon the very core of the political economy of language, a speciality so far hardly developed. Since a language has utility, it constitutes a good in the economic sense; but what sort of good? First, language is not consumed by being used. On the contrary, the more people use it, the better it serves each one of them. Language is freely accessible to all – no price can be exacted for using it. Moreover, a language cannot be created by one person alone; and not everyone need collaborate to create or maintain it (so no one has a veto). These characteristics define a language as a collective good.

But there is more: a language not only does not lose its utility when more speakers use it, all users actually *gain* from an increase in its use. A similar effect also occurs with standards for new products, as in the case of Apple or Window operating systems for computers, or VHS and Betamax for video-recorders: their value for each user increases with the number of their users – a phenomenon known as "external network effect" and also displayed by languages. However, while technical standards are incorporated in a consumer product that must be purchased, and that therefore allows those who will not pay to be excluded, no one can be excluded from a collective good such as a language. Languages, displaying as they do the properties of collective goods and also producing external network effects, thus constitute a special category: they are "hypercollective" goods.

This hypercollective quality can trigger a stampede from one language to another, although the desertion will be slowed down by the time and the effort it takes to learn the new language, and the tenaciousness of memory of the old tongue. Individual users will of course be tempted to switch from the old language to the new one as they assign it a superior Q-value. Acting in this way, they procure an advantage for themselves, but simultaneously reduce the value of the old language for those who continue to use it. The abandonment of a language can be prevented only when a critical mass of speakers is committed to preserving it, so that a minimal Q-value will be guaranteed. Conserving the Q-value therefore requires measures to prevent defections, necessitating either collective action by speakers of the language or compulsory state intervention. This argument provides the foundation for an economic theory of language politics (and of ethnic politics).

The hypercollective nature of a language applies also to its past. One might imagine that all communication leaves a sediment in the form of texts, either in human memory, written or printed on paper or recorded in digital form. The totality of these memorized, written, or recorded texts constitutes the cumulative cultural capital of that language, a capital accessible only through the language itself. This capital is hyper-collective in nature, for the simple reason that the more people contribute to it, and draw from it, the more useful it becomes for each one of them. Clearly, with the disappearance of the language the corresponding cultural capital would lose its value.

At this point one might envisage the elaboration of an economic theory of culture, of linguistic culture at the very least. Once again, two issues must be confronted: on the one hand, the individual temptation to defect and, on the other, the need for collective action or public constraint.

These findings may now be applied to the case of the European Union in its present state, as it finds itself in anxious expectation of future extensions. The European Union now boasts a common currency, but so far lacks a common language. In fact, there hardly is a language policy for the European Parliament, or for the Commission's bureaucracy, let alone for "l'Europe des citoyens", for civil society in the European Union. Of course, from the beginning the official language of each member state was recognized as an official language of the Community, and the subsequent Union. At the time, the six founding members contributed four languages: Dutch, French, German and Italian, an almost manageable number.

Without much discussion, French was accepted as the working language of the Community's budding bureaucracy, as it had been the language of diplomacy until the end of World War Two and the sole language of the European Coal and Steel Community that preceded the EC. In those postwar years, the Germans and the Italians kept a low profile and the Dutch (even when counting in the Dutch-speaking Flemish of Belgium) were not numerous enough to insist much on the use of their language in the administration; moreover, beyond the Low Countries Dutch hardly anywhere was taught in the schools.

The first great expansion of the European Community in 1973 brought in the British, the Irish (almost all of them native English speakers), and the Danes the vast majority of whom had learned English in school. In fact, English quickly became another working language of the Commission's bureaucracy and an informal lingua franca in the European Parliament. The Germans still did not much push their language and, being generally more fluent in English than in French, they may – wittingly or not – have helped to promote English.[8] So far, French is used more frequently in oral and written communication by the Commission's officials, except in contacts with states outside the Union, while the two languages are about equally current in the conversations among parliamentarians. German comes a far third, other languages hardly play a role in day-to-day communication.[9]

With the addition of Greece in 1981, of Portugal and Spain in 1986, and of Austria, Finland, and Sweden in 1995, the set of official languages in the European Union grew to nine and next to eleven, a quite unmanageable number that is bound to increase with many more languages once Hungary, Poland, the Czech Republic and subsequently central and eastern European countries join the Union. This prospect has prompted much alarm, but so far rarely any serious debate.

From the 1960s on, secondary education had been rapidly expanding throughout Europe. Quite independently from one another, the member states realized sweeping reforms of their secondary school systems, and in the process most of them reduced the number of compulsory foreign languages taught, henceforward prescribing only English, or leaving the choice entirely to the students who almost everywhere opted for English anyway.[10] As a result of the expansion of secondary education there are now more citizens in the Union who have studied one or more foreign languages than ever before. This applies to French, German, Spanish and Italian, but of course the numbers of English students have grown most spectacularly.

By the end of the twentieth century, 88 percent of secondary school students in the European Union (in 1992/93 and excluding Ireland and the UK) were taught English as a foreign language. French as a foreign language was taught to 32 percent, German to 19 percent, and Spanish to 9 percent (again excluding students in the countries where the language concerned is the medium of instruction). According to the most recent figures available, the great majority of high school students in Europe study a single foreign language (the all-European average is 1.2) and apparently the one language they learn in overwhelming numbers is

English.[11] Young people (15–24 years) in the European Union, asked (in 1997) what languages they speak well enough to carry on a conversation, mention English most often (55 percent), French (20 percent), and German (11 percent), another 29 percent answer that they do not speak any foreign language at that level.[12]

For the present purposes four levels of communication are to be distinguished within the European Union. In the first place, the official, public level: it consists mainly of the European Parliament in official session and of the European Commission in its external contacts. Here, the founding treaty applies, which recognizes all official languages of the member states as languages of the Union, and, moreover, requires that decisions by the UE should be published in all its languages, since they affect the laws of the constituent states. In the second place, there is the level of the Commission's internal bureaucracy, where the officials have more or less informally adopted a few "working languages" in their everyday contacts and in-house correspondence. Then, there is the third level, of transnational communication, neither official nor institutional, between the citizens of Europe, where several languages compete for predominance in various areas of the Union and in many different domains of communication. At this level too, English is paramount, no doubt, but it must still compete with French in Southern Europe and with German in Central Europe, where Russian has well-nigh disappeared.

The fourth level is that of domestic communication within each present (and future) member country. There, the official language is the mother tongue of a large if not a vast majority, taught in school at all levels, and protected by the national state in every way. Nevertheless, these "central" or national, official languages increasingly coexist with a supercentral language for transnational communication, at present and in all cases English, spoken by a quickly growing proportion of the population.

In fact, while the eleven official languages of the Union are used on the first level, for public and ceremonial occasions and for official documents, two languages, English and French, are used on the second level of informal communication in the corridors of Parliament and the meeting rooms of bureaucracy. German lags far behind, in third place. When it comes to the third level, that of civil Europe, statistics and survey data all concur that English is the first language of transnational communication, while French, German and maybe Spanish play secondary roles in the corresponding regions and for a limited scope of cultural or commercial exchanges.

At the fourth level however, within each member country, the national language will continue to function on most levels of domestic social interaction, while transnational functions will be provided by the supercentral languages that ensure all-European communication, again mostly English. As long as each state acts as the protector of its national language there need not be an immediate threat from the supercentral language, not even when a large majority of citizens have learned it as a foreign language. Hence, a state of diglossia, a somewhat precarious equilibrium between two languages in one society, will prevail.

Table 10.1 The voting cycle in EU language choices

Member states	Language repertoires						
	E	E&F	E&F&G	E&F&G&I	E&F&G&I&S	E&F&G&I&S&N	E&F&G&I&S&N&O
E+EI	1	2	3	4	5	6	7
F	7	1	2	3	4	5	6
G+A	6	7	1	2	3	4	5
I	5	6	7	1	2	3	4
S	4	5	6	7	1	2	3
N	3	4	5	6	7	1	2
O	2	3	4	5	6	7	1
(others, 5x)							
B	7	3	4	5	6	1	2
L	7	6	1	2	3	4	5

The languages are added to the repertoire from left to right in order of decreasing "Q-value" (cf. De Swaan, 1993). The higher the entry, the lower the preference. It is assumed (1) that member states prefer a language repertoire that includes their language above one that does not; and next, (2) that among these options they prefer a repertoire with fewer languages above one with more languages.

E refers to England and English, F refers to France and French, G refers to Germany and German, I refers to Italy and Italian, S refers to Spain and Spanish, N refers to the Netherlands and Dutch. O refers to all other member states of the European Union, and their respective languages: Portugal, Greece, Denmark, Sweden and Finland. Austria is assumed to vote like Germany, Ireland like the UK; Belgium supposedly prefers all combinations with F over those without it and all combinations with F & N over those with F only (combinations with N and without F are not put to the vote). Similarly, Luxembourg prefers combinations with F & G over combinations with F only, and combinations with F over combinations without it.

In this constellation the addition of any one language is opposed by all member states, except the one whose language is to be added. Conversely, the proposal to exclude a language receives the support of all member states except the one that stands to lose its language privileges. Thus, any series of votes on the language repertoires mentioned in the table will at some point produce "English only", which will then be defeated by the proposal "all languages" and at that point another cycle of eliminatory votes may start. Remarkably, if the single member states are allowed a veto (as they are on important issues in the Council of Ministers), none of the above proposals can defeat any other and the *status quo* will always prevail. This is probably a realistic rendering of the "official" and "public" language policy: complete paralysis in favor of the original policy of "all official languages in public". But otherwise, each single elimination proposal is accepted against the opposition of one or two votes only, except one: eliminate the "other languages" from "all languages", which is opposed by all the member states with "other" languages. This coalition could be split up if there was consensus on voting for the elimination of these "other" languages one at a time, against solitary opposition from the one country affected in each vote. Under these conditions, the *status quo* is especially hard to change by any kind of majority vote or when vetoes are allowed.

Note that except for England and France, preference curves are not monotonous, but for each country (except B and L) a sequence of repertoires, respecting the same cyclical order, may be found for which its preference curve is monotonous: the cycle starting with the smallest repertoire containing that country's language.

The European discussion, in so far as there is one, is defined by the dilemma between the conservation of a multiplicity of languages and the need for efficient communication at the all-Union level. In fact, a vicious cycle manifests itself in the European Union, this time in the guise of a latent "voting cycle". In principle, every proposal to abolish one of the eleven languages of the Union would be supported by a large majority (against the vote of the aggrieved member state). However, when the last proposal "use one language only" (English, most likely) would finally come to the vote, it would be defeated by a counterproposal "use all languages", since all members except the one with the language that lasted till the end will vote in favour of the latter proposal.[13] It is this latent voting cycle that explains the immobilism, the lack of action on the language issue in the EU.

The Union's mute immobilism is accompanied by a non-discussion, interspersed by an occasional conference or publication that necessarily must remain rather ineffectual. Nevertheless, on the rare occasions that the European language issue is raised nevertheless, a cabal of experts in the relevant disciplines and of representatives for the affected interest will use the occasion for a high display of convictions and commitments, most of them equally pious in their respect of the language rights of each and every party involved as pretentious in their ambitions for a grand scheme of European cultural *rapprochement*.

Public and official pronouncements on the European language question favor at one and the same time the optimal development of mutual understanding among the peoples of Europe and the maintenance of Europe's great linguistic heritage, "a wealth of tongues", without mentioning that the two objectives might be in conflict. Clearly, there is a desire to square the circle, the vicious circle of mutually reinforcing expectations that lead to a stampede towards English, and of a voting cycle that paralyses all policy at the Union level.

"The subject of languages has been the great *non-dit* of European integration."[14] Apparently, it turned out to be easier for the EU to settle upon a common medium of monetary exchange than on a common idiom for verbal exchange. But, in this case too, not taking decisions amounts to taking "non-decisions" – and these will affect the European language constellation as incisively and lastingly as any explicitly adopted policy ever could.

But as the language of the present collection of papers already demonstrates, in the absence of a commonly accepted alternative, Europeans will inexorably gravitate towards English.

Notes

1 Cf. for example Pierre Bourdieu (1982) *Ce que parler veut dire*. Paris: Fayard, published in English as (1991) *Language and Symbolic Power: The Economy of Linguistic Exchanges*), Cambridge: Polity Press.

2 Immanuel Wallerstein (1974) *The Modern World System*, New York: Academic Press.

3 Cf. Paulin Hountondji (1983) *African Philosophy: Myth and Reality*. London: Hutchinson.

4 Pascale Casanova (1999) *La République mondiale des lettres* (Paris: Éditions Du Seuil).

5 Johan Goudsblom (1988) Vanachter de doorkijkspiegel. In *Taal en sociale werkelijkheid* (Amsterdam: Meulenhoff).

6 Cf. Abram de Swaan (1988) *In Care of the State; Health Care, Education and Welfare in the Modern Era in Europe and the United States*, Cambridge: Polity.

7 Cf. Abram de Swaan (1993) "The evolving European language system; a theory of communication potential and language competition", *International Political Science Review* 14, 3: 241–55. Cf. for a more recent presentation and discussion: Abram de Swaan (forthcoming), *The World Language System; Political Sociology and Political Economy of the Global Language Constellation*, Cambridge: Polity.

8 Cf. Irene Bellier (1995) "Moralité, Langue et Pouvoirs dans les Institutions Européennes", *Social Anthropology* 3.3: 235–50, esp. 245; also, Ulrich Ammon (1996)

"The European Union: Status change of English during the last fifty years", in Joshua A. Fishman, Andrew W. Conrad and Alma Rubal-Lopez (eds) *Post-Imperial English; Status Change in Former British and American Colonies, 1940–1990*, Berlin/New York: Mouton de Gruyter, 241–67. Nevertheless, since at least 1991, the German government has regularly insisted on the adoption of German as the third language of the European Commission's bureaucracy, and in the Fall of 1999 it actually collided with the – then – Finnish presidency of the Union on this issue.

9 Cf. Michael Schlossmacher (1994) "Die Arbeitssprachen in den Organen der Europäischen Gemeinschaft. Methoden und Ergebnisse einer empirischen Untersuchung," in Ulrich Ammon, Klaus J. Mattheier and Peter H. Nelde (eds) *Sociolingistica, International Yearbook of European Sociolinguistics* vol. 8; *English only? in Europe.* Tübingen: Max Niemeyer Verlag, 101–22; see also Virginie Mamadouh, *De talen in het Europese parlement.* [Amsterdamse sociaal-geografische studies, 52] Amsterdam: Instituut voor sociale geografie, Unversiteit van Amsterdam, 1995.

10 Cf. Jean-Pierre van Deth (1979) *L'enseignement scolaire des langues vivantes dan les pays membres de la communauté européenne; bilan, réflexions et propositions.* Bruxelles: Didier.

11 *Key Data on Education in the European Union* (1999) Luxembourg: Office for Official Publications of the European Communities, 54–5.

12 *Les Jeunes Européens* [*Eurobaromètre*, 47.2], European Commission, 1997, 39 ff.

13 Abram de Swaan (1999) Keynote address, Conference on Institutional Status and Use of National Languages in Europe: Contributions to a European Language Policy (Brussels, March 24).

14 This has not changed at all: "There was much talk of milk pools and butter mountains, of a unitary currency, of liberalizing movements for EC citizens and restricting access for outsiders, but the language in which these issues were dealt with remained itself a non-issue," (cf. De Swaan (1993): 244.

References

Ammon, U. (1996) "The European Union: Status change of English during the last fifty years", in Fishman, J. A., Conrad, A. W. and Rubal-Lopez, A. (eds) *Post Imperial English; Status Change in Former British and American Colonies, 1940–1990*, Berlin/New York: Mouton de Gruyter: 241–67.

Bellier, I. (1995) "Moralité, Langue et Pouvoirs dans les Institutions Européennes", *Social Anthropology* 3, 3: 235–50.

Bourdieu, P. (1982) *Ce que parler veut dire.* Paris: Fayard. English (1991) *Language and Symbolic Power: The Economy of Linguistic Exchanges*, Cambridge: Polity Press.

Casanova, P. (1999) *La République Mondiale des Lettres*, Paris: Éditions Du Seuil.

De Swaan, A. (1993) "The evolving European language system; a theory of communication potential and language competition", *International Political Science Review* 14, 3: 241–55.

—— (forthcoming) *The World Language System; Political Sociology and Political Economy of the Global Language Constellation*, Cambridge: Polity.

—— (1988) *In Care of the State; Health Care, Education and Welfare in the Modern Era in Europe and the United States*, Cambridge: Polity.

—— (1999) Keynote Address: Conference on institutional status and use of national languages in Europe: Contributions to a European language policy, Brussels, March 24.

Goudsblom, J. (1988) "Vanachter de doorkijkspiegel", in *Taal en sociale werkelijkheid*, Amsterdam: Meulenhoff.

Hountondji, P. (1983) *African Philosophy: Myth and Reality*, London: Hutchinson.

"Key data on education in the European Union" (1999), Luxembourg: Office for Official Publications of the European Communities, 54–5.

Les Jeunes Européens [*Eurobaromètre*, 47.2] (1997), European Commission.

Mamadouh, V. (1995) *De talen in het Europese parlement*, Amsterdamse sociaal-geografis-che studies, 52, Amsterdam: Instituut voor sociale geografie, Universiteit van Amsterdam.

Schlossmacher, M. (1994) "Die Arbeitssprachen in den Organen der Europäischen Gemeinschaft. Methoden und Ergebnisse einer empirischen Untersuchung", in Ammon, U., Mattheier, K.J. and Nelde, P.H. (eds) *Sociolingistica, International Yearbook of European Sociolinguistics*, 8: *English Only? in Europe*, Tübingen: Max Niemeyer Verlag: 101–22.

Van Deth, J.-P. (1979) *L'enseignement scolaire des langues vivantes dans les pays membres de la communauté européenne: bilan, réflexions et propositions*, Bruxelles: Didier.

Wallerstein, I. (1974) *The Modern World System*, New York: Academic Press.

11 European sociology or a sociology of Europeans?

Dominique Schnapper

The sociological project

Sociology is a child of modern democratic society and therefore also a child of Europe and Europeans throughout the world, particularly in the United States of America. People have posed questions about their societies since the time of classical Greek philosophy, but the sociologist does not simply extend philosophical inquiry. As a particular intellectual discipline, sociology arose in Europe at a time when modern political thought and a recognition of the changes brought about by the Industrial Revolution were emerging. With its origins in the democratic revolution, as well as those of science and technology, sociology defines itself in opposition to philosophical and prescriptive traditions and their reflections on society. The intention of sociologists was to break with the philosophical tradition that since the time of Aristotle had contemplated the best possible political regime. Political philosophy no longer appeared to provide an adequate understanding of the political reality of modernity and the harsh transformations that were to be seen in the material conditions of life. A modern form of inquiry was all the more vital for sociologists because they were supporters of the scientific ideal of their century. They wanted to be in line with the aims of rational knowledge and to distance themselves from their own society in order to observe it objectively. Contrary to the philosophers, sociologists claimed themselves to be scientific and not prescriptive. They did not ask how society should function but instead they posed the question of how it does function. In a scientific society, they set themselves the task of being scientific, by analytically separating the cognitive and prescriptive and making a distinction between knowledge and action. Their task followed that of Spinoza's maxim "do not deplore, laugh, hate, but understand". This is why sociologists, as in any other scientific endeavor, base their analyses on inquiry in the widest sense of the term, such as an historical inquiry in the style of Max Weber, qualitative inquiries inspired by the work of anthropologists, or inquiries by questionnaires and statistical analyses.

There exists a direct line between sociology and political modernity. Knowledge of social practices is one dimension of the utopianism of the citizen. The desire to know and criticize one's own society that is specific to sociology is linked to the two key characteristics of modern society: democracy and science.

Modern society applies the goal of rational knowledge to the social reality and this knowledge in turn forms the political opinion of the citizen. The citizen has the absolute right to know and to decide. The inherent values of democratic societies give rise to the objective of establishing equality between individual citizens. Sociologists and statisticians are called upon to reply scientifically to political questions. During the thirty "golden years" (*les trente glorieuses*) that followed the end of the Second World War, when public debate influenced by Marxist criticism was centered on the degree and origin of social inequalities, sociologists were summoned to provide objective data in order to legitimize or condemn adopted policies. They were charged with providing arguments to the controversy that surrounded the respective virtues of liberal and communist political regimes in reducing inequalities. Today, they are called upon to comment on the process of "exclusion" for certain sectors of the population, a process which is at the forefront of political debate.

Sociological values and the values of citizenship

The implicit values of sociology are those of a society of citizens. This can be demonstrated by a critical appraisal of some of the most common methodological tools that that are frequently used in empirical research as part of the sociological tradition, such as mobility and marriage tables, and indices of segregation.

In the case of mobility, as is well known, a two-dimensional table is constructed where the rows are the social categories of the respondents ("sons") at a given moment and the columns the corresponding categories of their father ("fathers"). From such a table, it can be seen that a certain proportion of the social category of "sons" are close to those of their "fathers". Marriage tables are of the same type. A two-dimensional table is constructed with the social category of men who marry ("husbands") in the rows and the corresponding social category of the fathers of their "wives" in the columns. Such a table shows that a certain proportion of marriages takes place within or near to the same social group.

This type of analysis (the limitations of which will not be discussed here) consists of an implicit comparison of the observed reality with two abstract ideas: the absolute redistribution of chances that occur at each generation, measured through social mobility and marriage; and the absolute reproduction of the membership of social groups, together with the total social homogeneity of marriages. If it was found that the distribution of the data was random, this would mean that social chances are completely dispersed at each generation. However, if the distribution of the data in the social mobility or marriage tables was found to be clustered diagonally, this would mean a perfect association between immobility and social reproduction. All individuals would find themselves in the same social category as their fathers and they would marry with a person who belonged to the same social category as themselves. Such a finding would also imply that social structures are not transformed from one generation to the next. Of course, both cases are abstract ideas. How could it be that social status is totally independent of family socialization, which passes from one generation to another complete value systems (tacit or otherwise) and customs that are in part linked to social group membership? Conversely, how can absolute reproduction be possible in societies which practically apply the ideal of equality through legal and political systems, which promote mobility and exchanges, and which are dominated by the principle of equal rights? The two poles of the absolute redistribution of social chances and the complete social reproduction and perfect match that can be observed at each generation represent two methodological tools which tacitly reflect a utopia of citizens and equality for all individuals.

In the same way, indices of dissimilarity measure the distance between the actual distribution of populations in urban spaces and the idea (which is also a norm) of determining the nature of equity, as defined by the distribution of a group in a particular area (or any other spatial unit) proportional to its representation in the global population. If a certain group comprises 10 per cent of the population of a town, equity can be said to have been reached if 10 per cent of this group is found in each part of the town, and therefore the index of equity will be equal to zero. The index shows the number of persons belonging to a social group (defined by the sociologist) who must move from an area if equity is to be respected. If the index of dissimilarity is equal to 30, this would signify that 30 per cent of the social group must move in order for equity to be maintained (Schnapper 1998: 202). In this way the distribution of inequalities between individuals in urban areas can be measured with reference to social group membership and national or regional origins. It can then be compared with an abstract idea or ideal type to determine the random distribution of individuals in a town, an idea which stems from the ideals of equality in a democratic society.

The same type of analysis concerning these methodological tools can be used in the sociology of inter-ethnic relations – discrimination, segregation, mixed marriages, etc. They make possible a comparison between the social realities and the utopian vision of equal rights between individuals as measured by their equal dispersion in urban spaces, and through random marriages, all of which are utopias close to that of citizenship. These methodological tools of sociology are directly linked to the objective of social democracy, which is to ensure equality between individual citizens.

The national dimension of sociology

To be more precise, sociological research has often developed as a result of requests from political officials who are confronted with "social problems" that they can neither understand nor control. Sociological research has often been undertaken in response to this social demand. Research by the University of Chicago in the 1920s was a direct consequence of the riots of 1919 which caused the death of several Blacks who were newcomers from the Southern States. Sociology therefore, has always been directly linked to social problems and consequently national issues of modern society.

In consequence, there has always been a tension between this national dimension and sociology's aspiration towards rational knowledge which has become its vocation. The sociologists undertake research and build concepts within particular societies. At the same time they participate in a rational endeavor which is part of a universal horizon. This tension between the sociologists' national characteristics of their social experience, their research and their desire to rationally understand modern society is forever present in sociology.

In order to illustrate this inevitable tension inherent in the sociological project, I will discuss briefly here the example of inter-ethnic relations (Schnapper 1998). Concerning social subject matters and sociology, North Americans, English, French and all nationalities have different ways of treating the "Other" as well as approaching the same issues differently. These issues that are common to all democratic societies can be formulated in the following way: how can populations with different collective histories be made to live together given that democratic societies are united by the principles, the values and the practice of citizenship? How can the legitimacy of the principle of citizenship be reconciled with the freedom of citizens to retain their historical consciousness, culture and particular beliefs? Should the unifying principle of citizenship be invoked? Or should an institutional place be given in the public domain to particular groups by recognizing the value of their culture and establishment of their communities? Various social democracies and sociologists have replied in different ways, each of which reflect their national characteristics in respect of this fundamental question of social organization.

The United States

This issue lies at the heart of North American sociology. The initial goal of sociological research in the United States consisted of examining the integration question of their own society, founded by the WASPs and subsequently confronted with successive waves of migrants from Southern Europe, then Asia. At the time, this question was framed in the context of the past and contemporary behavior of these settlers towards the indigenous populations and the consequences of slavery for contemporary conditions of Afro-Americans.

For the sociologists of the Chicago school, American democracy allowed a resolution of the antinomy between the freedom of individuals to retain collective histories of their roots and full participation in their new nation. By examining the process through which diverse immigrant populations had created a unique and united society – a process termed as "assimilation" – they were also probing the very nature of American society. This entailed addressing the issue of how cohabitation and conflict between different ethnic and racial groups present in the population of the United States can be managed. Aligning themselves within the assimilation paradigm, sociologists set their objectives on an analysis of the cycles, size and direction of this process. Poles or Italians, for example, kept specific family behaviors that were influenced by Catholic codes of morality. The upward social mobility of the Jewish population appeared to occur at a quicker rate and to reach higher levels than the Italians, etc. For the sociologists of the Chicago school, North American democracy was not seen to eliminate particular cultures by coercion in the way that (according to them) the European nations had done. One of the goals of this assimilation approach was to understand the spontaneous and voluntary re-interpretation by migrants of their own traditions within the legal and political framework of the democratic nation state.

The discovery that ethnic groups constituted a huge sociological mechanism of defense that enabled immigrants to survive and adapt (groups which the second generation wished to escape from) represented a major finding of urban sociology between 1920 and 1930 (Burgess and Bogue 1964: 325). Sociologists wanted to see the progressive "assimilation" of all immigrants, whilst at the same time they wished to see the safeguarding of certain specific cultural practices and a reinterpretation of historical experiences and particular religions. They wanted to see immigrants fully participating in social life and adopting the universal values of American democracy. What better fate could there be for immigrants who had voluntarily come to the United States in search of freedom?

The paradigm of assimilation which implies the progressive but inevitable wiping out of ethnic forms had been adopted both by liberal authors and Marxist intellectuals. Its basis was fundamentally brought into question by the model that was to follow, known as "ethnicity", which from the 1960s onwards analyzed the failure of assimilation policies. Americans discovered, via sociologists, that the variety of populations which made up their country were neither assimilated at the same pace nor in the same way. Sociologists revealed the limits of the melting pot and showed that ethnic groups remained intact (Glazer and Moynihan 1963). In contrast to the generation of the 1920s and 1930s, sociologists who studied ethnicity during the period 1960 to 1980 no longer interpreted the existence of ethnic groups as a stage in the journey towards assimilation. Moreover, they thought that ethnicity was a permanent feature of American society and one which needed to be understood. The debate on the meaning of ethnicity has now replaced the analysis of assimilation in sociological discourse.

The majority of sociologists are opposed to the idea that inspired the researchers of the Chicago school, namely that assimilation represents a democratic means to ensure the participation of members of minority groups in community life without at the same time compelling them to give up their own culture. They have discovered all at once that the melting pot has failed, that it was reprehensible and that ethnicity exists and has a value. Moreover the project of the assimilation of populations and the universalist ideology of American democracy have been accused of having led to, according to the term used by French militants, "ethnocides". Instead, differences were to be celebrated. Every type of ethnicity became an expression of richness and every particular form of identity was judged to be valuable. The state should intervene to protect ethnicities, and failing to do so would lay it open to accusations of ethnocide. Thus the above discussion, with its point of reference being an analysis of American policies, and in particular the policy of affirmative action, shows how sociological research is an integral part of public debate.

European societies

European societies have addressed issues of national integration in different terms. This is because they are characterized by a history of conflicts that have placed them in opposition over many centuries, and a somewhat inhibited memory of colonization and wars of de-colonization. They are equally characterized by the tradition of nationalist movements (born in Europe) which have pursued the goal to make political unity and cultural identity congruent (Gellner 1983).

Europe is the place where nations were born. The history of political institutions and ideas of nationhood marks out each one of them. Every European country has a strong national tradition and a specific manner of treating inter-ethnic relations, and these traditions are linked to the political ways through which the national project has been developed. The very terms used to describe foreign populations or foreign origins shows how these concepts continue to differ, despite recent overlapping due to the same political necessity to integrate the children of the huge wave of immigrants following the Second World War. For Germans, the concept of "foreigners" is still in use; the British use the term "racial minorities" or more recently, "ethnic" or "cultural minorities"; the Dutch and the Swedish employ the term "cultural minorities"; the French have used the term "immigrants", and now "nationals" or "citizens". Through the words of social life the relation with the other expresses itself, together with the tradition of national integration and its forms, and more generally the concept of citizenship. Different ways of expressing the Other and policies directed towards foreigners within France could never be understood without reference to French *jacobinisme*, linked to a concept of the nation whose origins go back to the Middle Ages and which has been reinforced by the rationalistic universalism of the Revolutionaries, and then of the Republicans in the past hundred years. British "multiculturalism" has its roots in the system of parliamentary democracy which for a long time has recognized the representation of groups, classes and even the Scottish and Welsh "nations" in public life. The different approach to the "emancipation of minorities" that distinguishes the Swedes and the Dutch is due to their respective liberal and secular traditions. Up until 2000, the Germans were reluctant to allow some part of the *ius soli* to be incorporated in their national legislation because the notion of "German people" (*Deutsches Volk*) still exists as an ethno-linguistic entity. It was only in 2000 that the *ius soli* was recognized through the national legislation, whereas in France this issue was dealt with by legislation dating from 1889, that is more than a century ago.

Equally, it has been common to think of the two traditions of citizenship, *"à l'anglaise"* and *"à la française"*, as being in opposition. The individualistic concept of the citizen *"à l'anglaise"* that arises from Locke and other English philosophers, places an accent upon an equilibrium of power, political freedoms and the role of intermediaries. The citizens *"à l'anglaise"* are above all liberals. They demand the security of individuals, freedom of thought, speech and to act. Their liberalism in turn became democratized by the extension of political rights to all citizens. The British tradition places an emphasis on order, corporation, class, and on particular groups. English democracy has retained the idea that in order to safeguard free-doms, counter-balances of power must be produced through political representation of the main social forces. Pluralism is therefore construed as the "natural" expression of public freedoms.

The concept of the citizen *"à la française"*, which can be traced back to Rousseau, is based upon the unity of the political body, political participation, and the direct link between the citizen and the state. The citizens *"à la française"* are above all democrats, possessing political freedom which is ensured through participation of a collective sovereignty. For the French, democratic principles do not necessarily involve respect for fundamental liberties and liberal values. Intermediary bodies between the individuals-citizens and the state that prevent them from being free must be eradicated. The tradition of citizenship in France continues to be influenced by the Rousseau-like concept of a unified democracy, which in turn is reluctant about pluralism. Citizenship is, like the nation, indivisible.

French sociology and the refusal of "ethnicity"

In order to show how sociology has always been directly linked to political issues of national integration, I will touch on the example that I am most familiar with, which is the case of France. The starting point of French sociologists is the experience of "republican integration" which feeds the national mythology even when it is relativized or condemned. They situate their research in the history of immigration and a reflection on the integration of the nation, thereby extending the way in which Durkheim approached modern society. For Durkheim, the inclusion of "ethnic" dimensions in collective social life was in itself a way of casting doubt on the unity of the nation. Social issues considered in "ethnic" terms have not been considered in France until only quite recently (in the 1970s), after de-colonialization and the radical critique of the colonialist project of expansion, and under the influence of the North American sociological approach to ethnicity. This shift therefore took place in the climate of a radical questioning of the organization of political democracies, the nation state and the French Jacobite tradition. It was also the time when the consequences of the permanent installation of populations originating from the Third World who arrived during an economically prosperous period were debated. Throughout Europe, the question of the participation by these newly arrived persons in collective social life was also being posed under the form of and values of the new "multiculturalism".

Traditionally, the failure to take into account the "ethnic" dimension is explained by the fact that French sociologists, unlike their English speaking counterparts, have hardly studied specific relations between populations that are defined in terms of "race". French researchers have undertaken research on relations between populations with diverse national origins and they have studied the social conditions of immigrant workers. However, their surveys have been undertaken within the paradigm of the integration of the nation and the results have remained relatively marginal compared to mainstream and more widely recognized French sociology. In so far as they have uncovered issues relating to the large size of the immigrant population, these sociologists often resort to historical and political interpretations of their findings. The study of the characteristics of immigrants has found itself rapidly taken over by more theoretical analyses on the citizen, the nation or racism. The title of the book by Jacqueline Costa-Lascoux (1989), *From the Immigrant to the Citizen*, is a good case in point of the position of French sociology.

This perspective is of course, linked to the tradition of national integration, which does not recognize the existence of particular communities in the public space (Schnapper 1991). It was strengthened by the personal intervention of Emile Durkheim, who introduced sociology into academic institutions. Both a Jew and a republican, and a proponent of universalism, Durkheim anticipated the gradual weakening of the ethnic dimension of social life as a result of modern society. He was in favor of this evolution which he believed would liberate individuals from inherited attachments. This way of addressing the issue of "ethnicity" was in turn reinforced by the strong influence (direct or indirect) of Marxist thought since 1945. It explains why French researchers have hardly taken part in the debate over the meaning of ethnicity and why they willingly place an emphasis on the social and political dimension of relations between individuals. As Véronique de Rudder remarks, "the ethnic dimension of relations of co-existence is no longer often the most important of issues. Above all, what is important are the social, economical, cultural and political dimensions" (in Taguieff 1991, vol. 2: 163).

National relativity and the aims of rational knowledge

Sociological research, as we have seen, forms a part of wider social debates and the relationship between the two is often ambiguous. Sociologists deal with relations that develop between individuals and groups which refer to particular historical communities inevitably in a way that reflects their national context. In this view, each national society has its own peculiarities arising from a unique "political project" (Schnapper 1994: 51). Even the intellectual tradition has a national characteristic.

For this reason, in each national intellectual tradition, the concept of the "Other" is different and even specialists in the field paradoxically are often unaware of what other sociologists are doing. How many militants of "multiculturalism" do not know other languages? Different modes of thought between European countries should therefore be taken into account, in the same way that the approach of academics whose main language is English and should be considered as a contribution to universal knowledge. None of these contributions are a priori better or more correct than the others and they can all only be incomplete. But they differ, and therefore they present the opportunity to elaborate and debate different scientific viewpoints which can in turn enhance an understanding of social relations. Why would one want to ignore them if they conform to requirements of the sociological project and are based on inquiry and reflection? The viewpoint of a French or German or Italian sociologist has its origins in a particular historical and intellectual context. It must not simply be rejected on the pretext that it is "very French", "very German", "very Italian" or "ideological". We must realize that there is always a tendency to qualify as "ideological" the national way in which "Others" try to understand the social world. On these matters more than any others, the analyses of Alistair Crombie on "scientific style" as a specific way of "thinking" and "proving" are particularly relevant (Crombie 1994).

Whatever form the national characteristic of sociology takes, it should not give itself over to an absolute kind of relativism for to do so would be to discard the central aim of learning and understanding. The reason that sociology merges with the discourse of social actors is not because there can never exist absolute objectivity. Beyond its attachment to historical experiences and a particular national intellectual tradition, the task of understanding is part of the universal vocation of rationality. All rational research (that is to say research based on inquiry and reflection as well as being self-critical) contributes towards an understanding of social practices. What must be avoided is to confuse French, German, English or American approaches to sociology with sociology itself. The national character of each of these sociologies must be clearly recognized and always brought into question when applied other than within its own frame of reference. Can the North American analyses of "assimilation" be transposed as they are into European society? It is perfectly possible to be aware that all sociological reasoning has its roots in a particular national tradition and at the same time to conserve the universal horizon of rationality. In each national tradition, sociology contributes in its own way to the enterprise of a general understanding, which in turn must be conceived not as given but as a project or vocation.

Mutual criticism by sociologists in the context of different societies with different intellectual traditions should be one of the essential components of sociological inquiry. I do not try to hide, for example, that the theoretical propositions which I have put forward to reinterpret the way in which we think about inter-ethnic relations (Schnapper 1998: chapter 12) are the product of the French tradition of sociological inquiry, a tradition that has always emphasized the reflection on citizenship and on racist thinking rather than focusing on the relations between populations of different "races". However, this does not mean to say that they should be ignored. It is mostly Jewish intellectuals who work on anti-Semitism, but this is not a reason to ignore the results of their research or to deny their contribution, through the peculiar and extreme case of the Jews, to an understanding of the relations between different historical groups. We must not leave out the national experience of Afro-Americans if we are to understand the analyses of sociologists who focus on "Black issues" in the United States. Rather, by rendering their unique experience objective through sociology, these sociologists raise the general issue of the capacity of democratic societies to transcend, through citizenship, the social representations and the discriminations inherited from the past.

The search for a form of universality can only be undertaken on the basis of an understanding and critique of the results of each individual national research. Only by being aware of the national character of sociology, both our own and those of others, will the sociological project be able to contribute towards a knowledge whose universality can only be a goal or a project; in other words, a controlling idea in the Kantian sense.

European sociology

Since all sociology has national characteristics, it should come as no surprise that a European Association of Sociology has been formed at the same time as the European Union is being built. The same issues that are confronted in the political construction of Europe are to be found within European sociology: the link with the United States and the safeguarding of national traditions. The same cultural risks are involved, namely the reduction of European culture to its smallest common denominator symbolized by the use of pidgin English to communicate within Europe and equally within the European Association of Sociology.

I will leave aside the relations with the United States as I want to speak of the issue of Europe, which consists of resisting the elimination of national traits whilst at the same time transcending them, in social and political life as well as in sociology.

A European Association of Sociology can set itself two goals, one of which is modest and regional, the other more fundamental. One objective can be the study of the way in which particular social institutions function. For example, this could be an analysis of the relations between individuals and the tensions that exist within the enterprise or the family; the measurement of inequalities between social groups; an explanation of electoral practices; or more generally, the behavior of certain social groups. In these instances, there exists a European, even global sociology and Europe can be seen to be an excellent laboratory. European nations are close to each other through their principles of political legitimacy (citizenship), through their economic organization which has become increasingly integrated, and through their adoption of the welfare state, even though the way in which this latter is organized is not the same among all European countries. However, at the same time, they are distinguished by their different histories, secular conflicts and current rivalries, culture and language.

The Association could have as an objective the promotion of comparative research on these societies that are fundamentally close whilst also being so different that by passing through the English Channel or the North Sea, or by crossing the Rhine in whatever direction, one is exposed to an exotic experience. The European Association of Sociology will be able to encourage the development of these types of comparative research, through which we shall be able to understand better European societies and the workings of society in general. This project remains close to those of each regional association. It consists of a regional coming together of sociologists. Pidgin English, in this case, can be used as the means of communication between sociologists of Europe, in the same way as it is used by sociologists the world over.

However, if we wish to follow the primary objective of the sociological project, the European Association of Sociology can set itself a more ambitious task. This would be not only to compare the social worlds of the European societies, but also to keep (and to criticize) the national intellectual dimensions through which an intellectual project and a particular way of thinking is construed. We can only build Europe politically by taking into account national political traditions and moving beyond or transcending them, rather than by denying their existence. If the goal is to construct a European sociology that is not a province of a global sociology inspired by and in the style of the North Americans, we must take on board the national intellectual traditions of Europe. We must be aware of the betrayals that are evident in all translations. It is not the same thing to read Weber in German or in English, to read Pareto in Italian or in English, or to read Durkheim in French or in English.

The work of the founders of sociology can only be fully understood and appreciated if the national tradition within which they developed is taken fully into account, a tradition which is as much political as intellectual. Weber was an heir to German philosophy and scholarship. He lived in a time when nationalism flourished, and was a patriot who adhered in a restrained way to Pan-Germanic ideology. One only has to compare his written texts in German with their English translation to see the extreme simplification that the translation process carries with it, a simplification which in certain cases borders on betrayal. Durkheim was a child of the Third Republic, an assimilated Jew who was passionately aligned with Jewish patriots of the Republic, formed by the culture and rhetoric of the French. When he spoke of "Society", we should never forget that he had in mind the national French society of his era. Pareto was an heir of Machiavelli and Italian critical political philosophy.

We can, of course, take the attitude that the founders of sociological thought are out-dated and that our discipline is defined by a project that has become less philosophical and more "scientific", based as it is on comparative studies of the institutions and functioning of European societies. Many of us undertake these types of studies which are made possible through the financial support of European institutions, and which contribute towards collaboration between European sociologists. We can therefore profitably compare, for example, family forms, inequalities of income before and after tax, poverty and exclusion. I am quick to recognize the benefit of this type of research since I partake in it myself, as in the European program Effnatis which studies the comparative integration of the children of migrants in various European countries, and where I collaborate with my Dutch, English, Finnish, German, Spanish, Swedish and Swiss colleagues. But whatever their respective contribution, it seems to me that it would narrow the scope of inquiry if we restricted ourselves solely to these types of studies. To do so would be to give up that which represented the real ambition of sociology when it was created: to continue by other means – research in all its forms – the philosophical reflection on human life in societies.

It is clear that we are constructing a Europe in which English will be the language of communication. Sociologists are subject to this general principal as much as any other social actors. English is already and will inevitably become the language for communicating within the European Association of Sociology and for collaborative work between sociologists. After all, sociologists are also social actors. However, the language of rational knowledge and of sociological inquiry (which has universal aims) is not only a language of communication. If sociologists ignore the national dimension of their intellectual tradition, *ipso facto* they restrict their intellectual objectives. In this regard it seems important to me that the Association should be open to written texts in the major sociological languages of Europe, those of Weber, Durkheim and Pareto, thereby demonstrating its intellectual ambitions.

Recognizing the diversity of intellectual traditions is also to address the issue of the universality of sociological understanding. The European Association of Sociology can be more and something better than simply a regional coming together of sociologists. It can become the place where the fundamental issues of our discipline are discussed and where we can examine its roots in our respective national societies and its universality. It is the national intellectual traditions which give meaning and value to comparative studies, studies which are put on the agenda (and this is something to celebrate) by the construction of Europe. It is here that we can show how each national sociology contributes in its own way to a universal form of knowledge, something which is not a content and which must remain an objective or a project.

In any case, the European Association of Sociology will be a regional meeting place for sociologists dedicated to the study of neighboring countries. This has already been achieved and it is a notable success which we can celebrate. However, it can also be more than this by becoming the place where the fundamental questions of sociology are addressed and where an intellectual discipline that arose from the European nations can be renewed.

References

Burgess, E. W. and Bogue, D. J. (1964) *Contributions to Urban Sociology*, Chicago: Chicago University Press.

Costa-Lascoux, J. (1989) *De l'immigré au citoyen*, Paris: La Documentation française.

Crombie, A. C. (1994) *Styles of Scientific Thinking in the European Tradition: The History of Argument and Explanation Especially in the Mathematical and Biomedical Sciences and Arts*, London: Duckworth.

Gellner, E. (1983) *Nations and Nationalism*, Oxford: Blackwell.

Glazer, N. and Moynihan, D. (1963) *Beyond the Melting-Pot. The Negroes, Puerto Ricans, Jews, Italians, and Irish of New York City*, Cambridge: The MIT and Harvard University Press.

Schnapper, D. (1991) *La France de l'intégration. Sociologie de la nation en 1990*, Paris: Gallimard.

—— (1994, 1998) *Community of Citizens. On the Modern Idea of Nationality*, New Brunswick and London: Transaction.

—— (1998) *La Relation à l'Autre. Au coeur de la pensée sociologique*, Paris: Gallimard.

Taguieff, P.-A. (ed.) (1991) *Face au racisme*, vol. 2, Paris: La Découverte.

Index

www.ingramcontent.com/pod-product-compliance
Ingram Content Group UK Ltd.
Pitfield, Milton Keynes, MK11 3LW, UK
UKHW020858280225
455677UK00006B/87